A PLACE APART

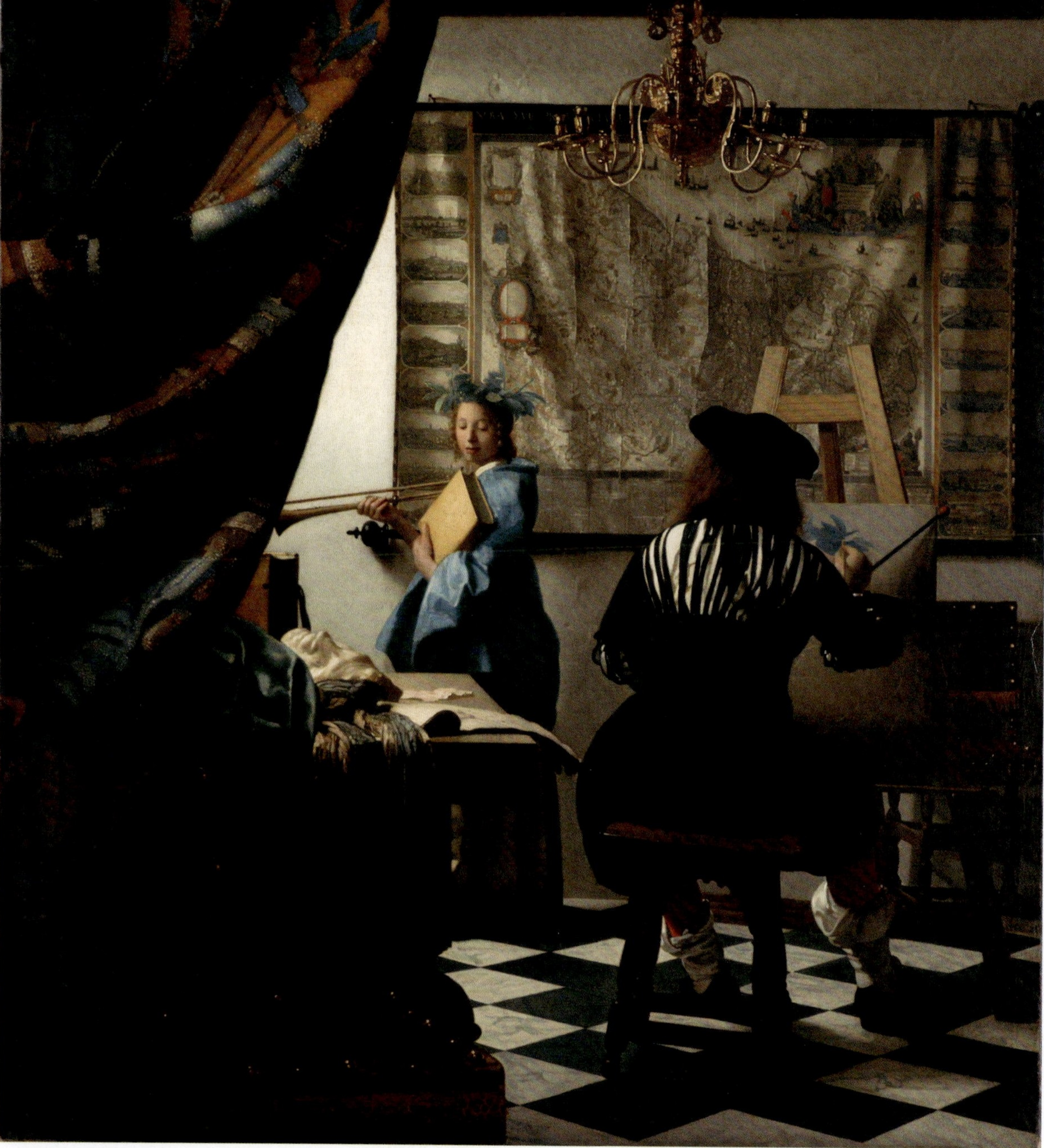

A PLACE APART

THE ARTIST'S STUDIO 1400–1900

CAROLINE CHAPMAN

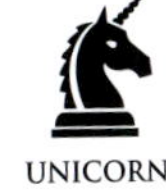

UNICORN

CONTENTS

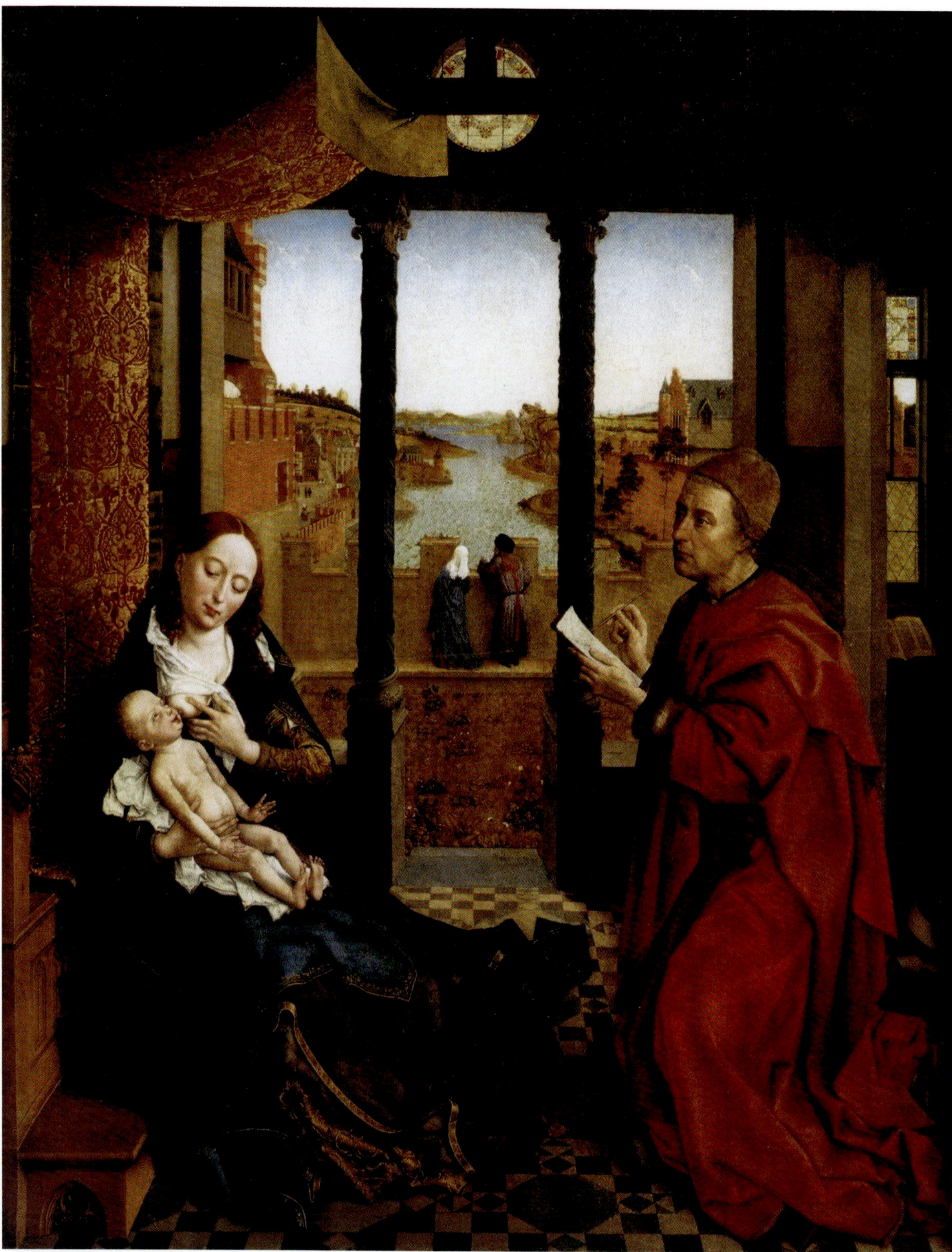

Introduction

Outsiders are always curious about artists and their surroundings; to them the sanctum sanctorum of the painter's house is the mysterious place ... It is the sacred meeting ground of a secret society, whose talk is a mosaic puzzle to the uninitiated – a laboratory in which ideas are melted down and boiled up, and turned out on canvas by magic, the paint-pot and brushes being the wizard's apparatus.[1]

PAINTPOTS AND BRUSHES are the very least of a studio's apparatus. Some ateliers were veritable Aladdin's caves that represent a lifetime of collecting objects that might one day be a source of inspiration. Reputedly, Picasso never threw anything away, even tickets for the Paris Métro. The entire floor of Francis Bacon's studio was so buried in knee-deep detritus that it is baffling how he found a place to put his feet. Only his easels reared above the rubble. ('I feel at home here in this chaos,' Bacon said, 'because the chaos suggests images to me.'[2]) Some studios record the owner's travels to exotic locations: Indian rugs, a statue of Buddha, a Turkish hookah, miscellaneous vases, a tiger skin and the occasional potted palm, its branches soaring gracefully above the clutter. Few lacked a couch or the ubiquitous plaster casts of classical statues: Apollo and the Venus de Milo peering down from high shelves; and the occasional bust of Plato to inspire philosophic musings. The studio of a military artist might boast a stuffed horse, a suit of armour and assorted instruments of death. Edgar Degas' Paris studio contained several of the objects that appear regularly in his paintings of women at their *toilette*: 'the tub, the dull-coloured zinc bath, the well-used *peignoirs* ...'[3] Édouard Manet held on to the bar behind which stands the girl with the inscrutable expression in his famous painting, *The Bar at the Folies-Bergères*.

Such studios gave no hint that they could also be battlegrounds where hopes were dashed, original concepts failed dismally in their execution

OPPOSITE: 1. Rogier van der Weyden, *Saint Luke Drawing the Virgin, c.* 1435–40

All Renaissance workshops had to belong to a guild. As Mary was believed to have appeared several times to St Luke and he made a portrait of her, he became the patron saint of artists. Here he is seen in his spacious studio drawing her with a stylus.

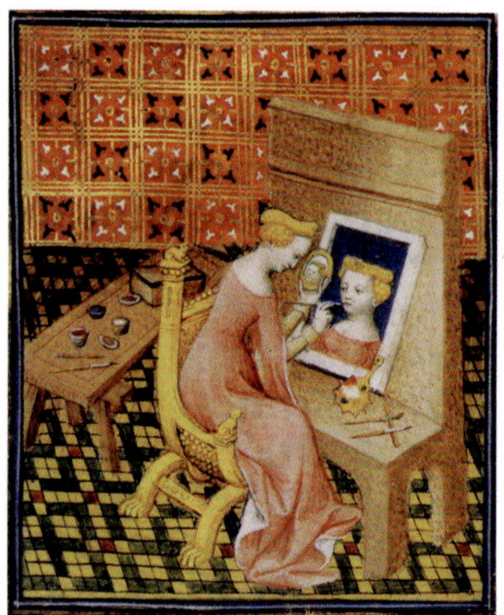

2. Illumination from Giovanni Boccaccio, *On Famous Women*, *c.* 1400

The pagan virgin Marcia, a famous painter and ivory engraver, holds a mirror before her as she paints her self-portrait. On the table to her left are some ready prepared pots of colour. To her right is a polygonal mirror and some spare brushes.

and paint refused to do what was asked of it. Such failures could lead to alienation, insecurity, depression, madness, even to suicide. Dominique Ingres and Henri Matisse both suffered from bouts of weeping, the latter to outbursts of fury. The Parisian art dealer, Ambroise Vollard, while sitting for his portrait to Paul Cézanne, recalled that the artist, in a fury because the work was going so badly, tore some of his watercolours from the wall and flung them into the stove. Conversely, studios could also be scenes of exhilaration, satisfaction, inspiration and conviviality.

The majority of artists, except those who had achieved fame and fortune, lived on the fringes of society. Many had their quirks, but they were allowable as society expected them to be eccentric. As Rudolf and Margot Wittkower acknowledge in their classic work, *Born Under Saturn*, 'there is an almost unanimous belief ... that artists are, and always have been, egocentric, temperamental, neurotic, rebellious, unreliable, licentious, extravagant, obsessed by their work, and altogether difficult to live with.'[4]

The evolution of the place in which an artist worked took until the nineteenth century before it became the 'studio' of popular imagination. Before that date, from the Middle Ages until well into the fifteenth century, artists were regarded as craftsmen. They were not concerned with 'personal' expression, but went wherever they could obtain work, be it church, chapel or castle, often remaining there for years until the commission was completed. In the early Middle Ages, workshops, known as *scriptoria* (writing rooms), were set up in monasteries where laymen worked alongside monks to produce Bibles and psalters for the monastery's own use. Paper was not available until the fourteenth century, so the artists worked on vellum made of calfskin which had been bleached, stretched, scraped and treated to form a surface of higher-quality than simple parchment. During the thirteenth century, illuminating manuscripts (literally, copies 'written by hand') became a commercial and secular enterprise, with workshops established in cities such as Paris, Oxford and Bologna. Wealthy patrons commissioned books to be made for them, such as the exquisite Book of Hours known as *Les Très Riches Heures du duc de Berry*.

A medieval and Renaissance workshop, or *bottega*, was a bustling, crowded space peopled by numerous apprentices and assistants all working on objects that could vary from a gold-encrusted altarpiece to a ceremonial banner. But first they had to learn to make every tool and material they used. 'The remarkable familiarity with materials possessed by all Renaissance artists, and their consummate technical skill ... remain monuments to the highly developed workshop structure ...'[5] Art was not a luxury then, but something that society wanted, needed and used.

In the course of the fifteenth century, the status of the artist rose:

INTRODUCTION

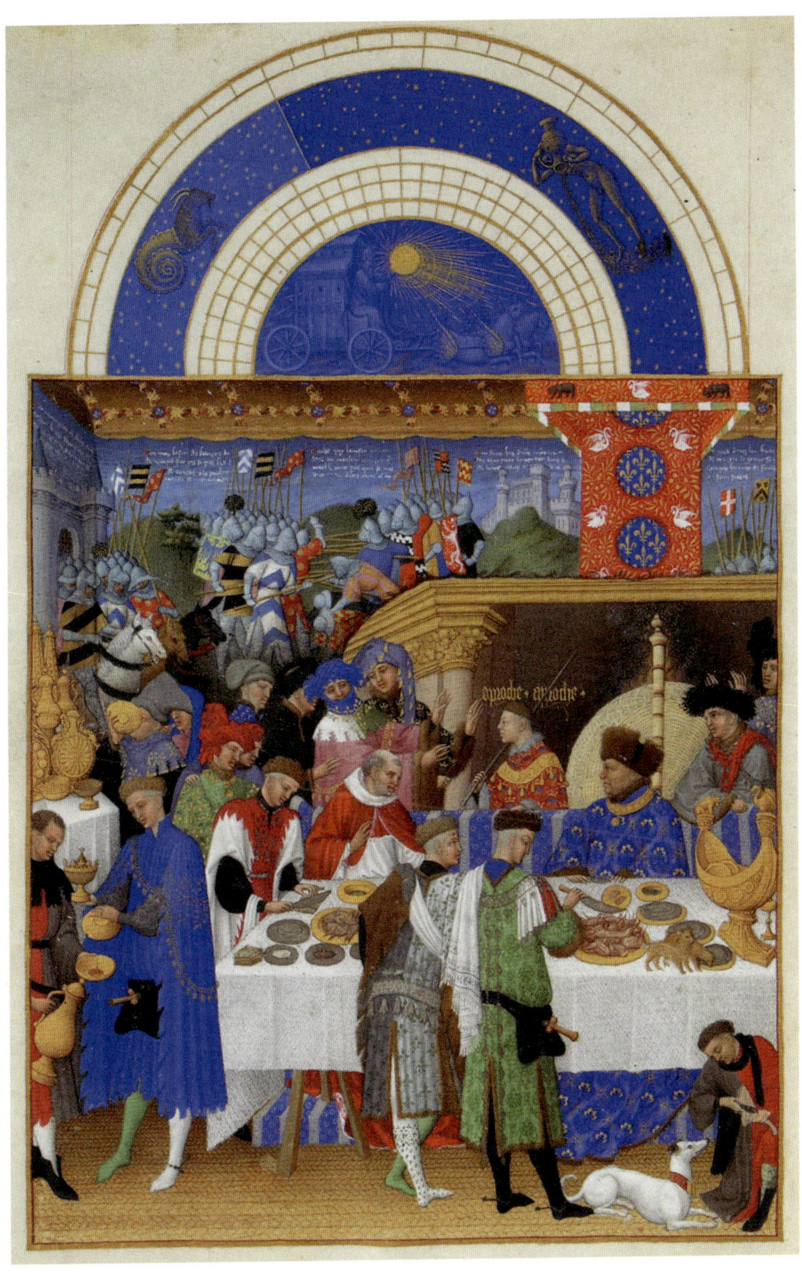

he was no longer an uneducated craftsman working with his hands, but a man of learning, working with his mind. This change in attitude was partly inspired by the writer and architect Leon Battista Alberti, whose treatise *On Painting* (1435) defined the Renaissance painter as an educated person who was on a level with his patron. Patronage, previously confined to the Court and Church, passed to the wealthy bourgeoisie, princes and popes who now did the buying and commissioning of works of art. Leonardo da Vinci, Michelangelo and Raphael all benefitted from such patronage, acting as propagandists

3. January from *Les Trés Riches Heures du duc de Berry*, c. 1416

The duc de Berry, his fur hat adorned with a huge diamond, receives numerous visitors who have come to offer him best wishes for the New Year. His pages, clad in sumptuous liveries, wait upon him. His little dogs are licking the plates. With its jewel-bright colours, this is International Gothic style at its best.

for popes and glorifying major figures of their time. At his premature death, aged thirty-seven, Raphael was a rich man, employing some fifty artists, the owner of a palace, two houses, a vineyard and land.

Cennino Cennini, the late fourteenth-century painter and theoretician, asserted in his treatise, *The Craftsman's Handbook* (*c.* 1400), that the artist should be regarded as a man of learning and distinction, and that his status 'is truly that of a gentleman and that it can be practised while dressed in velvet'.[6] Leonardo wore rose-pink tunics, fur-lined coats, jasper rings and boots of Cordova leather.[7] His hair, too, was beautifully coiffed, arranged in ringlets 'down to the middle of his chest'.[8]

In Leonardo's *Treatise on Painting,* he advocates that an artist should 'withdraw apart' as it enables him to think more clearly. He further advised that: 'Small rooms or dwellings discipline the mind, large ones distract it.'[9] Rather confusingly, he also wrote that 'the artist who withdraws completely courts madness'.[10] Such drawing apart is echoed by a plan for Michelangelo's house in Rome, dated about 1545, which shows a *bottega* (workshop) at the front of the house and a much smaller space labelled '*studiolo*' towards the rear.[11]

'Long before the word *studio* came to mean what it does today, the artist's space had been transformed into a space for study.'[12] A number of sixteenth-century paintings – by Dutch genre artists in particular – show a man, either seated at an easel or writing, surrounded by books and other paraphernalia associated with learning. What is significant is that he is alone, in a room separated off from the rest of the house.

Peter Paul Rubens (1577–1640), the greatest court painter of his age, also favoured a similar arrangement, preserving a small, private studio for himself – that he refers to as his 'secret *studiolo*' – in the summer house that he added to his Italianate palace in Antwerp. He used the ground floor of the building to paint his great canvases while the floor above contained a vast studio for his army of assistants.

In contrast to Rubens's hive of industry, Johannes Vermeer's *The Art of Painting* of 1666–68 (see frontispiece) shows the artist, often thought to be Vermeer himself, in an intimate and orderly studio with not a spare brush, paint rag or palette in sight. The image is light years from Bacon.

By the eighteenth century, art was no longer regarded as a trade but as a respectable profession. Sir Joshua Reynolds (1723–92) owned a large house in London's West End, a flashy carriage with gilded wheels and a villa at Richmond. The house contained a painting room (as studios were called then), an elegant room for his sitters and a gallery in which he could show his paintings. The latter was important, as before the advent of galleries and art dealers there were few ways artists could show their work. So respectable had the profession become that a few talented and ambitious women were able to surmount prejudice and

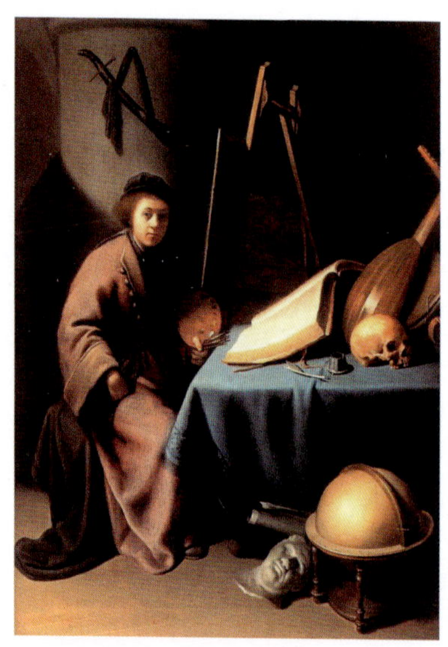

4. Gerard Dou, *The Painter in his Studio*, 1632

Dou has depicted himself cosily ensconced in his own space. He was so obsessed with dust permeating his paints that he would clamber into his studio through a trap door in the ceiling and then did not begin work until the dust, raised by this procedure, had settled.

INTRODUCTION

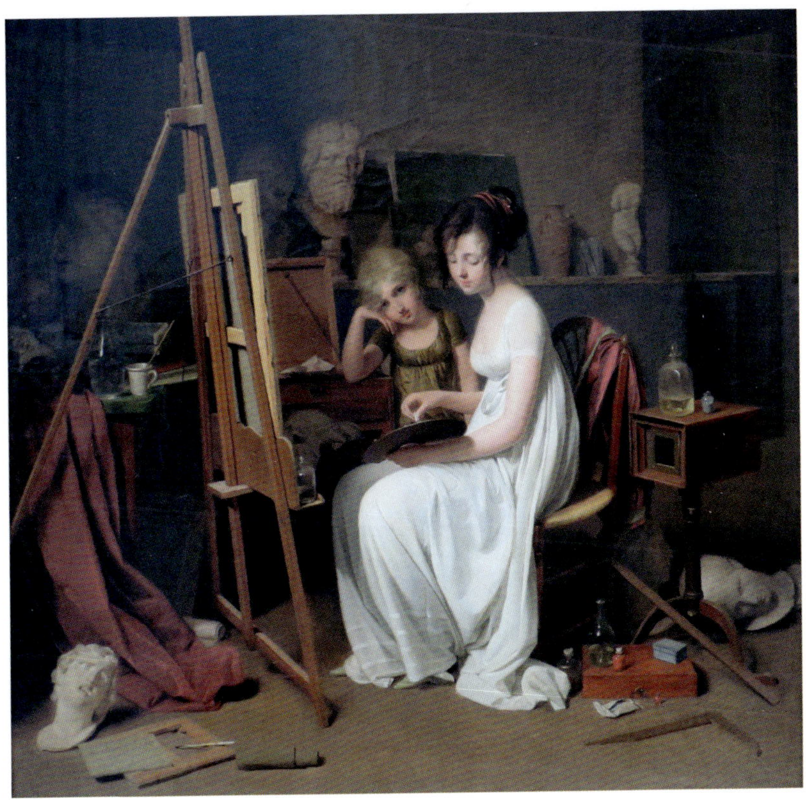

5. Louis-Léopold Boilly,
A Painter's Studio, c. 1800 (detail)

Boilly's charming scene of a female artist in her studio, attended by her daughter, is proof that by this date it was at last possible for a woman to become a professional artist. The classical busts and casts indicate the continuing importance of the classical ideal.

lack of proper training to make a living, their acceptance by society sympathetically recorded by male painters.

The word 'studio', used to designate the artist's workplace, only entered the English language in the nineteenth century. By then, studios had become more diverse and more spacious. The popularity of history painting and landscapes required more square footage in which to paint them. The Tenth Street Studio Building, constructed in New York in 1857, was the first modern facility designed specifically to serve the needs of artists. Some artists became celebrities, their studios vast showcases displaying their taste and status. By mid-century, *plein air* painters were more numerous, but they would still finish their paintings in the studio.

—— ♦ ——

My selection of artists may seem random and, in a sense, it is, but they have been chosen because they fulfil certain criteria: good stories, superb works of art and because there is information about their studios. The latter, as I have found to my cost, are often not described in artists' biographies. I have ploughed through vast tomes in search of such information and come out the other end none the wiser. This discrepancy apart, this book would not have been possible without the erudition of others – art historians, biographers, compilers of exhibition catalogues and essayists – whose knowledge I have distilled in my own way.

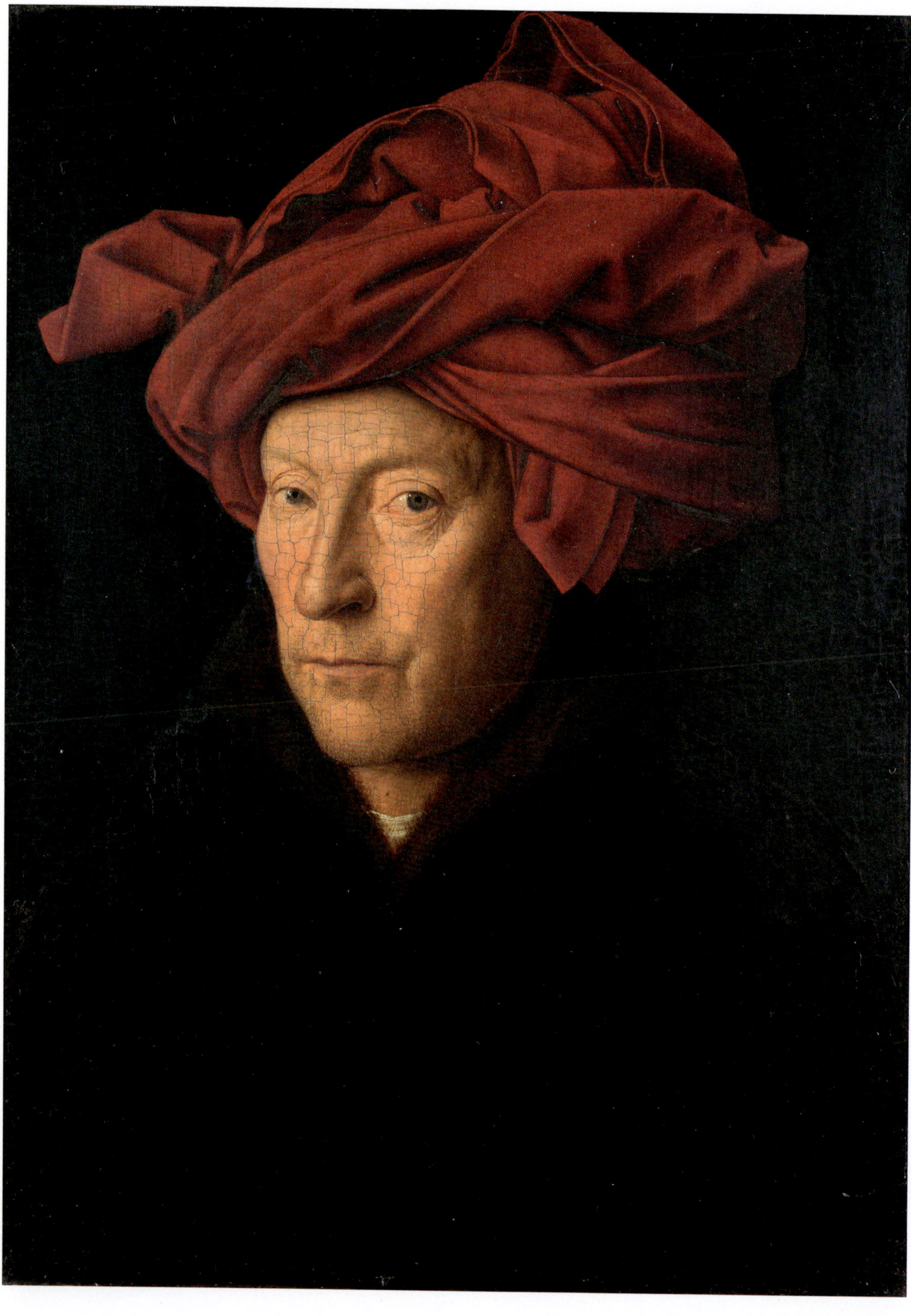

The Direction of a Master

The Renaissance Workshop

You, therefore, who with lofty spirit are fired with this ambition, and are about to enter the profession [of painter], begin by decking yourselves with this attire: Enthusiasm, Reverence, Obedience, and Constancy. And begin to submit yourself to the direction of a master for instruction as early as you can; and do not leave the master until you have to.
Cennino Cennini, *The Craftsman's Handbook, c.* 1400[1]

CENNINI HAD TAKEN HIS OWN ADVICE by serving a twelve-year apprenticeship under the direction of the artist Agnolo Gaddi (*d.* 1396), master of a Florentine workshop, or *bottega*. During those years he had become a moderate painter but had accumulated such in-depth knowledge of the materials and techniques used in a workshop that he compiled his famous treatise, *The Craftsman's Handbook* (*Il Libro dell' Arte*). Acting as a sort of manual, it contains everything that an aspiring artist needed to know, from gessoing to gilding, from frescoing to drawing, and from how to make goat glue to keeping miniver tails from becoming moth-eaten. He even has advice on 'How you should regulate your life', which includes consuming 'wholesome dishes, and light wines'. His sternest counsel, however, is on 'saving and sparing your hand, preserving it from such strains as heaving stones …' But, he adds darkly, 'There is another cause which, if you indulge it, can make your hand so unsteady that it will waver more, and flutter far more, than leaves do in the wind, and this is indulging too much in the company of woman.'[2]

The typical Renaissance *bottega* was a large open space opening on to the street, usually with living quarters at the rear or upstairs. The sixteenth-century print by Jan van der Straet depicts the Bruges workshop of Jan van Eyck (active 1422–d. 1441), but an Italian *bottega* would have been very similar. A successful commercial workshop, run by an active master adept at obtaining commissions, would have

OPPOSITE: **6.** Jan van Eyck, *Portrait of a Man with a Red Turban*, 1433

Together with his contemporary Rogier van der Weyden, Van Eyck was the most celebrated painter in Europe in the fifteenth century. His use of pigments bound not with eggs, as before, but with oil, enabled him to achieve the richness and depth of colour of this stunning portrait.

been crammed with apprentices, assistants and journeymen, all going about their different but interrelated tasks. These might include not only pictures but decorated saddles, altarpieces, silverwork, sculptures, bedheads, tombstones, painted *cassoni* (wedding chests), theatrical sets and costumes. The odours created by these endeavours would range from glue, leather, varnish, solvents and oil paint to the smell of terracotta clay and pine logs for the fire and kiln. Amid the sounds of sawing, hammering and grinding of pigments would be the clucking of the workshop's hens whose eggs supplied the main ingredient in the making of tempera. (A recent study suggests that egg yolk may also have been the key ingredient in oil paints used by the Old Masters because it helped prevent yellowing and wrinkling.[3])

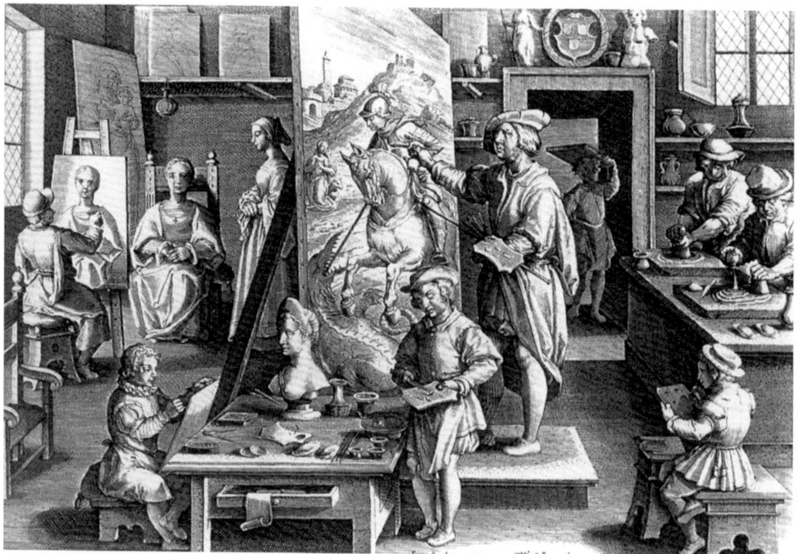

7. Jan van der Straet, *The Invention of Oil Paint, c.* 1590

This engraving illustrates some of the tasks involved in completing a painting. The studio master, elegantly clad in velvet, is completing his depiction of St George and the dragon while one of his assistants executes a lady's portrait. The assistants are busily preparing the various materials.

On the left of van der Straet's print a 'journeyman' – a skilled artist but not yet master of his own workshop – is painting a woman's portrait while her maidservant, with hands demurely clasped, waits on her mistress. In the centre, the master is putting the finishing touches to a large picture showing St George vanquishing the dragon. In his left hand he holds several brushes, a small palette and a mahlstick, the latter used to support his hand when he is painting detailed areas of the picture. In the foreground are three boys; judging by their youth, they have probably been taken on as apprentices. The boy on the left is sketching the objects on the table, while the one on the right is practising drawing eyes. In the centre, an older boy is preparing the master's palette. Standing on the right are two adult men grinding pigments into powder.

No artist could set up a workshop unless he was an approved member of a guild. The guild regulated the kind of work the master

    ONE / THE DIRECTION OF A MASTER

could accept, the materials used, relations with the patrons and the general organisation of the workshop. As well as assistants and journeymen, a master was allowed a number of apprentices. In return for board, lodging and some instruction, the apprentices prepared all the materials and kept the workshop scrupulously clean to prevent dust from permeating everything.

Despite strict guidance by the guild, some apprentices were poorly treated by their masters. The young artist Taddeo Zuccaro (1529–66) was apprenticed to Giovanni Calabrese, master of a workshop in Rome. Instead of being taught the various crafts, Taddeo was relegated to grinding colours all day. Calabrese's sadistic wife starved him of food and, should he be tempted to supplement his meagre diet, she kept the bread in a basket dangling from the ceiling with bells attached to warn her if it was touched. In the house, he was forced to make the beds, bring wood and water up from the cellar and to light the fires.[4] It seems strange that Calabrese was able to get away with treating Taddeo like an unpaid servant: a master was utterly dependent on his assistants and apprentices, since they did all the donkey work.

Objects created in the *bottega* were a collaborative effort, and such collaboration required a uniformity of style that the apprentice had to learn in order to be part of the team. Today, every artist or craftsman strives for individuality and originality, but during the Renaissance standardisation of types – altarpieces, for instance, fell into groups defined by shape, size or subject – was seen as a blessing, not a burden.[5] Even paintings could be the product of several hands, but supervised and corrected by the master who would then add his signature. This practice has caused nightmares for the art world: who painted what?

Leonardo da Vinci (1452–1519) is a case in point. He had been apprenticed to the Florence workshop of the successful sculptor-painter Andrea del Verrocchio (*c.* 1435–88) where he remained for at least three years. During that time, he is known to have painted a kneeling angel in Verrocchio's *Baptism of Christ*. In his seminal *Lives of Painters, Sculptors and Architects*, Giorgio Vasari (1511–74), states that 'although he was but a lad, Leonardo executed it in such a manner that his angel was much better than the figures of Andrea; which was the reason that Andrea would never again touch colour, in disdain that a child should know more than he.'[6] It is now thought that Leonardo also painted parts of the landscape in the background of the *Baptism* and a little tousled dog in Verrocchio's *Tobias and the Angel*. As a mere apprentice, however, Leonardo's work on both these paintings would not have been acknowledged: they would simply have been signed by his master, Verrocchio.

While serving as an apprentice in Verrocchio's workshop, Leonardo would have been taught drawing, or *disegno*, the fundamental skill

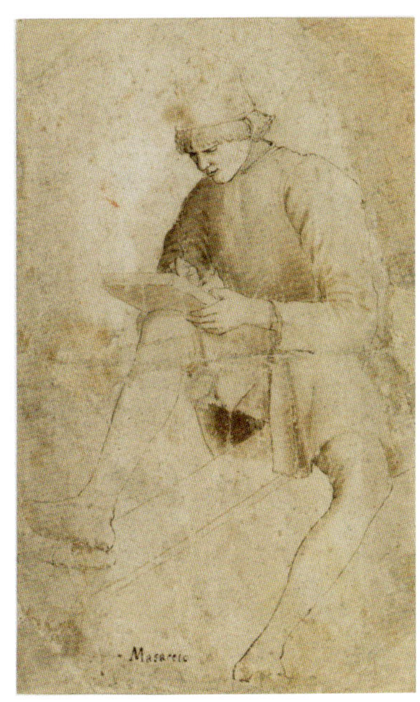

8. Workshop of Maso Finiguerra, *A Youth Drawing*, 1450s

Finiguerra was a goldsmith and designer who ran a workshop in Florence. This sketch of one of his young apprentices at work is one of several to have survived and is remarkable in that it has almost no corrections. Mastery in drawing meant mastery in all the visual arts.

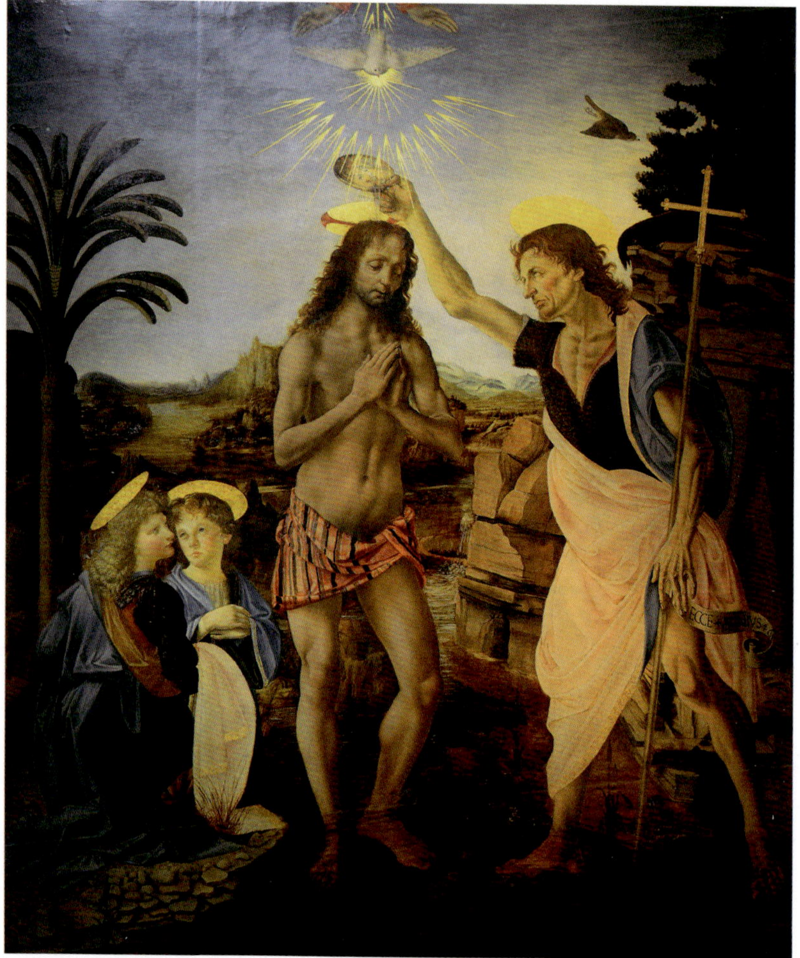

9. Andrea del Verrocchio, *The Baptism of Christ, c.* 1472–75

The painting depicts the baptism of Jesus by John the Baptist. Verrocchio ran a large and successful workshop in Florence. As one of his apprentices, Leonardo was made to study drawing, anatomy, sculpting and drapery. He painted the angel in the left-hand corner and also the landscape.

that all students had to master before they graduated to painting or sculpture. Cennini recommended that an apprentice should spend a year learning to draw, followed by six more years learning to prepare panels, apply gold and grind pigments. When Leonardo became the master of his own workshop, his pupils were not allowed to touch a paintbrush under the age of twenty.

Leonardo would have learned to draw by copying from model books – a sort of image bank and one of the chief treasures of a workshop – which contained studies of figures, animals, plants, faces and motifs. As apprentices repeatedly copied from the model books, they also assimilated the master's style. 'What does the pupil look for in the master?' wrote the Dominican friar, Girolamo Savonarola. 'I'll tell you. The master draws from his mind an image which his hands trace on paper and it carries the imprint of his idea. The pupil studies the drawing and tries to imitate it. Little by little, in this way he appropriates the style of the master...'[7]

ONE / THE DIRECTION OF A MASTER

The drawing implements used by pupils included pen and ink, chalk, silverpoint – a silver stylus sharpened at both ends – and charcoal, which was made from slowly roasted willow sticks (the lead pencil did not come into use until the early seventeenth century). The silverpoint was employed to draw on vellum, paper or on wood panels. The panel, usually made from poplar, had first to be sealed by using up to three layers of liquid size (water-based animal glue), often followed by a layer of linen fabric. Then came layers of thick gesso, a water-based paint made with chalk and size, resembling plaster of Paris. These were followed by layers of thin gesso, which then had to be smoothed down. It was up to the assistants to get the surface so finely burnished that it resembled ivory. The panel was then ready to be drawn on, painted or gilded. Before the appearance of India rubber in the late eighteenth century, mistakes were erased with the soft interior of freshly baked bread, or a feather.

Before any painting began, the master produced a full-scale drawing called a cartoon (a detailed preparatory drawing to scale). An assistant

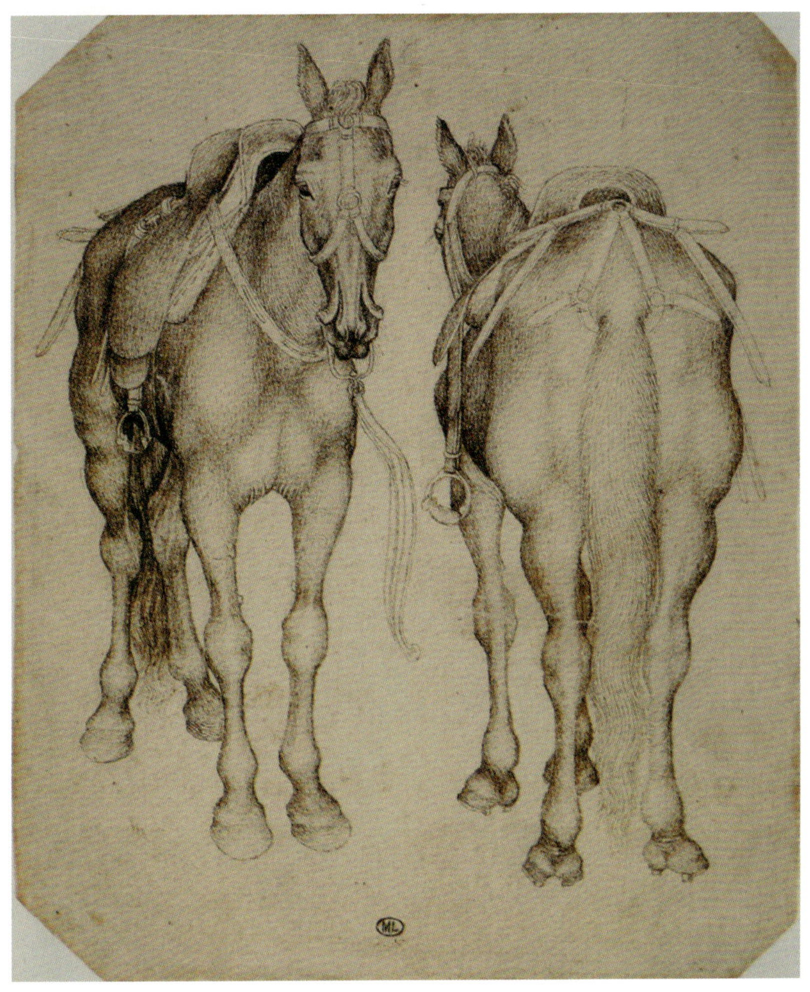

10. Antonio Pisanello, *Two Horses*, fifteenth century

By reproducing Pisanello's numerous drawings from his model books, his apprentices would not only absorb his artistic vocabulary but also learn his method of drawing, gaining the eye-to-hand skills to enable them to make life drawings of their own in their master's style.

11. Leonardo da Vinci, *Drapery Study
for a Seated Figure*, 1470–80

It is almost inconceivable what
breathtaking beauty Leonardo could
create with such drapery studies.
This investigation of drapery folds
was made possible by dipping a
length of fabric in clay slip and
arranging it over a figure made
of clay or wax. As the slip-soaked
textiles set, the results could be
studied from different angles and
lighting conditions.

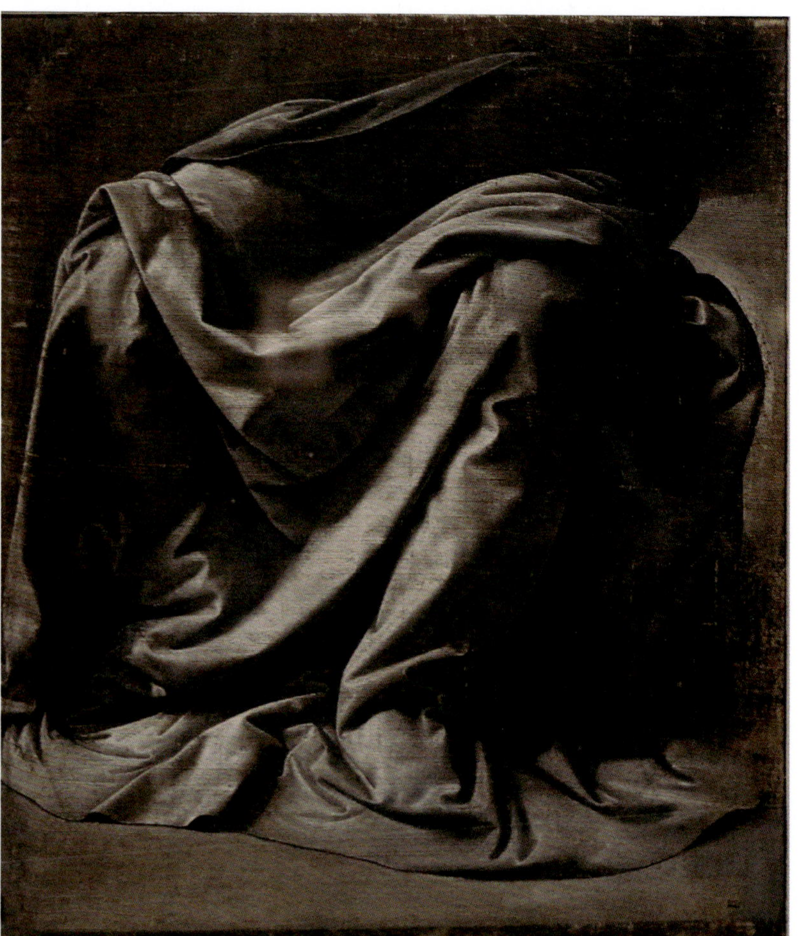

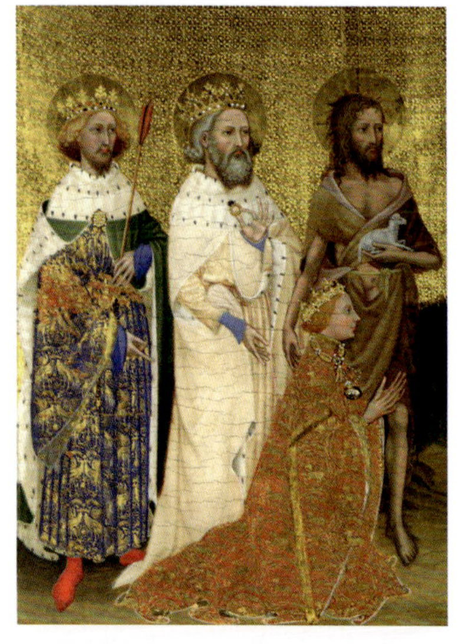

12. Anon, *Wilton Diptych*, c. 1395–99
(detail)

This small, portable altarpiece, made
for Richard II, is one of a handful
of English panel paintings to have
survived from the Middle Ages.
The panel shows Richard being
presented to the Virgin and Christ
Child. The exquisite incised and
punched patterns in the gold are
clearly visible.

pricked fine holes along the lines of the drawing, then placed the pierced
drawing on the prepared panel and pounced (dusted) powdered
charcoal through the perforations. This process left tiny dots of powder
on the surface beneath. An accurate copy of the drawing was made by
simply connecting the dots.

If areas of the gessoed panel were to be gilded, they were mapped
out and covered with red bole (clay) before successive sheets of wafer-
thin gold leaf were applied, which were then burnished. The gold was
often decorated with complex incised or punched patterns, especially
for haloes or details of costumes. When seen by flickering candlelight
in a dark church, the panels gleamed and shimmered. As an obviously
expensive commodity, gold was reserved for the most prestigious
commissions or the richest clients.

Until oil paint replaced it during the Renaissance, the paint
commonly used was egg tempera, a medium known to the ancient
Egyptians who used it to decorate their tombs and mummy cases.
It was made by binding ground pigments with egg yolks thinned

     ONE / THE DIRECTION OF A MASTER

with water. Cennini specified that 'When painting young faces, use the [light] yolk of a city hen,' but for mature faces the darker yolks of country hens was preferable.[8] (This sort of detail emphasises how well the Renaissance artist understood his materials.) Tempera dried very quickly, so it could neither be stored for future use nor blended on the painting's surface. The different shades had to be mixed in advance, then applied colour by colour with fine paintbrushes often made from the hairs of an ermine's tail. Michelangelo's unfinished painting of the Madonna and child with St John and Angels – known as the *Manchester Madonna* since its celebrated appearance in an exhibition in Manchester in the nineteenth century – shows the jigsaw-like process of a tempera painting to perfection.

The claim that Jan van Eyck invented oil painting – which had originated with Vasari – has long been discredited. Oil had indeed been used before, but as a transparent glaze applied over tempera. Van Eyck (and possibly his brother Hubert), however, proved that pigments bound with oil had a far greater flexibility, radiance, translucence and intensity of colour than tempera, which dries, with lightning speed, to a flat, dull surface. (Michelangelo remained unconvinced, declaring that 'Oil painting is for women, and slow and slovenly people.'[9]) Van Eyck's glorious *Portrait of a Man in a Red Turban* (see p. 12) – which is thought to be a self-portrait – brilliantly conveys the rich effects that are possible with oil paint. It has continued to be the dominant painting medium in Europe since the sixteenth century.

The pigments for both oil paint and tempera were bought from druggists and had to be ground to a paste with an egg-shaped muller on a grinding stone. If the artist was painting in tempera, the pigment was then added to an egg-water mixture. Every colour had its own characteristics and properties, and an apprentice had to learn how to deal with each one. Some minerals, such as lapis lazuli, were so hard that they had first to be reduced by pounding with a pestle and mortar. Preparing colours was one of the most skilled and labour-intensive tasks in a workshop. 'The great frescoes and panel paintings of the Renaissance are as much about materials as they are about form or subject.'[10]

The availability of some pigments and the subsequent introduction of others has helped shape the history of art. The pre-eminent pigment of early Italian painting was the vivid blue called *oltremare*, or ultramarine (literally, from across the sea), made by grinding the semi-precious gemstone lapis lazuli (Latin for 'the blue stone') to a powder. Prior to the eighteenth century, the sole source of lapis lazuli was mines deep in the mountains of Afghanistan from whence it travelled by donkey or camel along the Silk Road until it reached Syria, where it

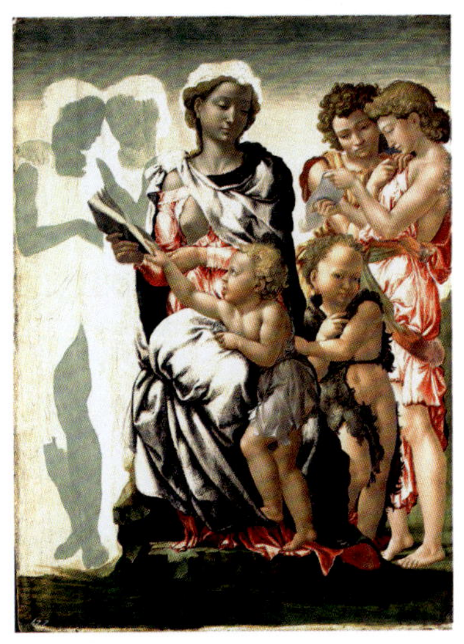

13. Michelangelo, *The Manchester Madonna*, c. 1494

This unfinished work shows how a tempera painting was built up. Michelangelo has made good progress with the Madonna, the Child and the infant St John the Baptist, but the *terre verte* that he used to underpaint flesh tones has only been applied to two of the four angels.

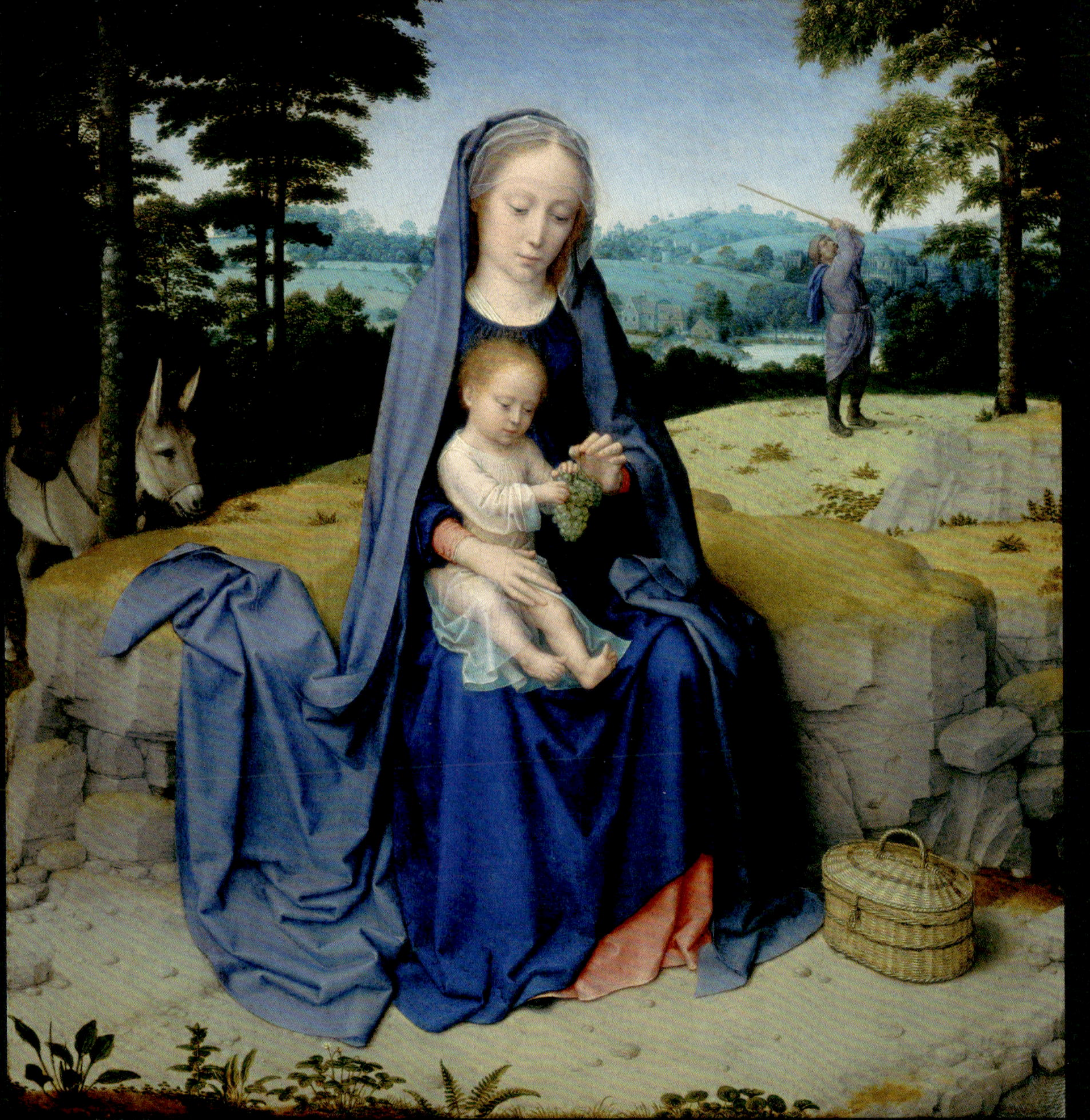

14. Gerard David, *The Rest on the Flight into Egypt*, *c.* 1510

From the Middle Ages, the colour most associated with the Virgin Mary was ultramarine, used here for her cloak. As valuable as gold, its use was a sign of the esteem in which the Virgin was held. Its precise use was a key point in many contracts drawn up between artists and their patrons.

was transported by ship to Venice – in all a journey of 3,500 miles. It is little wonder that it was fiendishly expensive and seldom used by artists unless they had rich patrons who could afford to pay for it. (Around 1704 a Berlin scientist accidentally discovered a way to make a blue that cost a fraction of the price of ultramarine. Named Prussian blue, it immediately became popular with artists throughout Europe.)

Certain pigments came from surprising sources: sepia was extracted from cuttle fish; purple from the shell of murex sea snails found in the Mediterranean; Indian yellow, although not imported to Europe from the East until the late 1700s, was said to be made 'from the urine of Indian cows that had been fed on mango leaves and then deprived of water' (a brilliant example of its use is J.M.W. Turner's *The Burning of the House of Lords and Commons* on page 101).[11] Vermilion, originally made by grinding the mercury ore called cinnabar, had been in use for 2,000 years; the rich red walls of luxurious dwellings in Pompeii are proof of its strength, durability and intensity. During the Renaissance, its regal colour was often reserved for the cloaks of cardinals and saints.

Until the collapsible metal tube was invented in 1841, each pigment in its powdered form was stored in a skin bladder, tied at the neck like a miniature suet pudding. Artists had to puncture the bladder with a sharp tack, then plug it up again after use. The metal tube revolutionised the way in which artists worked, both in the studio and out of doors.

Venice, with its trading tentacles extending to ports in the Adriatic and the Mediterranean, was an entrepôt for luxury items, which included the plants and minerals that formed the basis for an artist's colours; by the sixteenth century it had become renowned for the quality of its pigments. As a maritime power, the city was also rich in sailmakers who were able to produce huge linen canvas sheets of varying weights and weaves. Aided by the development of oil paint, canvas gradually replaced the wooden panels that had been used as a support throughout the Renaissance. It was cheaper, lighter, easier to store and paintings on canvas could be detached from their stretchers, rolled up and carried about. It was also simpler to prepare than wood panels, which required hours of laborious layering until the surface was fit to paint on. By the end of the sixteenth century, it had become the customary support for western painters. Two centuries later it was possible to buy commercially prepared canvases stretched to standard sizes.

As well as learning to draw, paint, gild and to prepare colours and mediums, linear perspective was another skill that an apprentice like Leonardo had to master. 'Perspective is to painting,' he wrote in his *Notebooks,* 'what the bridle is to the horse, the rudder to a ship.'[12] The Florentine architect Filippo Brunelleschi, who was responsible for the dome on Florence Cathedral, is credited with being the first to

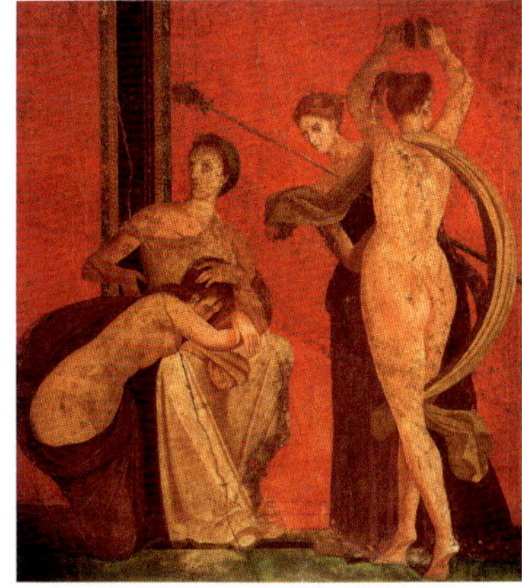

15. Fresco from the Villa of the Mysteries, Pompeii, before AD 79

Famed for its strength, richness and intensity, vermilion was used by the ancient Romans to paint statues of their gods and emperors on feast days. Here it decorates the walls of one of the luxurious dwellings at Pompeii.

invent perspective. The effect of this device in the first known work to use linear perspective, Masaccio's *Holy Trinity*, is dramatic: as Vasari commented, 'the coffered vault appears to recede so skilfully that the surface looks indented'.[13] It is difficult for viewers to believe that they are looking at a painted fresco on a flat wall.

Fresco was the great painting medium of the Renaissance. It was the quintessential product of the workshop's collaborative system, often involving its entire staff. For Cennini, it was 'the sweetest and subtlest technique that exists'.[14] Hundreds of churches, town halls and palaces provided artists with decades of work painting their walls. But painting a fresco had to be executed in situ – be it in a church, the interior of a palace or private house – and this required the artists and apprentices to take their workshop tools with them.

The drawing by Federico Zuccaro of his brother Taddeo painting the facade of Palazzo Mattei shows a fresco in progress. A scaffold has been built against the end wall of the palace, and an awning erected above the platform to protect the artists from the sun and to prevent the plaster from drying out. The word fresco means 'fresh' in Italian, which is the key factor in the process – known as *buon fresco* or true fresco – since it involved applying pure powdered pigments, mixed with water, straight on to a wet, freshly laid layer of lime plaster (*intonaco*). The artists had to work quickly on small sections at a time before the plaster dried, as the brushstrokes were immediately absorbed by the *intonaco*. The separate sections were called *giornate*, since each corresponded to a day's work. Some paintings were also made using *secco fresco*, in which paint was applied to plaster that had already dried.

Frescoing was particularly well suited to the private chapel, where large areas of wall space could be decorated quickly without enormous expense. One of the most famous examples is the Scrovegni,

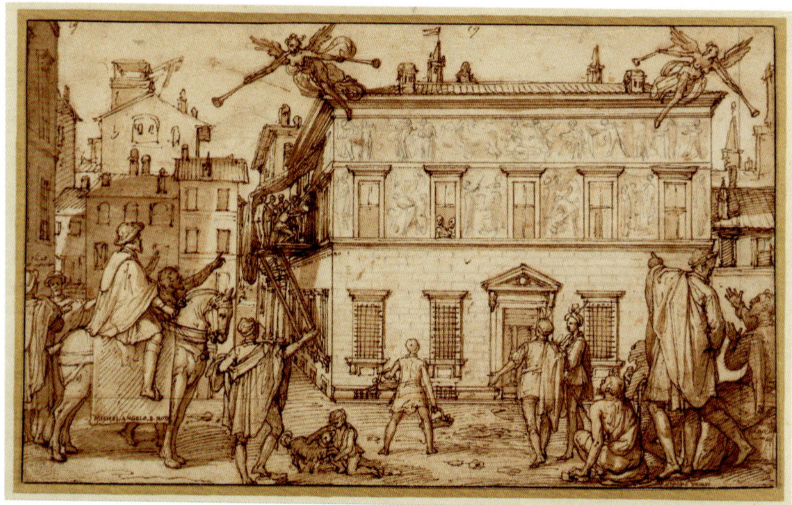

16. Federico Zuccaro, *Taddeo Zuccaro Decorating the Facade of Palazzo Mattei, c.* 1595

Taddeo sits precariously on the scaffolding, painting the fresco with a long brush. Michelangelo, mounted on a horse instead of his habitual mule, views Taddeo's progress. Vasari is deep in conversation on the far right. The facade was hailed as a masterpiece and cemented young Taddeo's reputation.

ONE / THE DIRECTION OF A MASTER

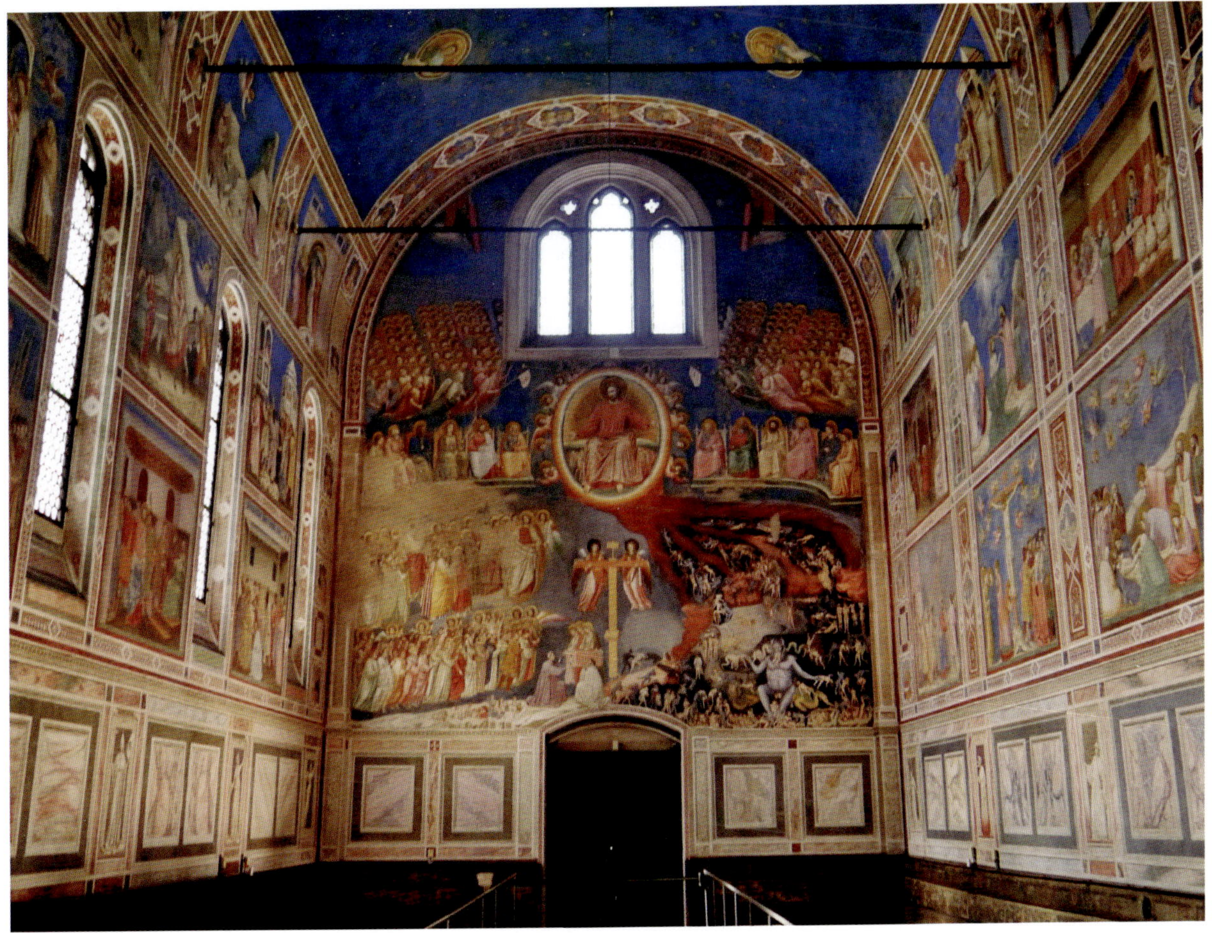

or Arena, Chapel in Padua, every sublime inch of which was painted in tempera by Giotto in around 1300.

Another glorious example of fresco is *The Procession of the Magi*, painted by Benozzo Gozzoli (*c.* 1421–97). It was commissioned by the Medici family for their private chapel in Palazzo Medici in Florence. Based on the biblical account of the three Magi, the artist has created a sumptuous procession of the Medici family, their allies and some of the important figures who had attended the Council of Florence several decades earlier. Festive processions were extremely popular in Renaissance Italy as they combined lavish display and fancy dress, thus providing a welcome distraction from everyday life.

The angelic figure riding a white horse is an idealised portrait of the ten-year-old Lorenzo (later to be known as Lorenzo the Magnificent) in the role of Caspar, one of the three Magi. Gozzoli has portrayed him as a beautiful youth whereas he grew up to be spectacularly ugly with bulging eyes and a flattened nose. The horse's bridle bears the Medici family devices of golden balls and ostrich plumes.[15]

17. Scrovegni Chapel, Padua, *c.* 1300

Giotto covered the Chapel's walls with frescoes showing episodes from the life of Christ in a dramatic way that was totally new. The postures of the figures are more natural, their expressions more realistic. Giotto used a fabulous amount of the costly lapis lazuli to paint the ceiling.

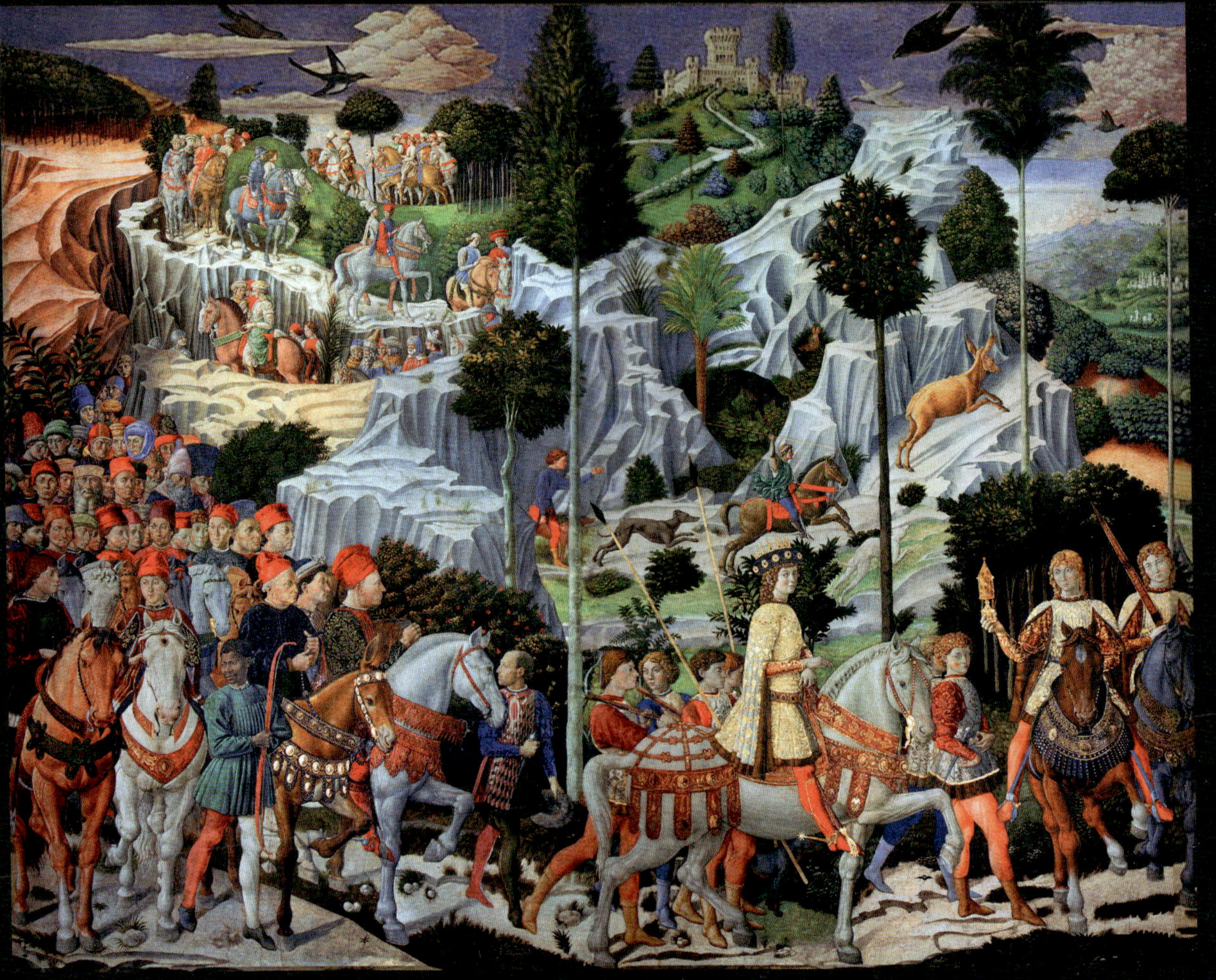

18. Benozzo Gozzoli, *The Procession of the Magi*, Palazzo Medici, Florence, 1459–63

Gozzoli covered three sides of the Medici family chapel with this glorious series of frescoes, each wall depicting one of the three kings accompanied by his train of servants. Riding his white charger, a youthful Lorenzo wears robes of velvet and brocade, interwoven with gold thread – all products of the thriving Florentine textile industry.

Blue was a particular problem, and skies and blue robes were often added *a secco* because neither azurite blue nor ultramarine – the only blue pigments then available – worked well in wet fresco. A letter from Gozzoli to Piero de' Medici, who had commissioned him to paint *The Procession of the Magi*, illustrates the difficulties of using blue. The artist had requested an advance so that he could buy the large quantities of the costly ultramarine that he needed for the fresco: 'I started applying the blue early this morning, the heat is great and the size is quickly spoiled.'[16]

Damp is the great enemy of fresco. It attacks the fabric of the *intonaco*, robbing it of its resistance and cohesiveness. As nitrates and other salts reach the surface, they destroy the colour and cause the paint to disintegrate and fall off in tiny flakes. This happened on a terrifying scale in 1966 when the River Arno burst its banks and swept through Florence. The only way to save the city's frescoes was to detach them from the walls, even though many of them were still wet. In all, 2,322.5 sqm were detached, restored and replaced.[17]

Renaissance artists were nothing if not flexible: they were able to paint studio portraits, altarpieces, cover walls with large areas of fresco and also create exquisitely decorated portable items. Included among this amazing variety were the *cassoni*, or storage chests. They were expensive and prized pieces of furniture, common in most Renaissance houses. The chest itself was made by a carpenter and then delivered to a *bottega* to be painted and gilded. Artists would decorate not only the sides but the outside and inside of the lid, so that wherever the chest stood, part of its decoration would be visible.[18] Although the *cassoni* were made for many occasions, the majority were for marriages and would accompany the bride and her dowry to her new home. Scenes from the Old Testament, the *Odyssey*, mythological and moral subjects were the most popular, the latter to encourage the newlyweds to live upright lives.

The products of the workshop to have survived in the greatest numbers are altarpieces. They took various forms, ranging from the single panel to diptychs, triptychs, even polyptychs that consisted of several panels often arranged in tiers. Some diptychs were portable

19. Giovanni di ser Giovanni Guidi (called Scheggia), *Cassone Adimari*, *c*.1450

The painting on this *cassone* shows an elegant wedding parade taking place in Florence. In the centre, a line of noblemen and noblewomen, wearing superb flowing garments, move in graceful dance steps under a colourful drapery, accompanied by musicians under the small loggia on the left.

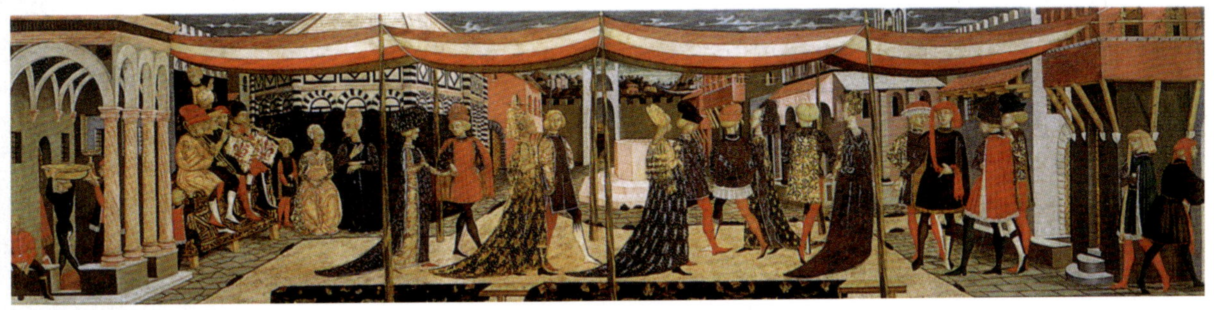

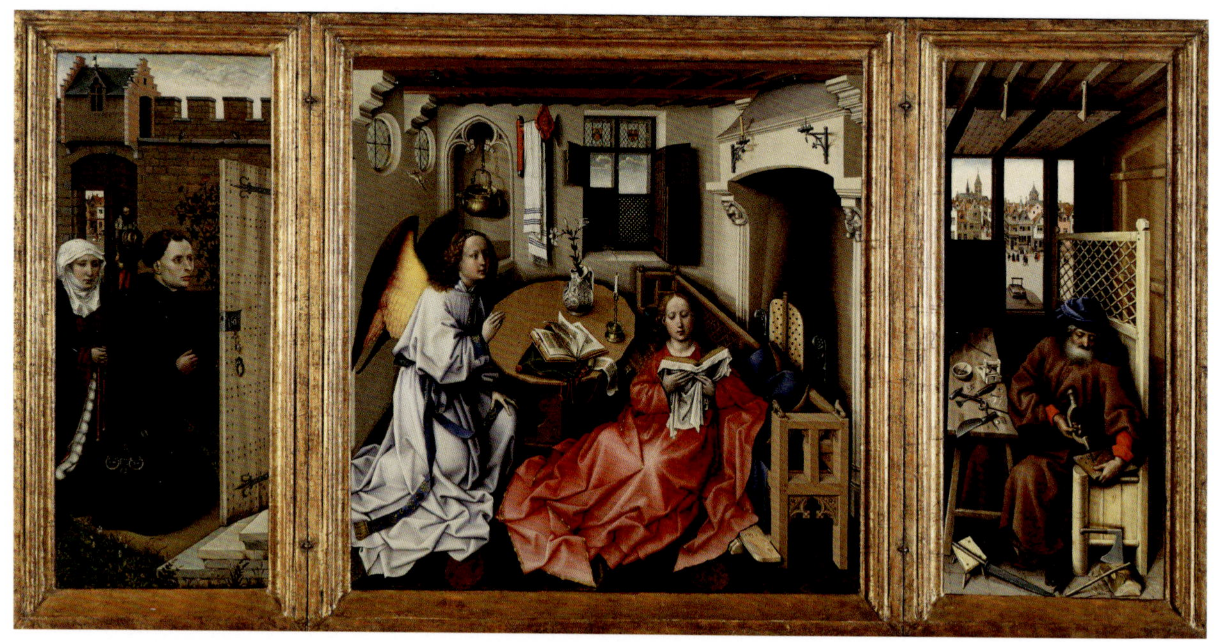

20. Robert Campin, *The Mérode Altarpiece, c.* 1427–32

A triptych like this was not intended for a church but served as a house altar. The patrons, kneeling on the left, would pray before it every day. The Holy Ghost is also in the room, signalled by the extinguished candle on the table. The centre panel shows one of the earliest known representations of a room in a bourgeois home.

as they could be folded in half and slipped into a pocket, available for private worship wherever its owner might be. Everyone had a personal saint to whom they prayed, as well as other saints to be called upon in times of need: for instance, St Apollonia was good for toothache, St Lucy for eye trouble, St Christopher for travellers. Life was permeated by saints and their particular stories to a degree that is hard to imagine today.

As altarpieces were often commissioned from major artists, many of them are remarkable works of art. Robert Campin's *Mérode Triptych* is a superb example. It shows the Virgin Mary seated in a typical northern European bourgeois interior, intent on her book. She seems as yet unaware of the arrival of the Angel Gabriel, or of the tiny child carrying a wooden cross who is descending on a beam of light in the top left-hand corner of the image. The child symbolises Mary's virgin pregnancy and Christ's death on the cross.[19] On the right panel, Joseph is busy drilling a hole in a piece of wood, oblivious that his life is about to undergo a radical change. On the left panel the husband and wife who commissioned the altarpiece – the donors or patrons – kneel in reverence of the scene before them.

During the Renaissance, patronage played an immeasurable role in the production of all types of art. A workshop's commissions came from many sources: public bodies and private individuals, sacred and secular institutions. Splendid furnishings – like *cassoni* – in a patron's house enhanced his prestige within society; commissioning a gold encrusted altarpiece or frescoes to decorate an entire chapel – as in the

ONE / THE DIRECTION OF A MASTER

Scrovegni Chapel – spread a patron's power and prestige far beyond the limits of his city. The son of an infamous banker, Enrico Scrovegni's magnificent gift to Padua was made in part to demonstrate his piety. Expiation of sins or guilt about the accumulation of wealth were often the motivations behind a donor's munificence. In short, he was trying to buy himself a place in Heaven.

In the Renaissance workshop, literally every pigment had to be ground, every brush assembled, every wood panel painstakingly prepared, every canvas cut to size and stretched on to its wooden frame, and it was here that these skills evolved and were honed to perfection. The quality and sheer craft of objects produced by the workshops 'are among the most beautifully made in the entire history of Western art'.[20] By the early eighteenth century the working lives of artists had been relieved of much of the drudgery of preparing the tools of their craft. Edgar Degas was later to declare that artists had lost these techniques: 'Beauty is a mystery,' he wrote, 'but no one knows it any more. The recipes, the secrets, have been forgotten.'[21]

From the late fifteenth century the artist began to be recognised as superior to the skilled craftsman. Art was no longer regarded as a trade, but more as a learned calling. Young men, who had served several years as apprentices learning strictly manual and technical procedures – as well as the practice of drawing – felt they needed more advanced teaching than they were able to receive from the master of a busy workshop. 'He is a poor pupil,' Leonardo wrote, 'who does not go beyond his master.'[22] This need was to be met by the newly formed academies.

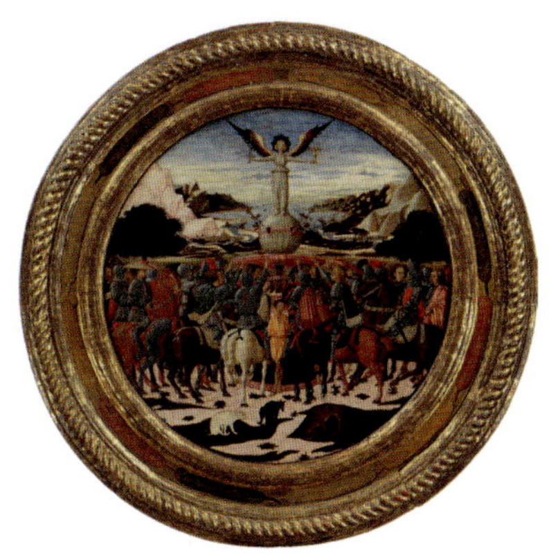

21. Giovanni di ser Giovanni Guidi (called Scheggia), *A Birth Tray*, *c.* 1449

Renaissance workshops produced an enormous range of beautifully crafted objects, both religious and secular. The latter included items such as 'birth trays' on which food was offered to expectant mothers.

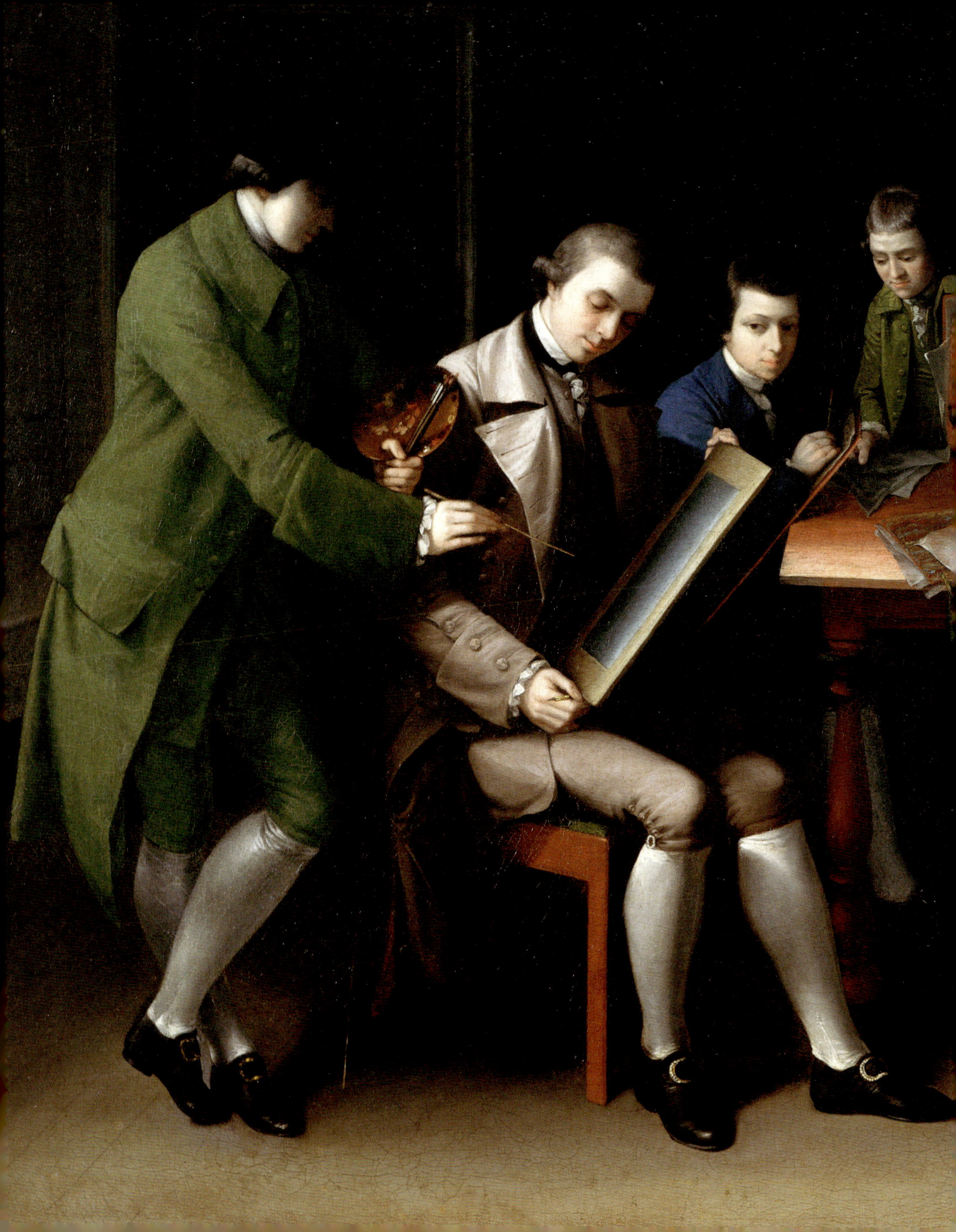

TWO

Nurturing Talent, Instilling Discipline

The Teaching Studio

THE MOST FAMOUS OF THE EARLY academies, and certainly the first public one, was the Accademia del Disegno, established in Florence in 1563 by Vasari under the joint patronage of Cosimo de' Medici and Michelangelo. Its title was significant: *disegno,* or drawing – especially 'after the life' – was the foundation of an artistic education, 'the master skill from which all other visual arts flowed'.[2] However, it was far more than just drawing lines on a piece of paper, but rather the creative inspiration that forms in the human mind. The artist was no longer an artisan, working with his hands, but a man of learning, developing his skills by reflection and experiment.[3] To this end, the academy's pupils also studied anatomy, the principles of antiquity, perspective, poetry and mythology. Leonardo was trained within a tradition of painting where 'every feature, the principals and the extras alike, the birds in the sky, the green forest and every single leaf of it, are all granted an equal and undiminished right to exist'.[4]

There were also private academies. As early as 1498 there is evidence that Leonardo had an 'academy' in Milan, but it was more of a debating society, a club, attended by men of science and the arts. The Carracci family of artists – the brothers Agostino and Annibale and their cousin Ludovico – established the most well-known private academy in Bologna in about 1582. They were all superb draughtsmen, and one of the first accounts of them records that even at mealtimes they had 'bread in one hand and a pencil or charcoal in the other'.[5]

OPPOSITE: **22.** Matthew Pratt, *The American School*, 1765 (detail)

This is the first major American studio picture. It depicts a scene in the London studio of the American artist Benjamin West, who is the figure standing at the left. The composition explores the academic tradition as carried out among Americans in late eighteenth-century London.

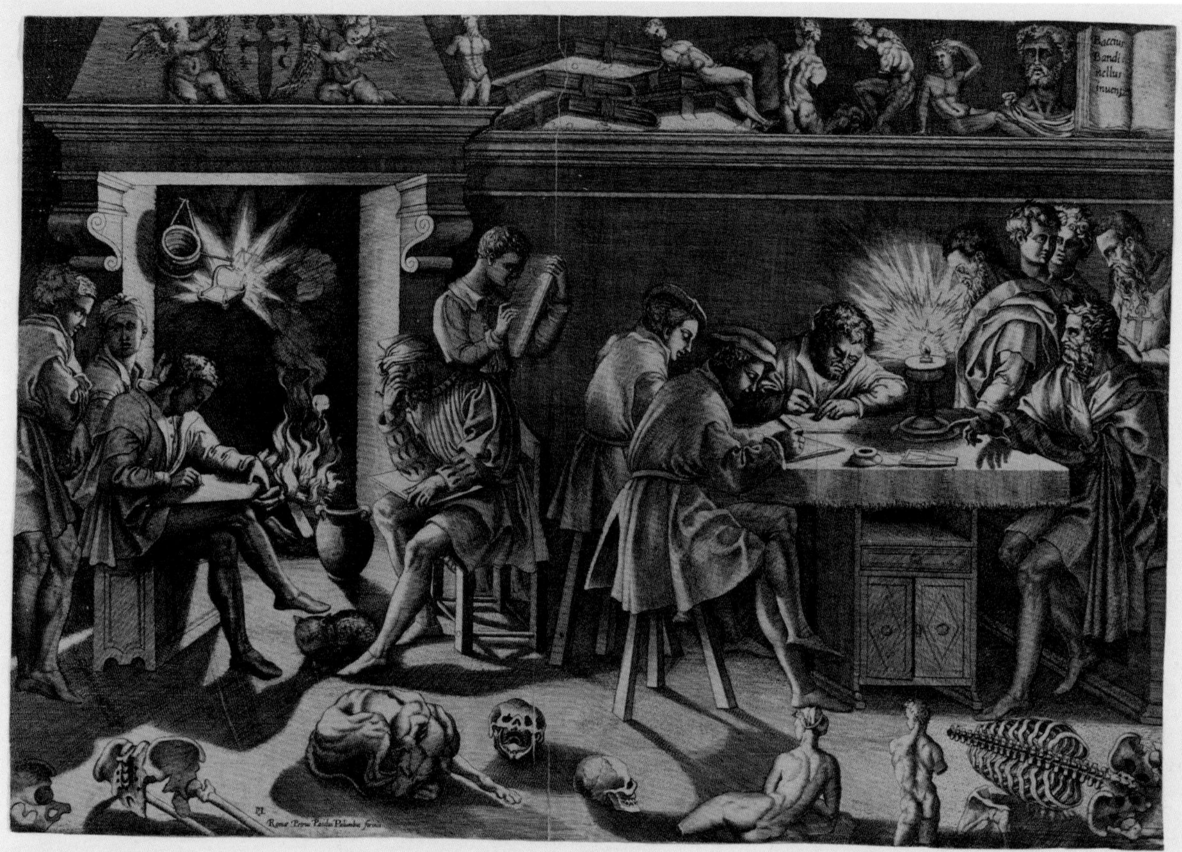

23. Enea Vico after Baccio Bandinelli, *Bandinelli's Night Class*, 1545–50

The Florentine sculptor, Baccio Bandinelli, established one of the earliest academies. The studio is equipped with books and antiquities, thus presenting the making of art as an intellectual enterprise, not simply an art school. The skulls and skeletons show the importance accorded to the study of anatomy.

Federico Zuccaro, whose *Early Life of Taddeo* is so revealing about the hardships endured by his brother during his apprenticeship, also founded a private academy, the Accademia di San Luca in Rome, which became the prototype for all European academies of art. Again, the basic message is consistent: that 'drawing is the father of all the arts'.[6] An etching of his Academy shows a group of artists receiving an anatomy lesson by dissecting a corpse. Artists were intensely curious about how things worked, especially the human body. Both Leonardo and Michelangelo dissected numerous corpses, the latter beginning the process in his late teens and continuing for most of the rest of his life. For obvious reasons, this gruesome procedure was scheduled for the winter months. Rotting corpses were known to have caused sickness and even madness among artists.[7]

An academy's pupils would draw on paper (made from pulped rags) which, by the fourteenth century, was being extensively made in Italy, its manufacture then spreading throughout Europe. However, it was still quite expensive, and artists tended to use every inch of both sides of a sheet of paper. Hence Leonardo's mixtures of wildly unrelated subjects, such as an intricate drawing of violets alongside his suggested technique

     TWO / NURTURING TALENT, INSTILLING DISCIPLINE

(plus diagrams) for soldering a lead covering on to a roof. Michelangelo, who was obsessively frugal, would scour the litter in his studio for paper that might still have some spare space which he could use.

Although academies proliferated throughout Italy during the sixteenth century, other countries were slow to follow suit. A Dutch artist, Michael Sweerts (1618–64), opened an academy in Brussels in 1659 and a painting of it (see page 47) shows the students drawing from a partially nude youth. However, artists like Rembrandt and Rubens were taught by the master of a workshop and, subsequently, set up workshops of their own. One source estimates that Rembrandt taught over fifty students during the course of his career, stowing them away in cubicles in the attic of his house in Amsterdam. As their parents had to pay a considerable fee for their instruction, and as Rembrandt sold their paintings and prints profitably, he was making good money from his students.

Judging by the large number of images of pupils attending one of Rembrandt's life classes, the nude model played a dominant role in his teaching. There is a series of pen and wash drawings which show the same skinny boy in different poses. (As a studio master, Rembrandt was allowed to hire nude models, a practice that was otherwise illegal.[8]) Apparently, he was a hard taskmaster, once reducing his pupil Samuel van Hoogstraten to tears when he corrected his work.[9]

When the Académie Royale de Peinture et de Sculpture – along with the École des Beaux-Arts – was founded in Paris in 1648, it too proved to be a hard taskmaster, maintaining rigid control of the teaching methods and establishing a strict hierarchy of genres. History painting – the depiction of scenes from ancient literature, mythology and history – was deemed the most prestigious, followed some way behind by portraiture, genre, still life and landscape. (This hierarchy became so deep-rooted that artists were still fighting to get free of it three centuries later.) The pupils began by drawing from drawings, then drawing from plaster casts and, finally, were allowed to draw from the live nude model. The curriculum culminated in a competition for the coveted Grand Prix de Rome, the winner being awarded a scholarship to study in Rome.

The somewhat rigid curriculum and teaching methods of the academies were venerated and adhered to throughout the eighteenth and nineteenth centuries, and it is scarcely surprising that they came to be criticised as stultifying by increasingly innovative and inventive young artists. The Irish critic and novelist, George Moore, who attended a private art school in Paris in the 1870s, attacked the sterile teaching at the École. The obedient student, he wrote, would spend up to ten hours a day being 'taught to measure the model with his pencil, and

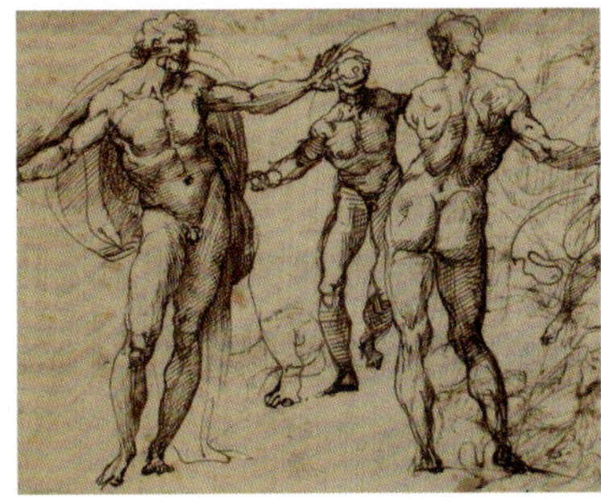

24. Agostino Carracci, *Male Nudes and Other Studies*, *c.* 1590 (detail)

The teaching at the Carracci family's academy in Bologna was principally based on drawing from the live model, nude and clothed, supplemented by drawing from plaster casts of classical sculpture. By hatching and cross-hatching, Agostino has added tone and weight to his figures.

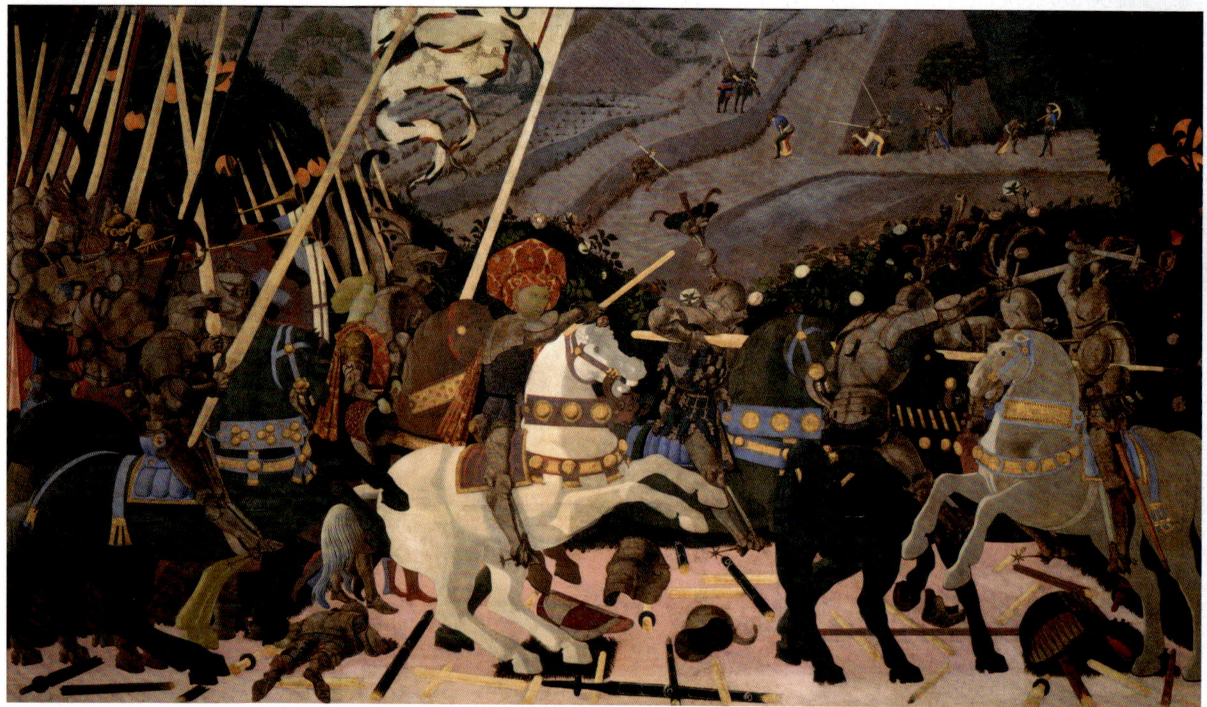

25. Paolo Uccello, *The Battle of San Romano*, 1456

Academies taught their pupils perspective and foreshortening. Uccello was obsessed with both techniques. The dead soldier in the left foreground of the battle must have caused a sensation at the time as it is possibly one of the earliest examples of foreshortening.

OPPOSITE: 26. Charles-Joseph Natoire, *Life Class at the Royal Academy of Painting and Sculpture*, 1746

Natoire was a professor at the Royal Academy in Paris. In this drawing, he depicts himself in a red cloak correcting a pupil's sketch. Other students are drawing from the two life models posing on the table in the centre. The paintings on the walls and casts of antique statues serve as time-honoured prototypes.

how to determine the movement of the model with his plumb-line. He is taught how to draw by the masses rather than by the character, and the advantages of this teaching permit him, if he is an intelligent fellow, to produce at the end of two years' hard labour a measured, angular, constipated drawing, a sort of inferior photograph.'[10] Moore makes no mention of the anatomy lessons provided by the École, however. John Shirley Fox, who joined the École when he was only fourteen, had an unnerving experience when the lecturer promised them a new and 'most admirable subject' to study. 'I was unfamiliar with death at that time,' recalled Shirley Fox, 'and it came somewhat as a shock to me to find that the body … was that of a young Italian whom I had known quite well by sight as a model during his life. The poor fellow had contracted pneumonia and died very quickly.'[11]

Claude Monet, a student at the private school run by Charles Gleyre, railed against the insistence that when drawing from life, the model should end up looking like a classical statue. Woe betide those who actually painted what they saw. Monet has left this account of how Gleyre used to reproach him: 'You've a dumpy little man there, and that's how you've gone and painted him! He's got big feet, so you gave him big feet! … Just remember this, young man: when you do a figure study, always have the antique in mind.'[12]

Although Gleyre's own paintings were largely in the academic tradition, he encouraged his pupils to try painting outdoors. This

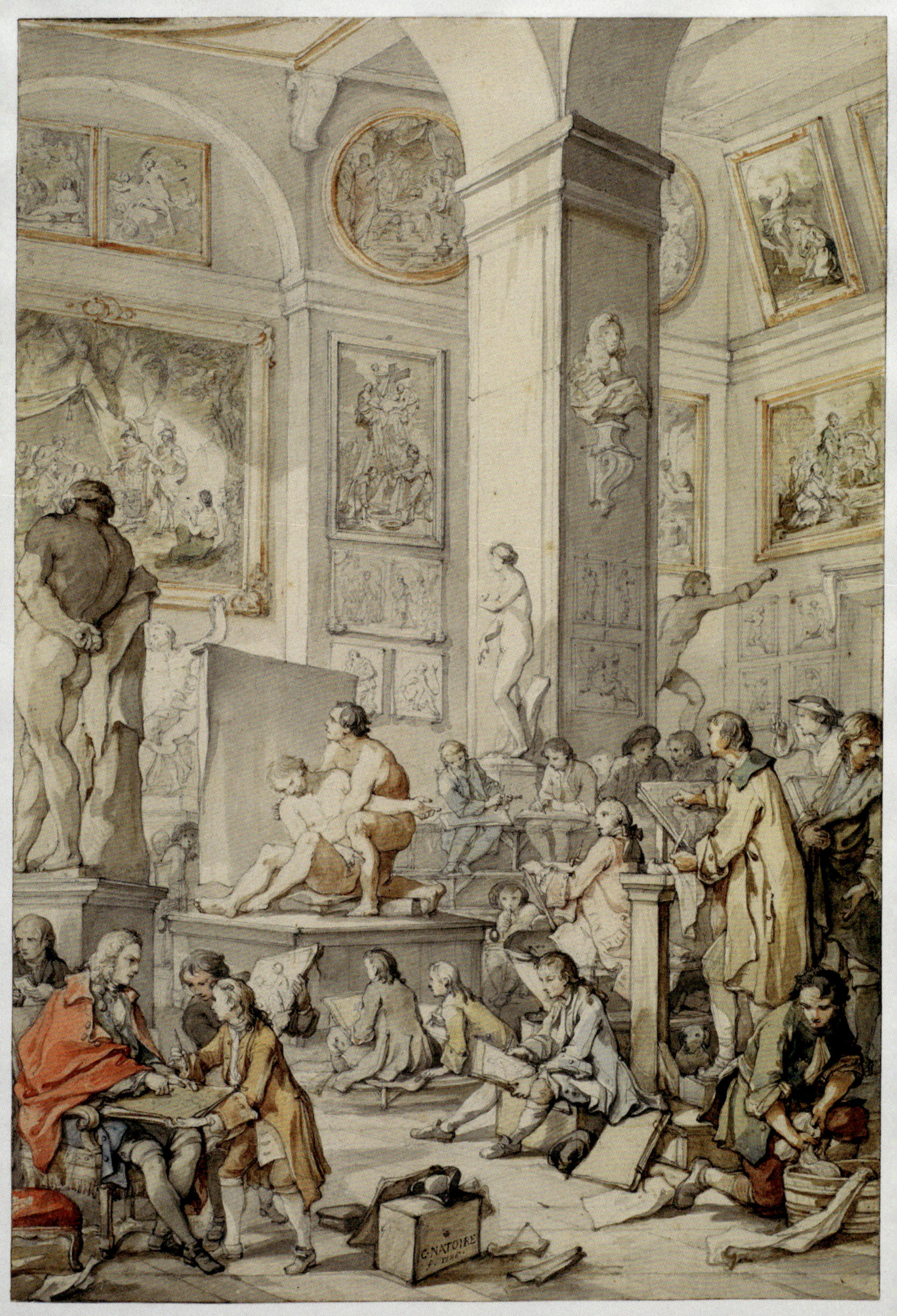

C. NATOIRE
f. 1746.

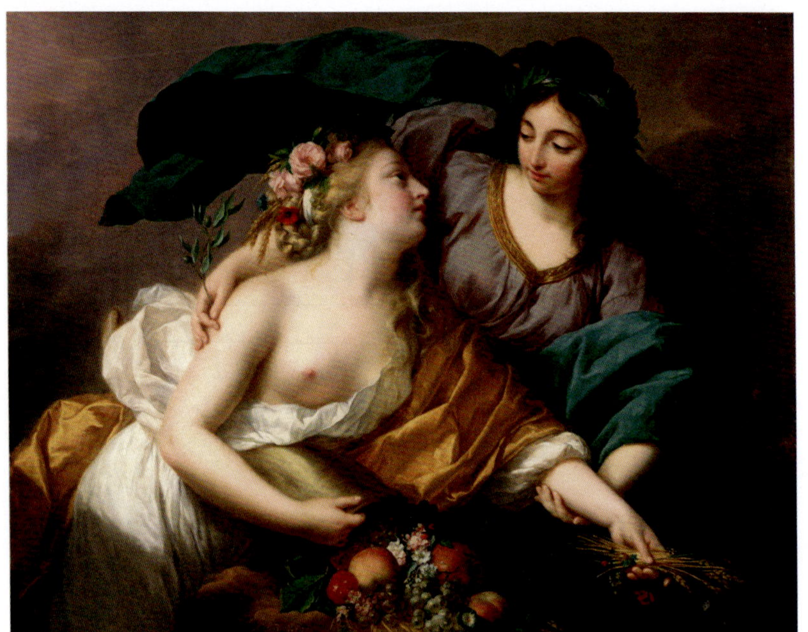

27. Élisabeth Vigée Le Brun, *Peace Bringing Back Abundance*, 1780

Painted while France was embroiled in the American War of Independence, the signing of the peace treaty in 1783 underscored the relevance of the painting's subject matter. Her submission of it as her reception-piece at last gained her membership of the Académie Royale.

was to have a long-term effect on not only Monet, but three of his fellow pupils: Renoir, Alfred Sisley and Frédéric Bazille. They became close friends and would later be counted among the leaders of the Impressionists.

Judging by students' accounts during the mid-nineteenth century, the treatment of new pupils at the École was similar to that of a new boy at an English boarding school. The pupil might be required to sing a song while stark naked or be hung upside down from the rungs of a ladder for a prolonged period. The moment French artist Jules Breton entered the studio to which he had been assigned he was surrounded 'by faces whose expressions, bantering, menacing, or strange, absolutely terrified me', all the while being beaten over the head with cushions.[13] This initiation ceremony seems mild when compared to a friend of the artist Ernest Meissonier whose treatment could have ended in his death or impalement. 'He had to jump from a considerable height, out of a loft, from which the ladder had been carefully removed, after the floor had been piled with studio stools, turned legs upward.'[14] However, it was the mighty École des Beaux-Arts which won the dubious prize for initiation ceremonies. 'One poor fellow was tied nude in a basket hung from a hook in the ceiling, left all night, and was found dead in the morning.'[15]

Women artists were barred from joining the Académie until 1682, when seven of them were admitted. Élisabeth Vigée Le Brun, who was Marie-Antoinette's chosen portraitist and on her way to becoming an international celebrity, was accepted as a member in 1783. Ten years later, in the wake of the Revolution, the Académie was abolished. When it reopened in 1795, women were excluded from membership altogether. They were not to regain admission to the École until 1897 although, by then, its dominance in the world of artistic training was on the wane.

Beginning in 1667, the Académie sponsored the annual Salons, held in the Salon Carré of the Louvre. At that date, it was the only venue artists could exhibit their work – provided it had survived stringent scrutiny by the jury. Open to all comers, the exhibitions rapidly became the most important public entertainment in Paris, and heterogenous scrums as a result. The history paintings caused some bafflement among those who had not benefitted from a classical education. Louis-Sébastien Mercier in his *Tableaux de Paris* (published in the 1780s) describes the bemusement of some spectators: 'A typical idler takes the characters of myth to be heavenly saints, Typhoeus to be Gargantua, Charon to be St. Peter, a satyr to be a demon, and Noah's Ark to be the Auxerre coach.'[16] (It is a sobering thought that today's spectators would suffer from the same bemusement.)

It took Britain over a century to catch up with France, founding the Royal Academy of Arts in London in 1768. It had various homes before finally settling in its superb location on Piccadilly, with the statue of Sir Joshua Reynolds – its first President – resplendent on its plinth in the courtyard. Pupils attending the Academy's Schools followed much the same drawing course as was taught by the École des Beaux-Arts. The Schools' schedule also included lectures on anatomy, geometry and perspective, architecture and painting. What is surprising is the

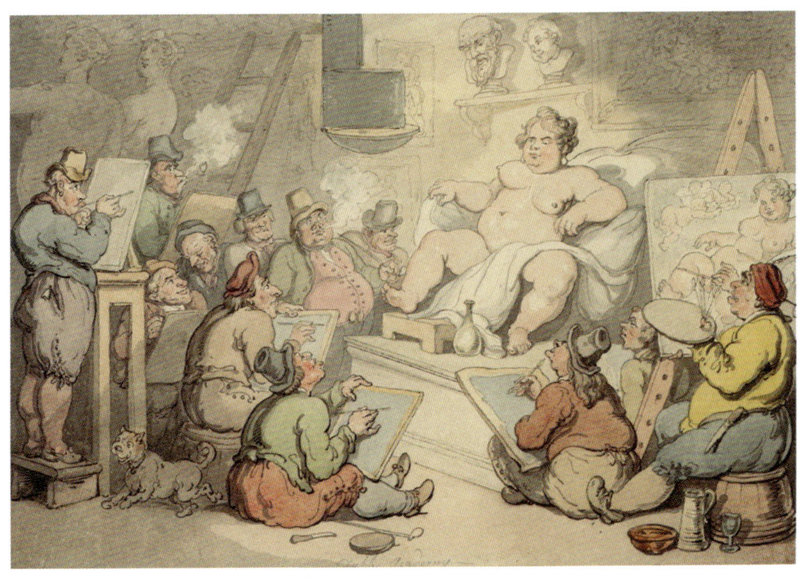

28. Thomas Rowlandson, *A Dutch Academy, c.* 1792

Rowlandson produced several views of life classes at the Royal Academy, although this painting satirises one in Holland. While a student at the Academy, he had upset the naked model by firing a pea at her from his peashooter. The pea had found its mark.

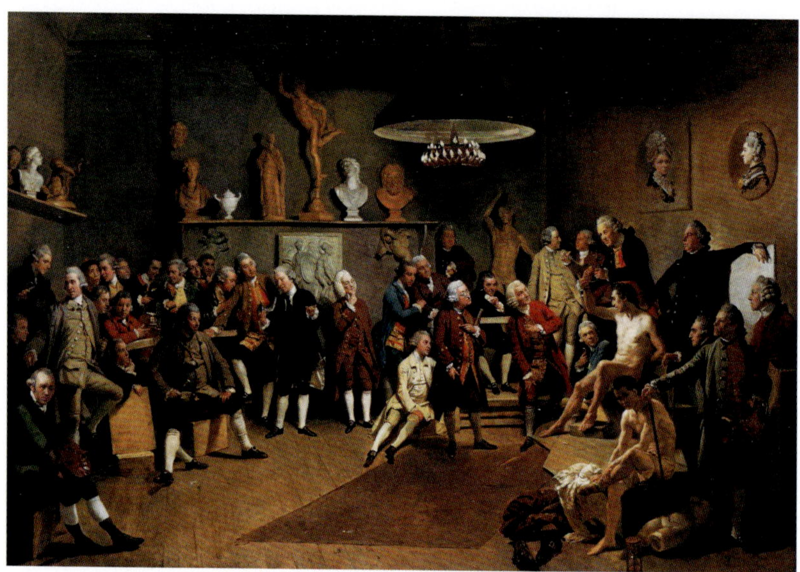

Zoffany's famous painting shows the founding members of the Academy attending the Academy's life class. Sir Joshua Reynolds is the standing figure wearing a black velvet suit, white stockings and holding an ear trumpet, as he was very deaf.

Academy's insistence on promoting history painting, as this type of painting had no pedigree in Britain where support had been found for only one type: portrait or 'face painting' – a term used by some portraitists.[17]

The Academy's emphasis on drawing is illustrated by the *Academicians of the Royal Academy* by Johann Zoffany (1733–1810) that imagines all the members assembled in the life class. The Keeper of the Schools is setting the pose by adjusting the knotted cord used to support the model's hand. The first model, the young man in the foreground, is getting dressed.

Drawings of the male nude often hid the genitalia under a piece of handily floating drapery or sometimes omitted them altogether. That this delicate dilemma persisted into the nineteenth century is indicated by the Academy's Council passing a resolution to the effect that the students were showing 'needless fidelity' when drawing the genitalia and they wished to 'dissuade' them 'from bestowing unnecessary attention on unimportant parts ...'[18]

The two female artists elected as founder members of the Royal Academy, Angelica Kauffman (1741–1807) and Mary Moser (1744–1819), were unable, on grounds of decency, to be present at the life class in person. Instead, the two women are represented by rather dim, unfinished portraits hung high on the wall, behind the group.

As in Paris, the Academy held annual summer exhibitions (which continue to this day) which attracted not only royalty and fashionable society but a potpourri of humanity who came to see who else was there as much as they came to look at the pictures.

By the end of the eighteenth century every large European city had its official art school or academy. In America, the first to open was the Pennsylvania Academy of the Fine Arts in Philadelphia, founded in 1805. All of them stressed the importance of drawing from the Old Masters, classical statues and the live model. Although many artists were later to criticise this rigid, traditional type of teaching, most major artists of the nineteenth century – including Degas, Seurat, Van Gogh and Matisse – had studied at an academy, either at a public or, if they could afford it, a private one.

Although France's most famous neoclassical artist, Jacques-Louis David (1748–1825), had been a pupil at the École des Beaux-Arts, he abandoned its strict curriculum when he established his own private teaching studios in the Louvre, stressing instead the importance of drawing from the live model. An admiring former student described his teaching methods: 'He sought to utilise the particular faculties that nature had given to each of his disciples. In a word, he developed their talent instead of seeking to transmit to them his own. This is what

30. Jean-Henri Cless, *David's Studio*, *c.*1804

This is one of David's two teaching studios in the Louvre. The student on the ladder is adjusting the lighting so that it falls on the live model. The woman posing on the right is a plaster cast of a Greco-Roman statue. David himself is instructing a student on the extreme left.

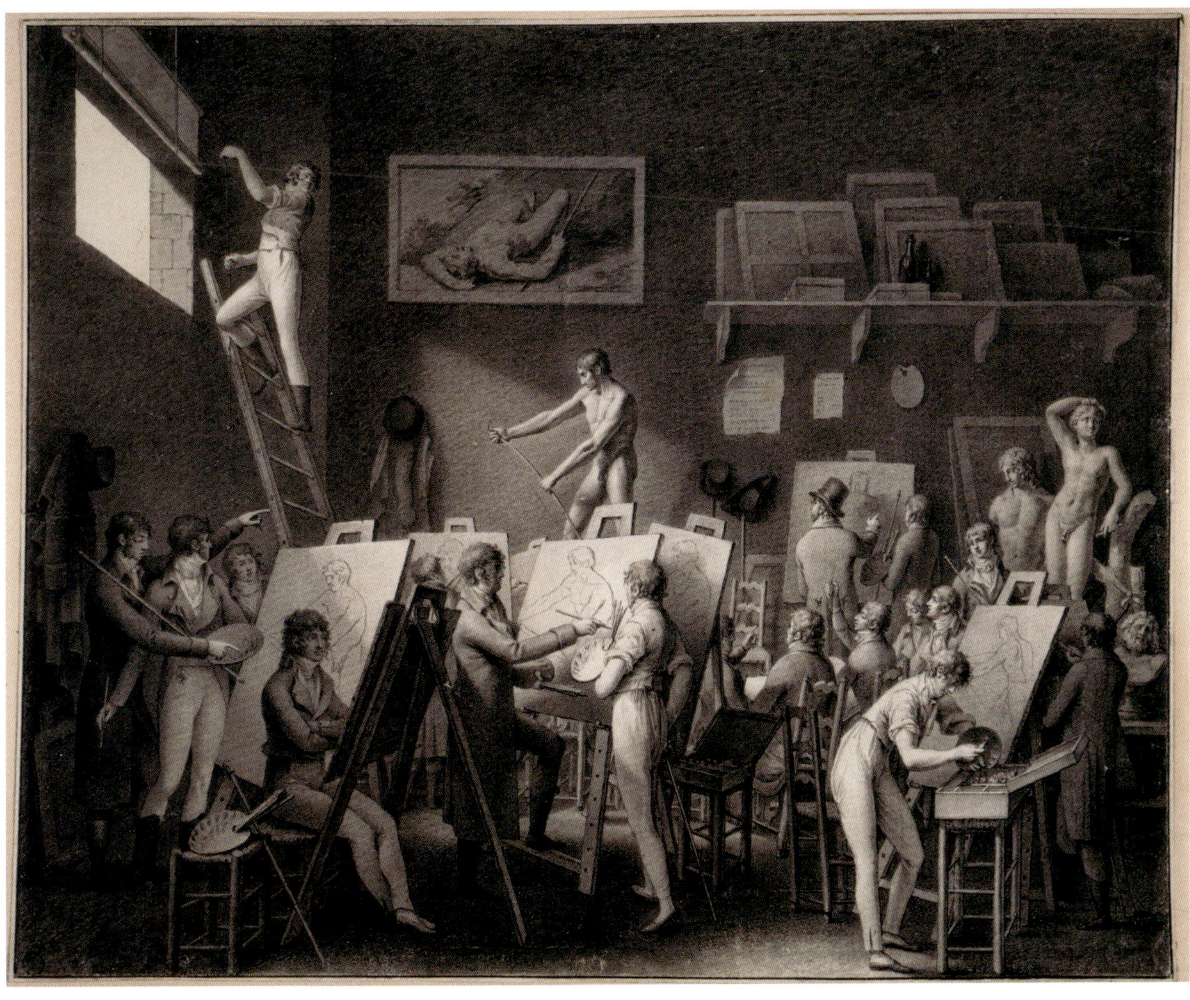

characterises his school, and has rendered it incontestably superior to all others of the same period.'[19] David allowed his most talented students to paint parts of his compositions, such as the drapery or details in the background, but he always reserved the most important areas for himself.

David formed a whole generation of artists, among them Antoine-Jean Gros and Jean-Auguste-Dominique Ingres. He was also one of the first to take on female students, setting up a separate studio for them in the Louvre – an innovation for which he was severely reprimanded by the Louvre authorities. David responded that the women were not only segregated from his male students but that their morals were 'beyond reproach', adding, 'I myself have too much self-respect to keep them for an instant if their conduct were otherwise.'[20] Despite his protestations, it appears that David was obliged to close his studio to women soon after this clash with the authorities.

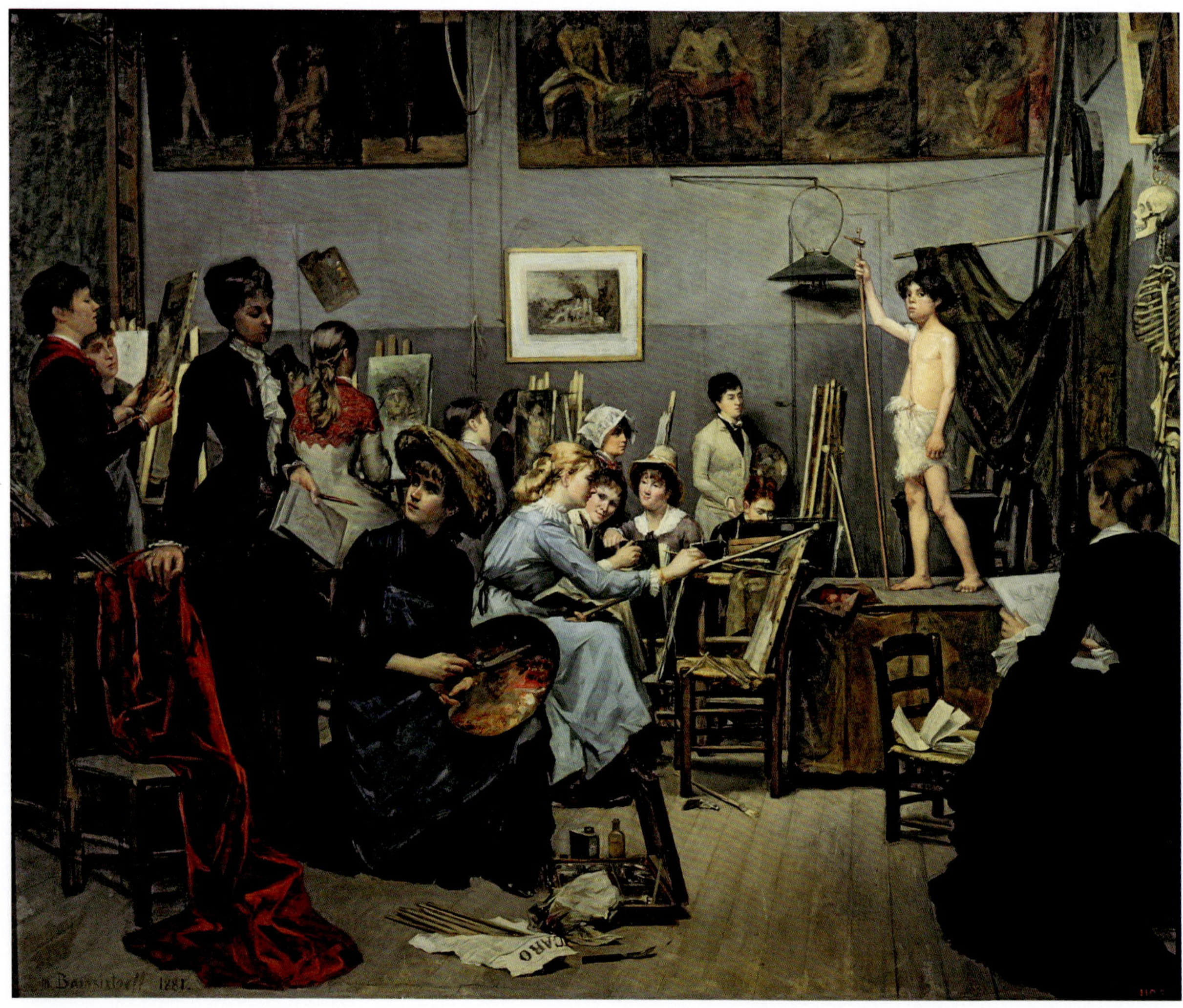

David was not the only artist to be granted permission to have a studio in the Louvre. 'Since the reign of Henri IV, twenty-seven coveted workshops and apartments in the Grande Galerie had been placed at the disposal of artists and artisans for their entire lives,' often passing from one generation of a family to the next. 'One of the glorious oddities of the Louvre is that much of the art on view – at least that of French artists – was produced in the very building in which it is now displayed.'[21] David had several well-known neighbours: Jean-Baptiste-Siméon Chardin, Jean Honoré Fragonard and Maurice-Quentin de La Tour among them. The first woman to be allocated lodgings within the Louvre's hallowed walls was the French artist Anne Vallayer-Coster (1744–1818), but then only because her most prestigious patron, Marie Antoinette, interceded on her behalf.

The quality of the artist's Louvre apartments varied according to the success they had achieved in their careers, ranging from the baronial splendour of the history painter Charles-Antoine Coypel, whose numerous rooms were stocked with rare wines and bejewelled snuff boxes, to the apartment occupied by the sculptor Edmé Dumont which was a 'hovel, a complete rat's nest without any furniture'.[22]

During the chaotic years of the Revolution, ateliers of every kind had sprung up and the palace had become a shambles. Moreover, it was rumoured to be a centre of anti-Napoleonic intrigue, while the gardens had become an open-air brothel. A visit by Napoleon in 1805 put an end to two centuries of occupation by artists. 'Get them out of there!' he thundered.[23]

During the second half of the nineteenth century independent academies, or ateliers, proliferated in Paris. The city became a magnet for young artists, male and female, bent on obtaining the high-quality teaching they were unable to find in their own countries. They came in their hundreds from America, Britain, Europe, Scandinavia and Finland, roosted in tiny apartments, worked long hours in the art schools, ate in ridiculously cheap student restaurants and made lifelong friendships.

For women students, distanced from parental control, these were years of blissful freedom. As single women, however, there remained certain taboos: they could not frequent cafés, set up their easels in the street, visit the Louvre unchaperoned or travel on the top floor of an omnibus as they might reveal a flash of ankle as they mounted the stairs.

One of the most popular private art schools was the Académie Julian, run by Rodolphe Julian, who accepted both male and female pupils, the latter in the belief that women deserved to receive the same standard of tuition as men. Furthermore, he enabled them to study from the nude live model, a concession for which women had long yearned and fiercely campaigned. The Irish writer and critic,

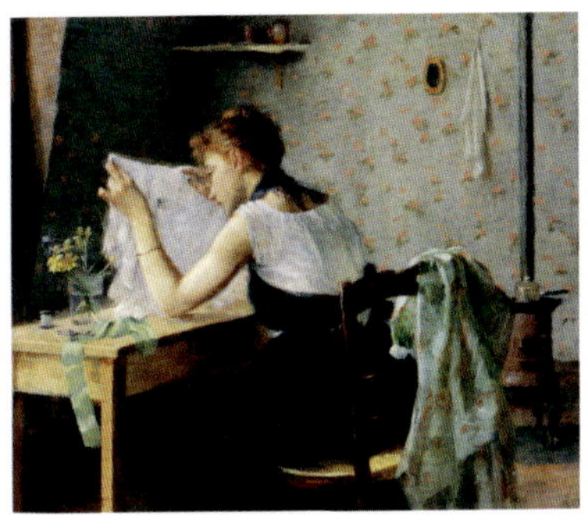

32. Maria Wiik, *In the Attic Studio*, 1889

In the second half of the nineteenth century, eager foreign students flocked in their hundreds to Paris, bent on obtaining serious instruction in the city's private art academies. The Finnish artist Maria Wiik has shown her sister at work in a typical attic apartment.

33. Édouard Manet, *Eva Gonzalès
Painting in Manet's Studio*, 1870
Gonzalès, Manet's only formal pupil,
was a successful artist, one of the
four women Impressionists and a
regular exhibitor at the Salon. The
long period she spent sitting to
Manet profoundly influenced her
style of painting. She was also a
brilliant pastellist.

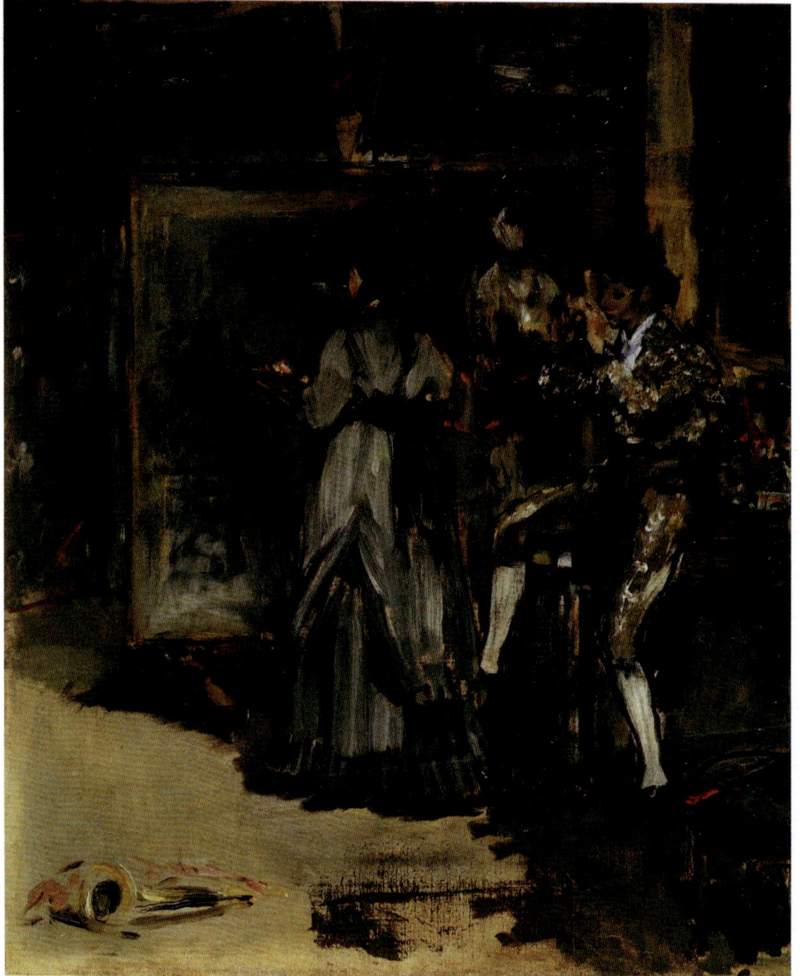

George Moore, who had attended Julian's, later grew sceptical of his style of teaching: 'That great studio of Julian's is a sphinx, and all the poor folk that go there for artistic education are devoured ... After two years they all paint and draw alike ...'[24]

Julian had so many applications by women to join his académie that he had to open a second studio. One of his students described it: 'Four weary flights of stairs led to the atelier, a huge brick-floored room whose one light from the sky-window filtered down upon the model's head as through the bung-hole of a hogshead.'[25]

To promote his académie, Julian persuaded one of his students, the beautiful and wealthy Russian, Marie Bashkirtseff (1858–84), to paint one of his female classes at work. *In the Studio* shows the room crammed with young women painting a rather limp youth supporting himself with a long staff. Although his loins are discreetly girded, the male nudes in the paintings on the wall above him are proof that Julian did indeed provide them for his female students.

     TWO / NURTURING TALENT, INSTILLING DISCIPLINE

Julian's most direct rival was the Académie Colarossi, which boasted students from America, Europe, Russia, Japan and even a black Haitian. One of Colarossi's students, the Russian artist Marevna Vorobieff (always known as Marevna) gave a vivid description of the studio's stifling conditions:

> We were positively melting in an inferno permeated by the strong smell of perspiring bodies mixed with scent, fresh paint, damp waterproofs and dirty feet; all this was intensified by the thick smoke from cigarettes and the strong tobacco of pipe smokers. The model under the electric light was perspiring heavily and looked at times like a swimmer coming up out of the sea.[26]

Another great resource for artists was the Louvre. Copying paintings by revered masters of the Italian Renaissance, of Holland, Flanders and France was an inspiration and a challenge. Renoir acknowledged his debt to the hours he had spent, squatting at his easel in its endless galleries. 'It is in the Museum that one learns to paint … One must make the paintings of one's own time. But it is there … that one develops the taste for painting, which nature alone cannot provide.'[27]

A few artists took on private pupils. Édouard Manet taught one only, the French artist Eva Gonzalès (1849–83), who became one of only four women to be considered part of the Impressionist group. His life-size portrait of her (in the National Gallery) depicts the young artist dressed from head to toe in white, seated at an easel, working on a still life. The painting gives the impression that she is just a 'lady amateur' whereas she was an intensely serious artist who produced a substantial body of work in her brief life – she died in childbirth at the age of thirty-four.

Another of the four women Impressionists, Berthe Morisot (1841–95), who was a close friend of Manet's and had sat for some of his iconic paintings, became a little jealous of the length of time he had spent painting Gonzalès' portrait. He seemed to be prolonging the sittings by washing out the head with soft soap every evening. 'The portrait is no further forward,' Berthe wrote to her sister Edma, 'he tells me it is now the fortieth sitting and her head has just been scraped off again. He himself is the first to laugh.'[28]

In the latter half of the eighteenth century a number of professional women artists taught female pupils. Although she only accepted a handful, Élisabeth Vigée Le Brun taught purely to make money, whereas the portraitist Adélaïde Labille-Guiard (1749–1803) did so out of conviction. She boldly demonstrated her commitment to teaching in a huge self-portrait that includes two of her pupils,

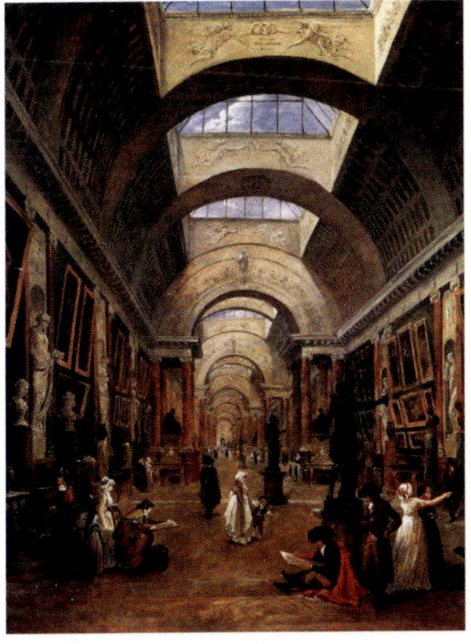

34. Hubert Robert, *The Grande Galerie in the Louvre*, 1796

Robert painted a series of views of the interior of the Louvre. This one shows artists copying some of the paintings, a practice considered essential for art students to complement their studies at art school.

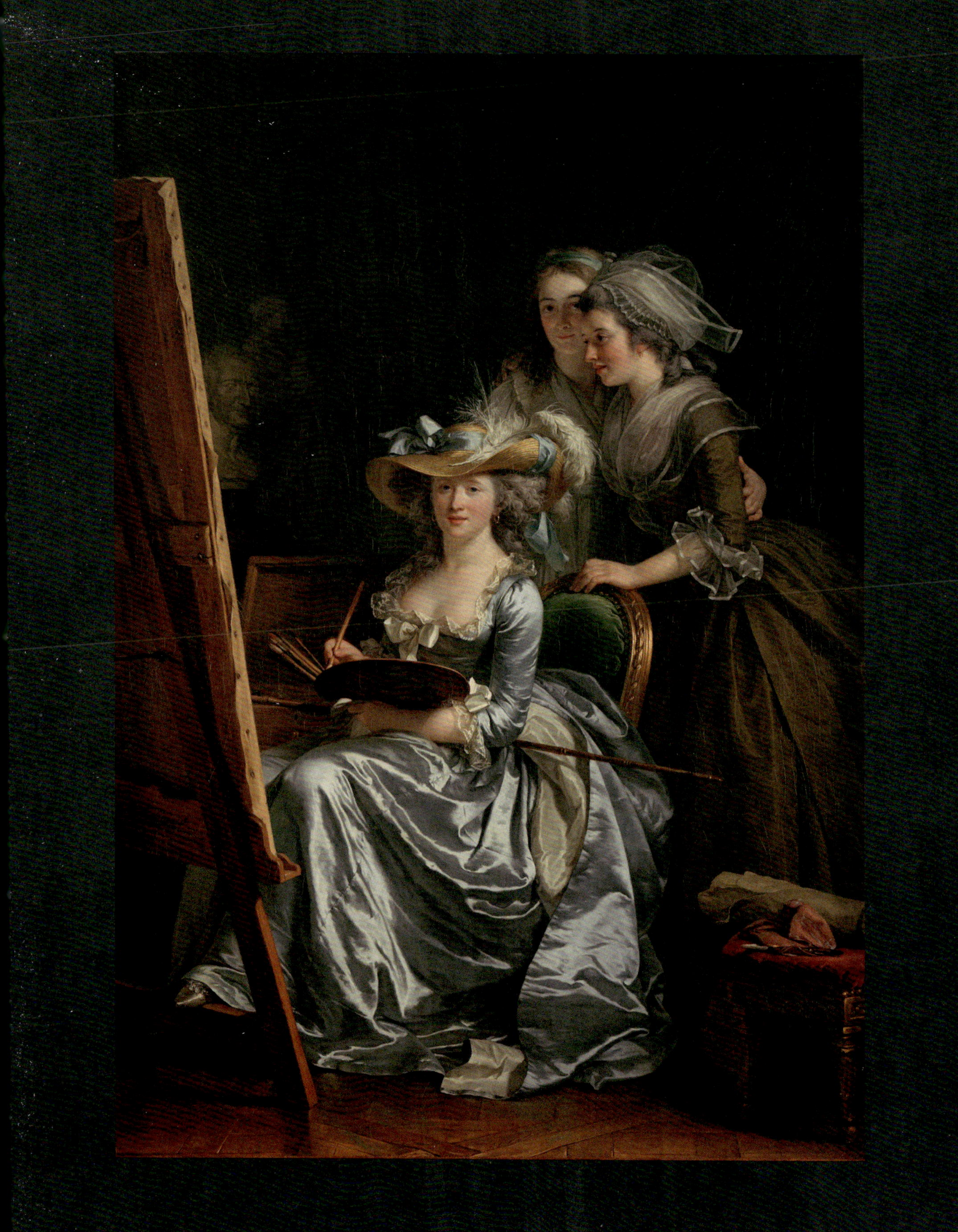

Marie Gabrielle Capet and Marie Marguerite Carreaux de Rosemond. However, her championing of women artists was frowned upon in some quarters: when she applied to the Louvre for an apartment and a studio, she was refused on the grounds that she taught female students and 'no-one wanted the Galeries du Louvre to be overrun by young girls'.[29]

Throughout this chapter the emphasis has been on the importance of drawing from the live human model as the foundation of an artistic education. Some of these models came to mean a great deal more to certain artists than just a naked form on a dais: they became an inspiration, a muse. Not all models were human, however, and some artists went to extraordinary and surprising lengths to recreate historical events, which sometimes entailed using the strangest of models.

Splendidly arrayed in impractical satin, the artist advertises her teaching of female pupils with this huge painting. For one of the pupils, Marie Gabrielle Capet, Labille-Guiard's tuition transformed her life and she became a distinguished miniature portraitist.

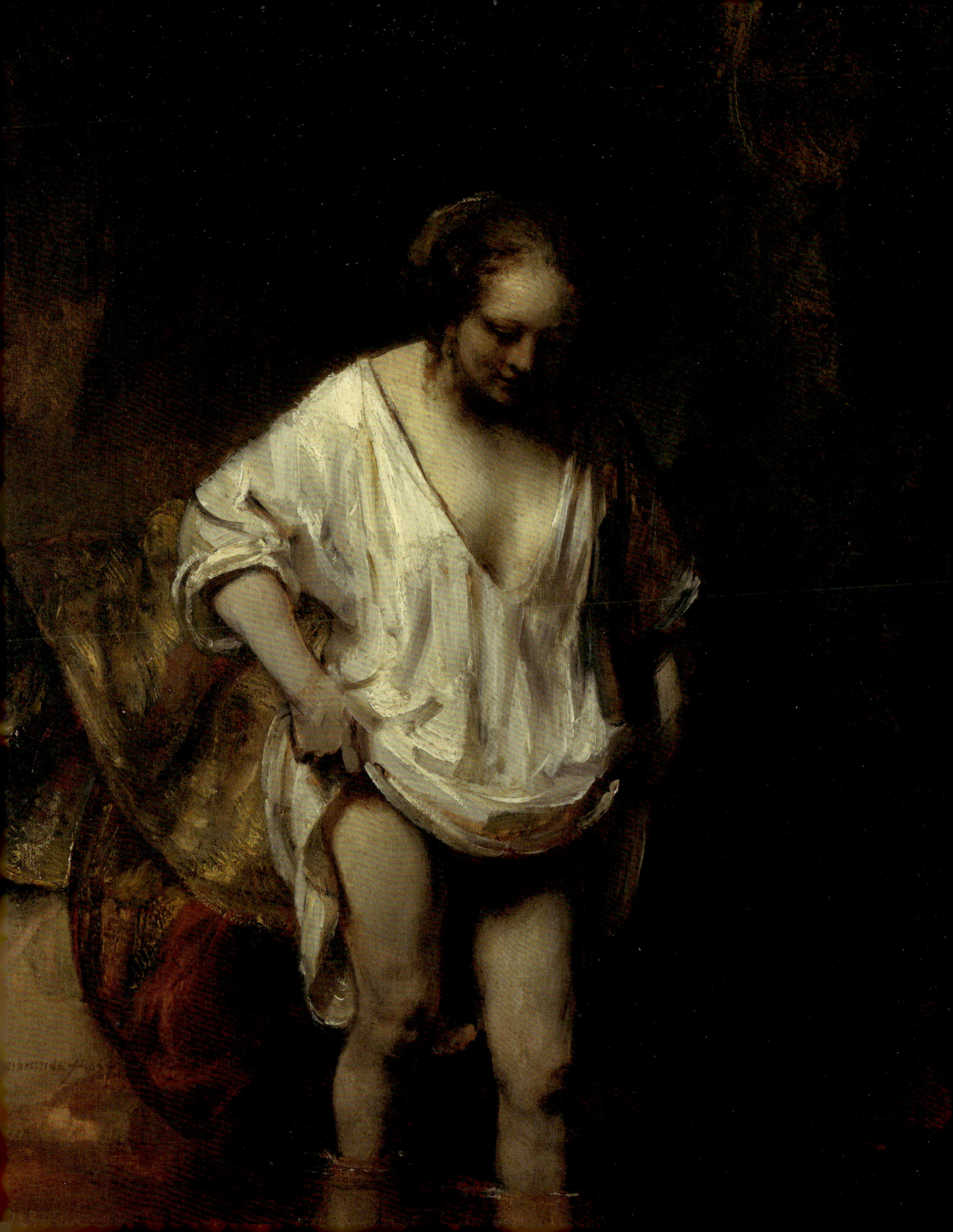

THREE

From Inspiration to Obsession

Models and Muses

[The] silent rituals of the life class; the fetid atmosphere, the smoke and heat of the oil lamp, the naked model, transfixed by the slow trickle of sand through the hour glass and the collective gaze of male art students.[1]

THE PREVIOUS CHAPTER ESTABLISHED that the three central aspects of an artist's academic education were the study of classical statues, anatomy and the live model. The statues – Venus and Apollo were the favourites – seldom fail to appear as shadowy forms in the background of images of artists' studios and art schools. But to study an inflexible figure with a surface of dull plaster or cold marble gives an artist no sense of a warm, breathing human being, or of what lies beneath the skin.

In search of anatomical knowledge, both Leonardo and Michelangelo dissected human cadavers. Leonardo, who dissected more than thirty bodies during the course of his career, boasted of his finesse with the scalpel, but speaks feelingly of 'the fear of living at night-time in the company of these dead men, dismembered and flayed and terrible to behold'.[2] (Although controversial, dissection was permitted under licence.) In the days before refrigeration and preservatives, it was wise to carry out dissections in the winter months. Leonardo notes that: 'As a single body would not last long enough, it was necessary to use several bodies in succession, so as to arrive at a complete knowledge [of the veins].'[3] The image of the artist, alone at night, peeling back the skin and muscles of a rotting corpse, is chilling but also reveals what he was prepared to endure to fully understand the human body.

In Martin Gayford's view, expressed in his magisterial *Michelangelo: His Epic Life,* anatomy for Michelangelo was 'simply a utilitarian stage

OPPOSITE: 36. Rembrandt van Rijn, *Hendrickje Bathing*, 1654

Finding good models was a perpetual problem – and expense – for artists, and many economised by using their friends and relations. Here, Rembrandt's mistress and companion of his later years has posed for this intimate and tender painting.

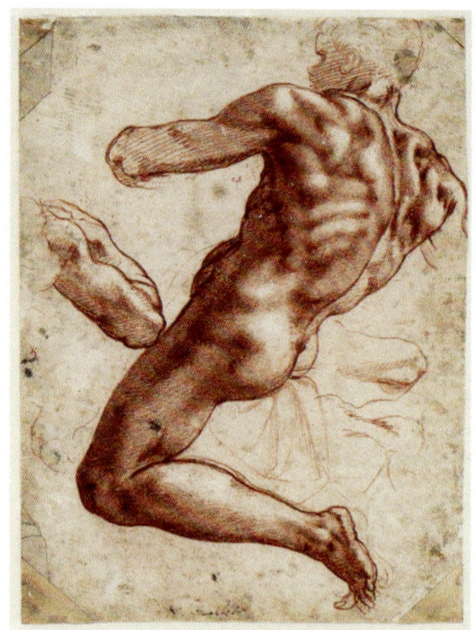

37. Michelangelo, *Study for an* Ignudo *for the Sistine Chapel,* *c.* 1504–05

This study is for one of the twenty male Ignudi (nudes). Since they have no narrative or symbolic meaning, Michelangelo could give free reign to their depiction. Leonardo perhaps had such a study in mind when he advised against making muscles too conspicuous, as they risked looking like 'a sack of walnuts'.

towards the creation of the final result, which was the carving or painting of transcendentally beautiful figures'.[4] Leonardo, however, is thought to have been sniping at his younger rival when he wrote: 'You should not make all the muscles of the body be too conspicuous, unless the limbs to which they belong are engaged in great force of labour ... if you do otherwise you will produce a sack of walnuts rather than a human figure.'[5]

Michelangelo's women, both sculpted and painted, often appear to have the bodies of athletic men. His feelings about the female body were possibly revealed in a burlesque poem he wrote that ended with the line, 'When I look down upon each of your breasts they look like two watermelons in a bag.'[6]

Renaissance writers in general are oddly silent about female nude models, although Vasari mentions several in his *Lives of Painters, Sculptors and Architects,* some of them by name. Many models doubled as prostitutes, which perhaps explains why they remain faceless. Another reason for the ignoring of female models is that Renaissance treatises, which laid down much of what was taught in art schools until well into the twentieth century, dictate that the nude body that artists should study is male. Male models were able to strike more extreme poses and their muscles were more prominent.[7]

It seems perfectly natural – and perhaps taken for granted and thus not recorded – that young men working as apprentices in a Renaissance workshop would have modelled for many figure types, both male and female. They were on the spot and did not have to be paid. (The Italian Baroque artist Artemisia Gentileschi complains in a letter about the expense of models.[8]) Whilst working on his statue of Perseus, Benvenuto Cellini (1500–71) records that having 'no assistants except some little shop boys, among whom was one of great beauty ... I made use of the lad as a model, for the only books which teach this art are the natural human body.'[9] The female nude model may have been ignored by Renaissance writers, but the drawings, paintings and sculpture of the period speak louder than words.

Also on the spot and free of charge were members of an artist's family. Rembrandt (1606–69) painted his wife Saskia and his mistress Hendrickje Stoffels. The latter posed for him at least five times in various states of undress and half-dress. In the achingly sad *Bathsheba* she is completely nude; in *Hendrickje Bathing* (see page 44) she is wearing an undershift which she raises above her knees as she steps tentatively into the water.

Rubens painted his two wives and his children, his first wife Isabella Brant partially nude and his second, Helena Fourment, completely nude. In one of the latter – in which parts of her body, but not her

THREE / FROM INSPIRATION TO OBSESSION

breasts, are invisible beneath a fur coat – she is adopting the pose of an ancient statue of Venus. 'Only through such mythological allusion could an essentially nude figure be made acceptable.'[10] Kenneth Clark, in his classic work *The Nude,* credits Rubens with creating 'A new complete race of women ... He takes the female body, the plump, comfortably clothed female body of the north, and transforms it imaginatively with less sacrifice of its carnal reality than had ever been necessary before.'[11]

The employment of male models in academies of art is documented in England in 1673.[12] A painting by the Flemish painter Michael Sweerts of a nearly nude youth posing for students in his art school shows that they were able to study life drawing in Brussels as early as 1660. The Italian and French academies of art that were established in the sixteenth and seventeenth centuries had excluded the study of the female nude; it was only in the late eighteenth century that the situation began to change.

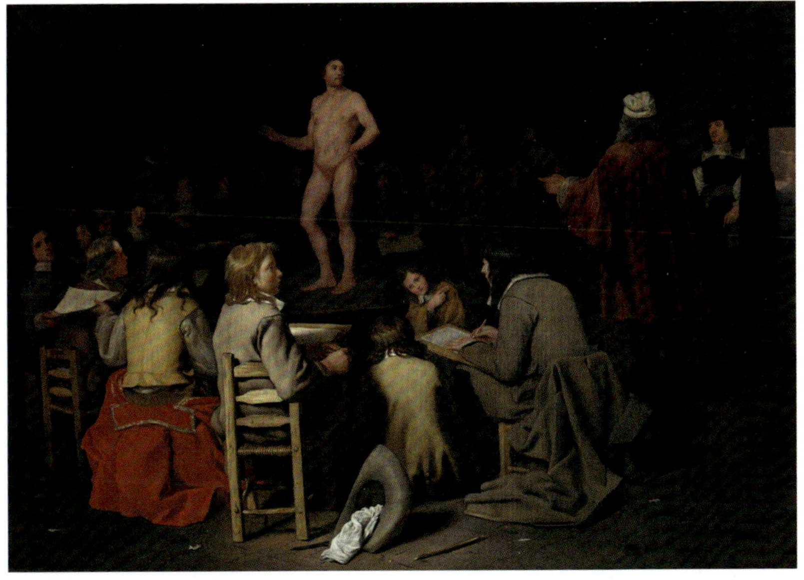

38. Michael Sweerts, *The Drawing Class,* 1660

Sweerts opened an academy in Brussels in 1659. His painting is one of the earliest representations of a life class in which the pupils are studying a model who is not pretending to be a character from the Bible or mythology, but is a partially clothed youth.

When London's Royal Academy was founded in 1768, four male models were hired for the Academy Schools, thus recognising them as professionals and respectable employees in a royal institution. A year later male *and* female models were supplied. However, no unmarried man under the age of twenty was allowed to draw from the nude female, and when she was posing, only Academicians or students were admitted to the life room. The standard shift for posing was two hours, the time measured by an hourglass.

Male students were taught anatomy by Dr William Hunter. Hunter supplied an *écorché* (flayed) body of a smuggler who had been hanged at Tyburn, then cast in plaster in the pose of the Roman sculpture, the

Dying Gladiator. (Nicknamed Smugglerius, a cast of him can be seen today in the Royal Academy.)

Reynolds's favourite model was George White, whose magnificent physique was the result of a life spent laying paving slabs. There were other named models at the Academy: Guardsman Higgins, who had fought at Waterloo and was described as a 'perfect Achilles', and Samuel Strowger, who had been in the Life Guards but became both a model and a porter at the Academy. Soldiers made excellent models because of their good physique and their ability to remain still for long periods.[13]

Lady Elizabeth Butler (1846–1933), the first woman to paint military subjects, preferred policemen as models, as they did not wear moustaches. Obsessive about accuracy, she used models for every picture when she painted on location. Horses were made to charge, fall, then struggle to rise again; 300 men in uniform, carrying knapsacks, were put through appropriate exercises to enable her to sketch them. For her painting *The 28th Regiment at Quatre Bras* she even purchased part of a field of tall rye grass, then had it trampled by some local children. One of her paintings required a model to be trussed up in a suit of armour: 'He was consequently allowed frequent rests, when down his trembling arm would clatter and the instrument of torture on his heated forehead [the helmet] came down with a great thump on the table.'[14]

In 1868, America's principal art school, the Pennsylvania Academy of the Fine Arts, established a Ladies' Life Class that allowed women to study a live model, but only if it was female. Studying the male nude was a step too far: even the Academy's male classical statues were adorned with 'a close fitting, but, inconspicuous fig leaf'.[15] When one of the Academy's professors, Thomas Eakins – who firmly believed that a woman should be the guardian of her own virtue – removed the loincloth from a male model while teaching the Ladies' Life Class, there was an uproar and he was forced to resign. His daring innovation, however, had been far in advance of the Royal Academy, which did not allow female students to draw from a male nude until 1893, and even then the model's loins had to be wound about with a 'cloth of light material 3m long by 1m wide'.[16]

Having an attractive body was not the only criterion for being a good model, male or female, particularly as much of the work was for fully-clothed or character models. Punctuality and dependability were essential; for male models, so was arriving sober. Tractability was more useful than intelligence. Being able to hold a pose, often a painful one, for long periods without fidgeting or fainting was fundamental. Above all, a good model had to be prepared to submit himself or herself to whatever the artist required. At some art schools a new model was routinely subjected to all manner of indignities by the students.

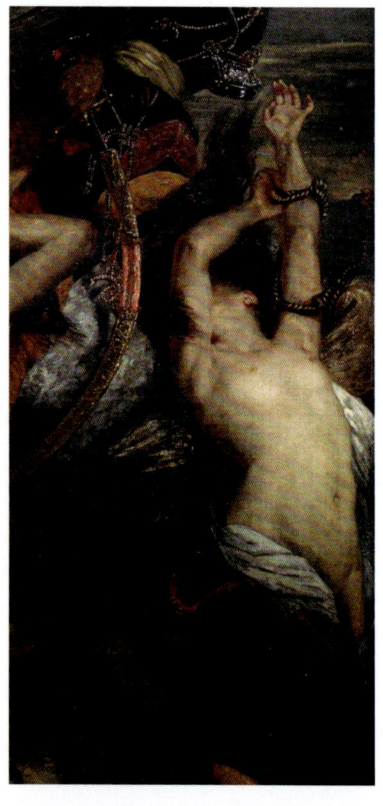

39. Eugène Delacroix, *The Massacre at Chios*, 1824 (detail)

This is a detail of the artist's huge painting depicting a scene from the war between the Ottomans and the Greeks. It caused a sensation when it was exhibited at the Salon in 1824. Delacroix has used his favourite model and one-time mistress, Émilie Robert, for the magnificent nude torso.

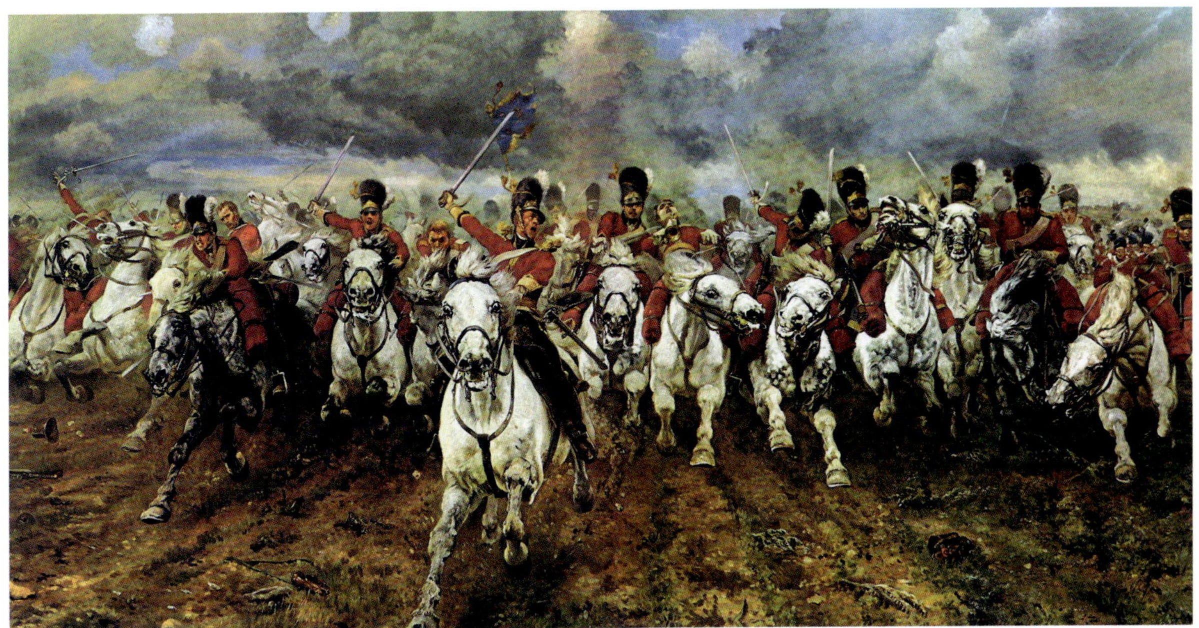

Italian models were considered the best in both figure and temperament. Their feet came in for particular praise: English women tended to have bad feet because they wore pointed shoes, but the feet of Italian models, bare in childhood and then clad in simple sandals, kept their shape. In his inaugural lecture at the Slade School in 1871, Edward Poynter assured students that he would provide them with the best Italian models as they were 'not only in general build and proportion, and in natural grace and dignity, far superior to our English models, but they have a natural beauty, especially in the extremities which no amount of hard labour seems to spoil'.[17]

In Paris, models congregated around the gates of the École des Beaux-Arts. They came in all shapes and sizes: old men with patriarchal beards who would make an ideal Joseph or saint; others would be perfect Madonnas; another a Pysche or a Wood Nymph. The most resourceful models were able to satisfy all demands: 'Mlle Nina poses angels and virtues at four francs a session. N.B. Payment for capital sins by arrangement to be agreed between the parties.'[18]

Mlle Nina's 'extras' emphasise that female models seldom escaped the whiff of immorality attached to their occupation. Fashionable artists like Sir Frederic Leighton did their best to keep everything respectable by requiring his models to enter his Kensington house through a special door. George Romney's model was always accompanied by her mother. The actions of certain artists, however, only served to confirm the public's view that female models did more for their wages than just pose. In their quest to depict absolute reality in their paintings,

40. Elizabeth Southerden Thompson (Lady Butler), *Scotland Forever!*, 1881

Lady Butler was the first woman artist to concentrate almost exclusively on military subjects, and the first painter to celebrate the courage and endurance of the ordinary British soldier. She prided herself on her accurate representation of the movement of a horse's legs.

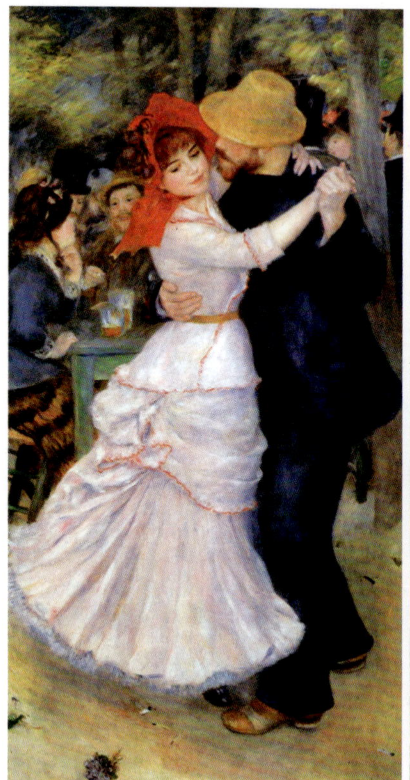

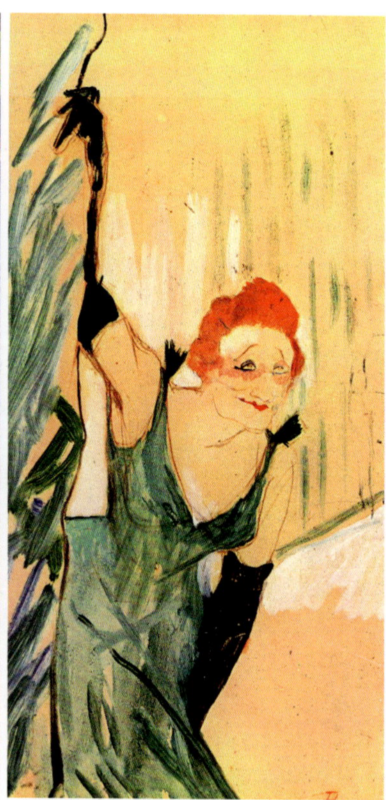

Dante Gabriel Rossetti and his fellow Pre-Raphaelites needed models as they could not paint anything without them, but they preferred to use ordinary people rather than professionals and scoured the London streets for likely candidates. When Rossetti rented a studio in Red Lion Square, his landlord posted a notice in the hall stipulating that visiting models must be 'kept under some gentlemanly restraint, as some artists sacrifice the dignity of art to the baseness of passion'.[19]

In Paris, from mid-century onwards, an artistic community flourished whose adherents were not only prepared to live outside bourgeois society – although many of them had been born into it – but revelled in its exclusion: bohemians. The artists' models became their friends, lovers and partners in the creative process, and occasionally their wives. A young striving artist like Gwen John, sister of the ultra-bohemian Augustus, struggled to make a living as a professional painter when she first went to Paris in 1904, but did not hesitate to supplement her income by modelling. Suzanne Valadon, despite her seamy, impoverished childhood in Montmartre, became one of the leading avant-garde women painters, not by attending art school but by modelling for artists such as Pierre-Auguste Renoir and Henri de Toulouse-Lautrec and learning as she posed.

While some women never posed for a painter in his studio, they were so captivating that they became a source of inspiration for certain artists, especially for a brilliant draughtsman like Toulouse-Lautrec who could capture their allure in a few swift strokes from across a crowded room. The sketches were later worked up in Lautrec's studio on rue Lepic, a steep hill leading to the summit of Montmartre, surrounded by the bars, cabarets and brothels which he frequented. (It was said that he drank so steadily that his moustache never dried.[20]) A photograph of 1890 shows Lautrec in his dim, hangar-like studio, a diminutive figure crouched on a low stool as he puts the finishing touches to a large picture. Here he painted in complete silence, far removed from the throbbing rhythms and frenzied gaiety of nightclubs like the Moulin Rouge. The studio also boasted the unusual luxury of a bathroom, as well as a rowing machine to exercise his legs, which had been deformed since childhood.[21]

Lautrec's huge vibrant posters, plastered on the walls of Paris, immortalised Belle Époque celebrities like the singer Yvette Guilbert, with her trademark long black gloves; the dancer La Goulue, who created the French can-can; and the red-headed dancer Jane Avril. He was as fascinated by these women who performed in the city's hot spots as he was drawn to the brothels and the artistic riff-raff of Montmartre.

Models were not always human. In an eighteenth-century echo of Leonardo's passion for knowing what lay beneath the skin, George Stubbs (1724–1806) spent some eighteen months dissecting horses. Having established a studio in a lonely farmhouse in Lincolnshire, he began operations on the first of some twelve horses. The dead horse was suspended from the ceiling of his studio by means of a special tackle so that he could manoeuvre it into different positions. The carcass could hang for six to seven weeks, or as long as it was fit for use, enabling him to strip away layer after layer of skin and muscle until he came to the skeleton. His only assistant was his common-law wife, Mary Spencer. Throughout this macabre procedure, he drew and made notes. Engravings made by Stubbs from the drawings were published in 1766 as *The Anatomy of the Horse*.

On occasion, equine models could be temperamental. Stubbs was commissioned by the Marquess of Rockingham to execute a life-size painting of his horse Whistlejacket. During one 'sitting', Stubbs removed the painting from his easel and leant it against a wall. The horse, being led about by his stable-boy, caught sight of it and began to 'stare and look wildly at the picture, endeavouring to get at it, to fight and to kick it'. Stubbs had to come to the boy's rescue and pummel Whistlejacket with his palette and mahlstick before the horse could be calmed down.[22] (Stubbs's magnificent painting is in the National Gallery, London.)

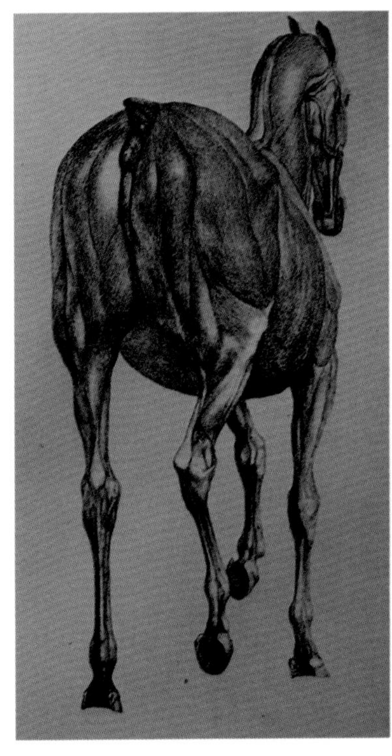

43. George Stubbs, *Anatomy of the Horse*, 1766

Stubbs revolutionised the painting of horses and other animals with his rigorous investigations of their anatomy. For his book *Anatomy of the Horse*, he lived for eighteen months with the putrefying carcasses of horses slung from the ceiling, analysing and mapping their anatomy in accurate and beautiful drawings.

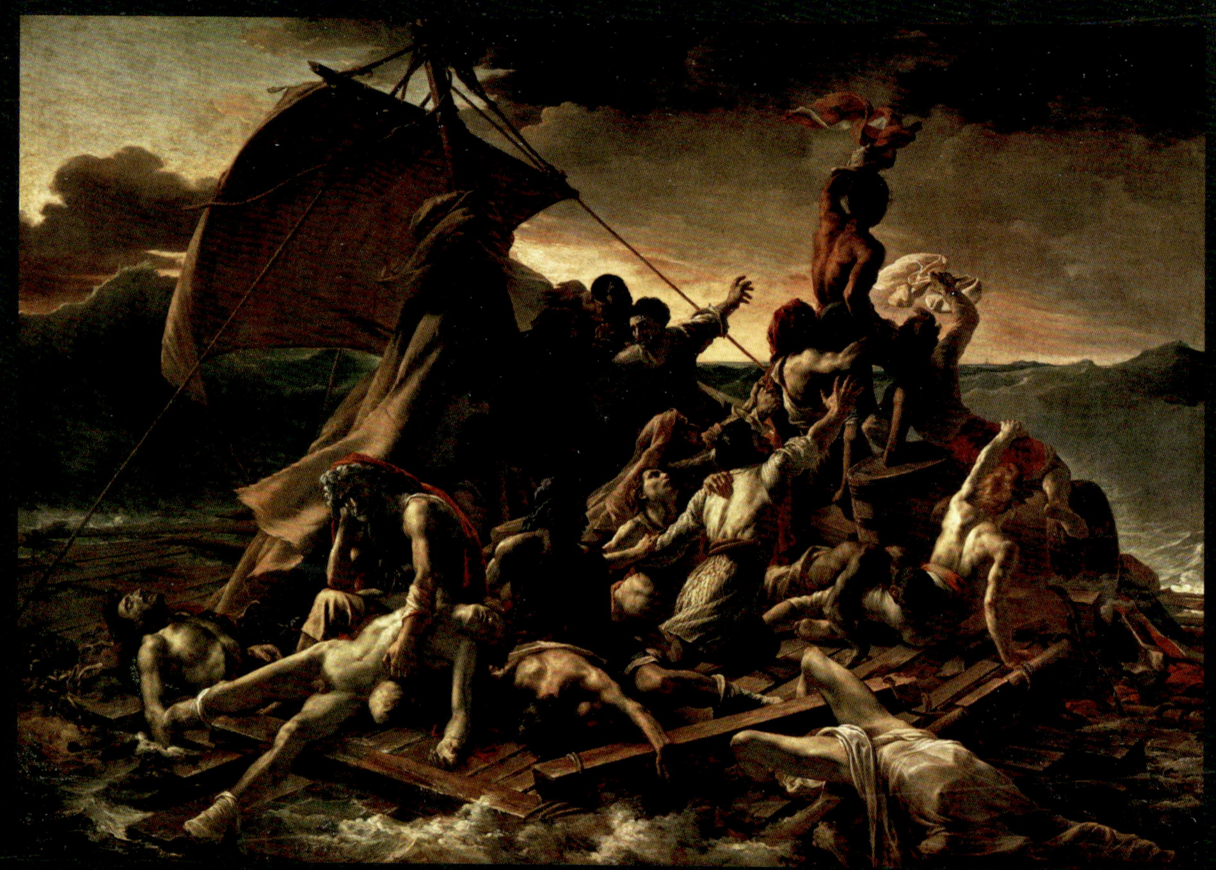

44. Théodore Géricault, *The Raft of the Medusa*, 1818

The artist went to fantastic lengths to recreate the tragic shipwreck. Some of his friends acted as models for the figures. Delacroix is the one lying face down with his arm outstretched – an extremely uncomfortable position to maintain for any length of time.

Some artists went to immense lengths to recreate historical events, assembling in their studios all manner of 'props' and models. Théodore Géricault became obsessed by the tragic story of the wreck of the French frigate *Medusa*, which struck a reef off the coast of Mauritania in 1816. Of the 147 people set adrift on a hurriedly constructed raft, all but fifteen died in the thirteen days before they were rescued. Those who survived had endured starvation, mutiny, madness, dehydration and cannibalism.

Some of the survivors of the disaster were still alive and able to tell him their stories. One had been the ship's carpenter and he constructed a detailed scale model of the raft on which Géricault positioned wax models to represent the survivors. He visited hospitals and morgues so that he could study the colour and texture of the flesh of the dead and dying and brought severed limbs back to his studio to study their decay, plus a severed head which he borrowed from a lunatic asylum and stored on his studio roof. He made and discarded numerous sketches and struggled to choose the best moment of the disaster to illustrate.

Géricault first shaved his head so that he would not be tempted to go out, then closeted himself in his studio for eight months until the picture was finished. Absolute silence was essential: the sound of a chair being moved was enough to break his concentration. For such a monumental painting (491 x 716 cm), in which the figures in the foreground are almost twice life-size, it is remarkable that he apparently used only small brushes. His marathon, however, paid off: at the age of twenty-seven he had produced a work that established the international reputation he craved and which has since become an icon of French Romanticism.

Another actual event, the execution by firing squad in 1867 of Maximilian I, Emperor of Mexico, inspired Édouard Manet to embark on a series of three large oil paintings, a smaller oil sketch and a lithograph. The execution caused a furore in France and the news media bristled with accounts – and photographs. (The advent of photography had made artists more conscious of getting things right. In their quest for total accuracy, they often found themselves competing with the camera itself.)

The *Execution* paintings were created in Manet's studio which, by that date, was in a former fencing school on rue de Saint-Pétersbourg near the Gare Saint-Lazare. One of his many visitors described it as a 'vast room panelled in old, dark oak with a beamed ceiling ... A pure, soft and absolutely even light comes from the windows looking out onto the Place de l'Europe. The trains pass very close by, whirling their plumes of white smoke. The floor shudders and quivers underfoot like the deck of a boat in motion.'[23] Rather to one visitor's surprise, the studio was 'of a monkish simplicity – not a useless piece of furniture, not a knickknack,

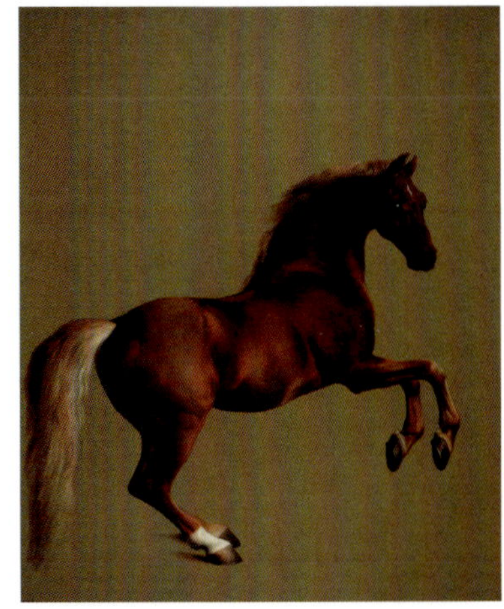

45. George Stubbs, *Whistlejacket*, *c*.1762

Commissioned by the 2nd Marquess of Rockingham, Stubbs painted Whistlejacket, an Arabian chestnut stallion, almost life-size. It is now considered to be one of the most important British paintings of the eighteenth century and Stubbs's masterpiece.

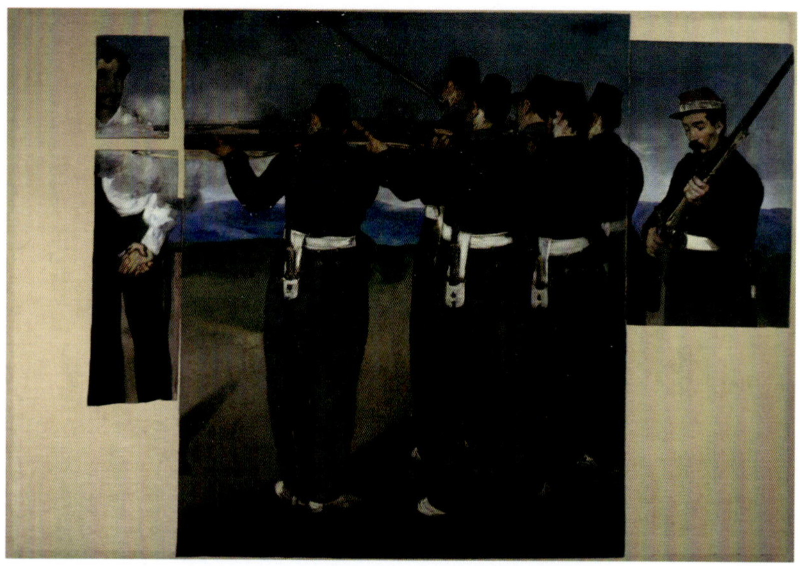

46. Édouard Manet, *The Execution of Emperor Maximilian*, 1867–68

After Manet's death this painting, the second version of the series, was cut up and sold in three separate parts. Outraged by this desecration, Degas later tracked down and eventually reunited the parts of the painting. Manet's composition echoes that of Goya's *The 3rd of May* of 1808.

but everywhere the most brilliant studies on the walls and the easels'.[24] Another feature was the split-level gallery, once used for judging fencing bouts, which Manet had screened off and hung with crimson satin curtains. This mysterious partition led to much speculation about what went on behind the curtains.

Allegedly, whilst he was working on the *Execution*, Manet told the writer and art critic Émile Zola: 'I can't do anything without a model. I don't know how to invent.'[25] Thus it is no surprise that he arranged for a squad of infantry from the local barracks to model for him. Two friends posed for the principal characters, although Manet altered their faces. To capture the likeness of Maximilian and the other victims, he used photographs.

Zola gave an illuminating insight into Manet's way of working when he sat to him for his portrait: 'Sometimes in the half sleep of posing I saw the artist who, with tense face and radiant eyes, was completely absorbed in his work as he stood before the canvas. He had forgotten me; he no longer knew I was there; he painted me like he would have painted any other living creature, with an attentiveness, an artistic conscientiousness, that I have never seen anywhere else.'[26]

Given the intensity and focus that artists such as Manet brought to their work, it is scarcely surprising that for some painters and sculptors their female models ceased to be just an attractive face or a shapely body and became a source of inspiration, a vital stimulus, the key to their creativity. Their muse. Occasionally, however, a muse could become an obsession.

According to Georgio Vasari, the Florentine painter Andrea del Sarto was so obsessed with his wife's beauty that even when he

   THREE / FROM INSPIRATION TO OBSESSION

used other models, they all ended up resembling her. While Vasari is complimentary about del Sarto as a painter and as a man, he has nothing good to say about his mistress Lucrezia del Fede, who became his wife when she was widowed. 'And then,' Vasari adds darkly, 'he had more than enough to do for the rest of his life ...'[27] He was forced to prostitute his matchless technical skill to make enough money to keep his worthless wife happy and 'harassed' by jealousy over her constant infidelities and by her 'tyrannising arrogantly' over his pupils in the studio, which made 'all their lives a burden'.[28] He remained so blinded to her vixenish ways that he could see nothing odd in painting Lucrezia's features on a Madonna or a saint.

The Viennese artist Gustav Klimt contracted syphilis at an early age, which may have been one of the reasons why his relationship with Emilie Flöge is thought to have been platonic – although it did not prevent him from being a serial womaniser with several illegitimate children to his name. His bond with Emilie was one of intense friendship. They went everywhere together, their lives intertwined. He painted many of Vienna's most beautiful and glamorous women, while she was a successful fashion designer, creating revolutionary, strikingly patterned, smock-like dresses which were all the rage. When they were apart, he wrote her numerous postcards, sometimes eight in a day, and nearly 400 letters during the years they were together.

Egon Schiele (1890–1918) left this account of Klimt's studio in Vienna: 'At the end of a garden ... stood a small, low house with many windows, shaded by high trees. One made one's way through flowers and ivy.'[29] A photograph of the artist in the garden shows him dressed in his habitual floor-length garment (which a friend suggested he should wash more often) and felt shoes. In the studio itself, free love reigned. A journalist described the scene: '... here he was surrounded by enigmatically naked women, who, while he stood silently at his easel, wandered up and down the studio, lolled about, lazed and blossomed through the day – always ready for a wave from the master'.[30] His countless cats played amongst the hundreds of drawings strewn about the floor, despite his friends regularly doing away with them to prevent them causing too much havoc.[31]

After years of speculation, it is now thought that Klimt's *The Kiss* shows Klimt himself in a passionate embrace with Emilie. The painting, which has since become a twentieth-century icon, was a symbol of eternal love and a remarkable tribute to Emilie, his companion and muse for twenty years until his death.

Another muse, Joanna Hiffernan, was immortalised by James Abbott McNeill Whistler (1834–1903) in *Symphony in White, No. 1: The White Girl* (the first of three *Symphonies* for which she modelled). Born in

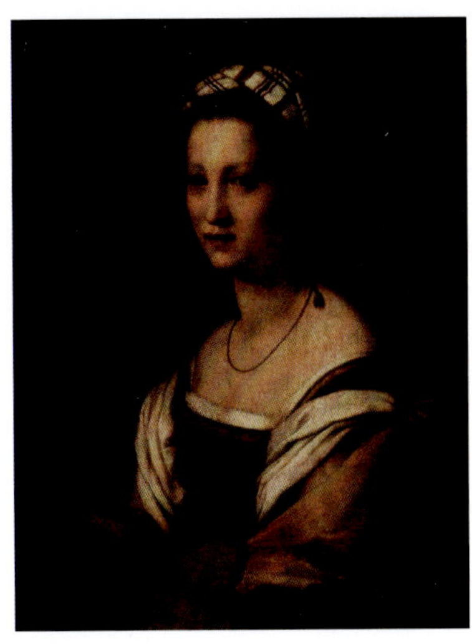

47. Andrea del Sarto, *Lucrezia di Baccio del Fede, the Artist's Wife, c.*1514

Lucrezia was Del Sarto's model for several years, and he eventually married her. She brought him property and a useful dowry, but she also brought him trouble. She was faithless and jealous, but he was so besotted with her that he put up with all the difficulties she caused.

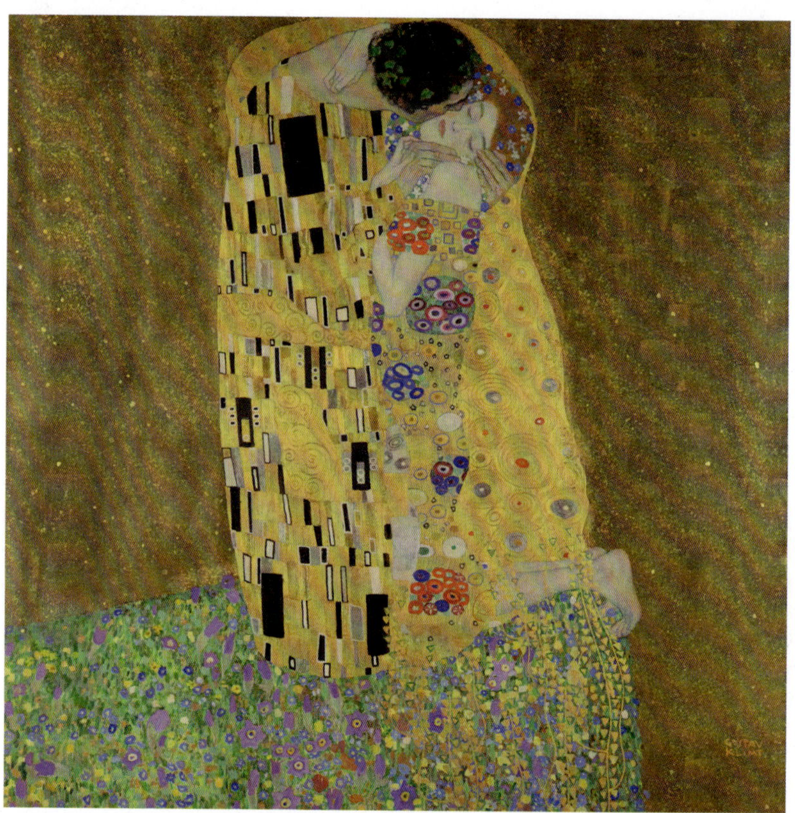

48. Gustav Klimt, *The Kiss*, 1907–08
This famous painting is now thought to represent the artist and his intimate friend Emilie Flöge. Klimt had been trained at an art school in Vienna, where his course had included the study of mosaics. Here he indulges his love of Byzantine mosaics and gives full rein to his taste for gold leaf.

America, trained in Paris, Whistler had settled in London in 1859. He was eccentric, glamorous, a showman, an egomaniac and a virulent racist. He made enemies as fast as he made friends. The index of one biography lists no less than five different people that he had 'knocked down', ample evidence of his fiery temper. In his book of essays on art, *Nothing if Not Critical* (1987), the Australian art critic Robert Hughes said of him: 'His mannerisms were effeminate, and when excited he pranced about like a peahen on hot bricks.'[32] His dandified appearance was augmented by his monocle and tuft of white hair. He was also a serious and committed artist. Probably his best-known painting is the portrait of his mother. The image of the old lady sitting sideways to the viewer, dressed in funereal black, her hands crossed in her lap, has a stillness that is mesmerising.

An Irish immigrant, Joanna met Whistler in London in 1860 and within a year had become by turns his principal model, mistress, common-law wife and partner. In 1861 she accompanied Whistler to Paris. *The White Girl* (an allusion to Wilkie Collins' phenomenally successful novel, *The Woman in White* of 1859–60) was painted in the studio he rented at 18 boulevard Pigalle. He bought materials from a colour merchant in Saint-Germain-des-Prés, hired an easel for four months and set to work. Joanna had to stand for long sessions, dressed

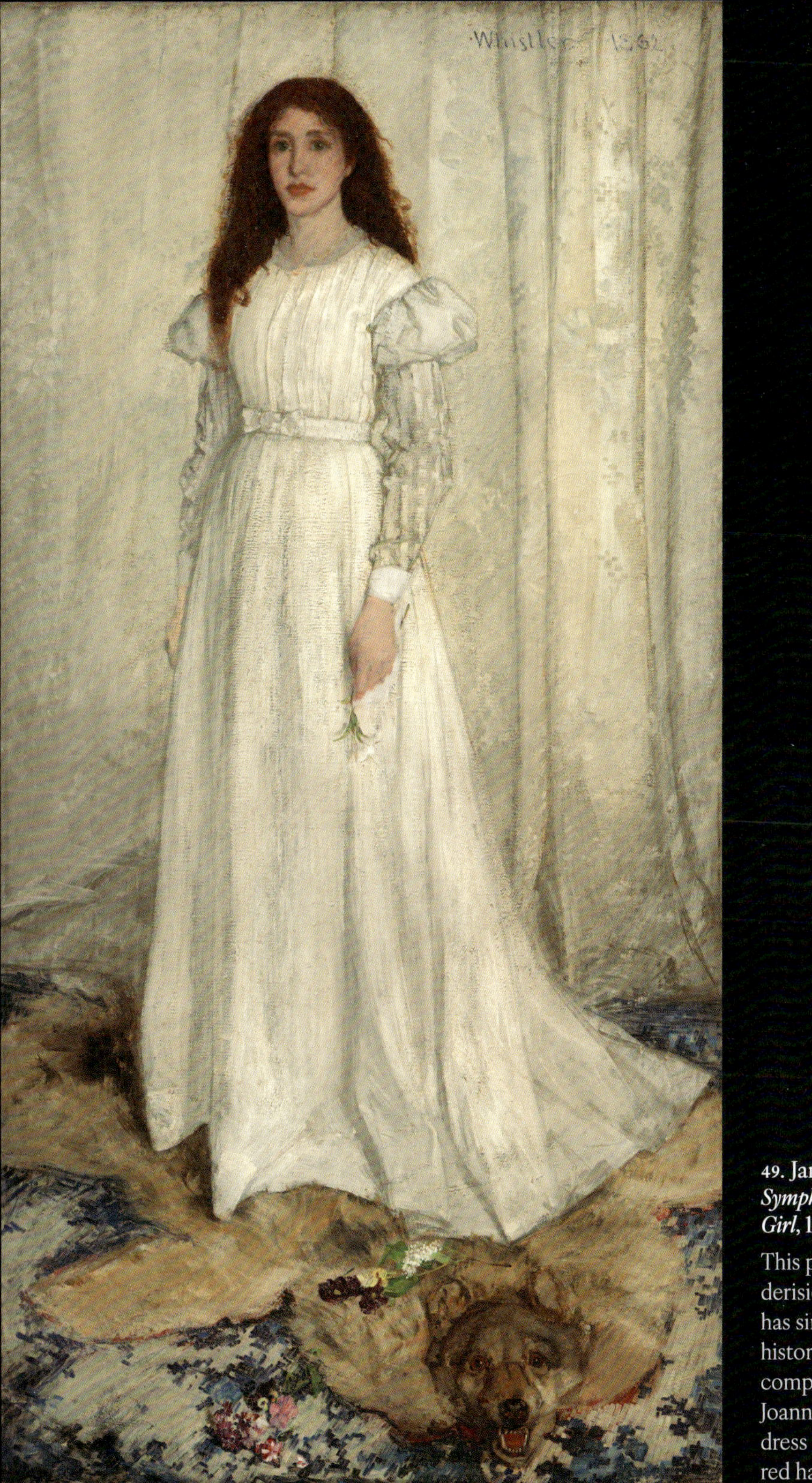

49. James Abbott McNeill Whistler, *Symphony in White, No. 1: The White Girl*, 1862

This painting was met with derision when it was exhibited but has since become an icon of art history. Whistler's muse and loyal companion throughout her brief life, Joanna Hiffernan, poses in her white dress in front of a white curtain, her red hair flaming around her.

– in the middle of winter – in flimsy white cambric. They were both adversely affected by the fumes of the solvent and lead white paint that Whistler used in the painting. (Judging by the recollection of another of Whistler's models, the twelve-year-Cicely Alexander, Joanna must have had a tough time of it. 'I considered that I was a victim all through the sittings, or rather standings,' she wrote, 'for he never let me change my position, and I sometimes stood for hours at a time. I would get very tired and cross, and often finished the day in tears.'[33])

Joanna, however, was enthusiastic about the end result: '... the W[h]ite Girl has made a great sensation – for and against. Some stupid painters don't understand it at all while Millais for instance thinks it splendid, more like Titian and those old swells than anything he has seen – but Jim [Whistler] says that for all that, praps [sic] the old duffers may refuse it altogether.'[34] The 'old duffers' – the selection committee for the Royal Academy's 1862 Summer Exhibition – most certainly refused it, and it was singled out for particular abuse when it appeared at the Salon des Refusés in Paris a year later. It, too, has now joined the ranks of art history's iconic images.

Although they never married, Hiffernan managed his Chelsea studio when he was abroad and looked after his illegitimate son by another woman. She was to remain an integral part of Whistler's life until her death from bronchitis in 1886 at the age of forty-six, her lungs hopelessly compromised by London's fogs.

The poet Robert Graves maintained that wives cannot be muses, 'that certain disqualifications – excessive familiarity for one – prevent an artist's wife from inspiring her mate'.[35] Graves seemingly ignores the fact that having a favourite model available at all times was a major advantage to an artist. Paul Cézanne painted his wife Hortense – known to his friends as 'The Dumpling' – up to thirty times, and posing for Cézanne could be an endurance test, as he sometimes paused for twenty minutes between brushstrokes. Pierre Bonnard painted his wife Marthe 385 times. He painted her not in his studio but in the bed, on the bed, with or without clothes, pouring coffee, sewing, feeding the cats and in the bathroom. Picasso's biographer, John Richardson, described Marthe as the artist's 'amphibious wife,' as she spent much of her time in a bathtub, apparently in the belief that hydrotherapy would cure her numerous ailments.[36] Neither Cézanne nor Bonnard needed a studio for these images, as they painted them against the backdrop of various rooms in their own homes.

The French artist Édouard Vuillard painted his widowed mother, a pious, hard-working Parisian seamstress, more than 500 times, acknowledging to his biographer in 1920 that *Maman, c'est ma muse.*'[37] As he lived with her for sixty years until her death at the age of

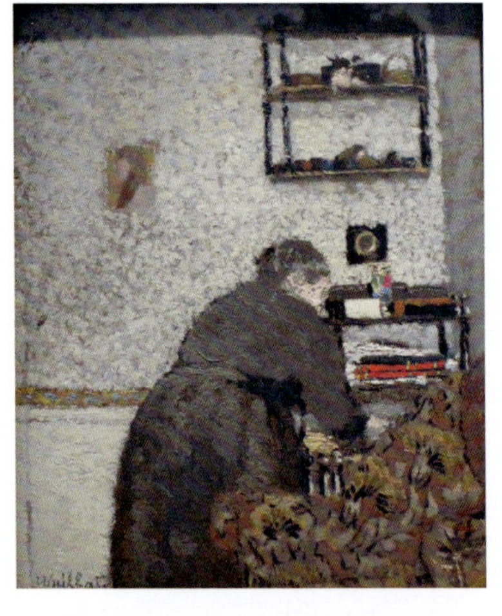

50. Édouard Vuillard, *Mme Vuillard in a Drawing Room*, 1893 or 1898

This is typical of the informal, unposed images that the artist painted of his mother. They generally show her busy with some task in their shared home in Paris, a dumpy figure with her hair done up in a bun.

   THREE / FROM INSPIRATION TO OBSESSION

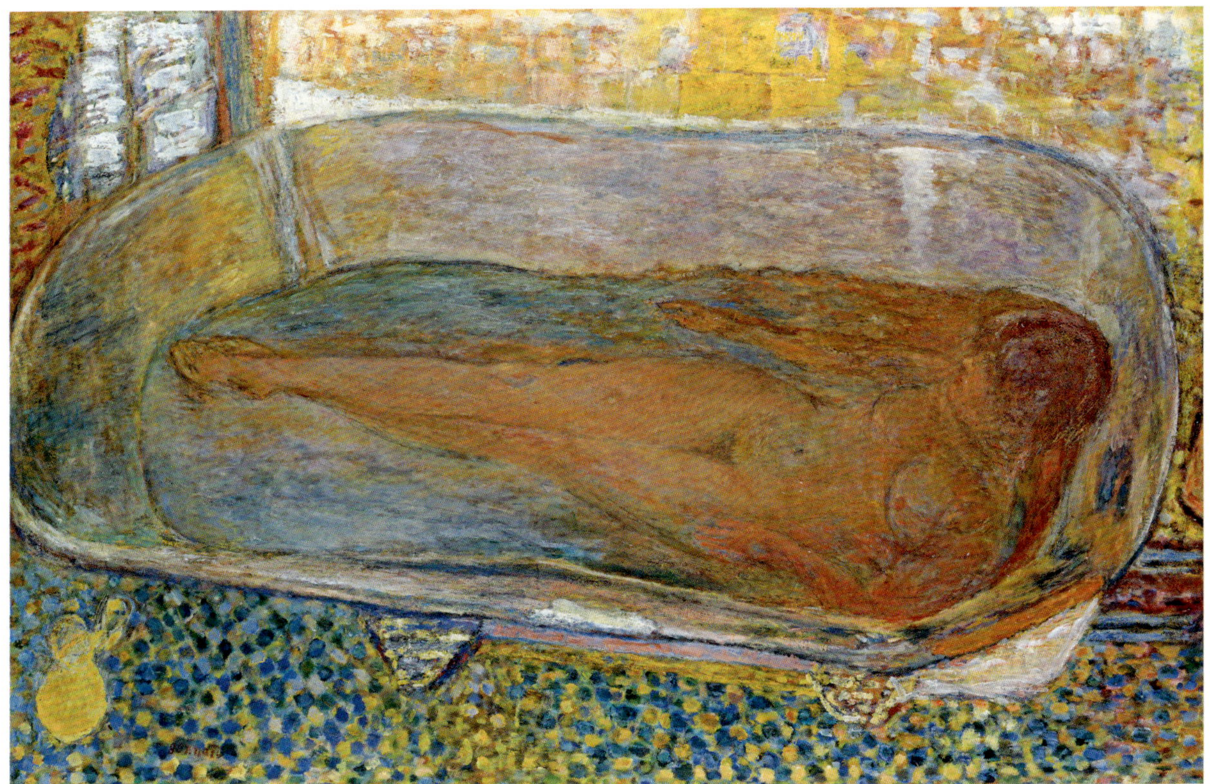

eighty-nine, she was endlessly available and, naturally, free of charge. Like Bonnard's images of Marthe, Vuillard painted his mother about the house, engaged in domestic tasks, taking tea with friends or toiling in her dressmaking workshop. She is recognisable only as a rather dumpy presence, her features seldom defined. These images are snapshots of daily life. They are not portraits.

Whether in the studio, at home, or out in the world, artists relied on models to realise their vision and to stimulate their imagination. Many models were 'professionals' and therefore had to be paid but, where possible, artists used their spouses, friends, relations or lovers, who were free. Some artists even turned to animals, corpses or professional soldiers to conjure historic scenes. Certain models became not only useful but essential to an artist's creativity, their muse. Drawing inspiration from life around them allowed artists to create evocative glimpses of domesticity, convey character and personality, and to populate religious and historical scenes with real people.

51. Pierre Bonnard, *La Grande Baignoire*, 1937–39

Bonnard specialised in intimate domestic interiors, flooded with light. Increasingly reclusive in his later years, his isolation was blamed on his wife – shown here in her bath – who suffered from paranoid delusions. But she was a willing model, appearing in nearly 400 of his paintings.

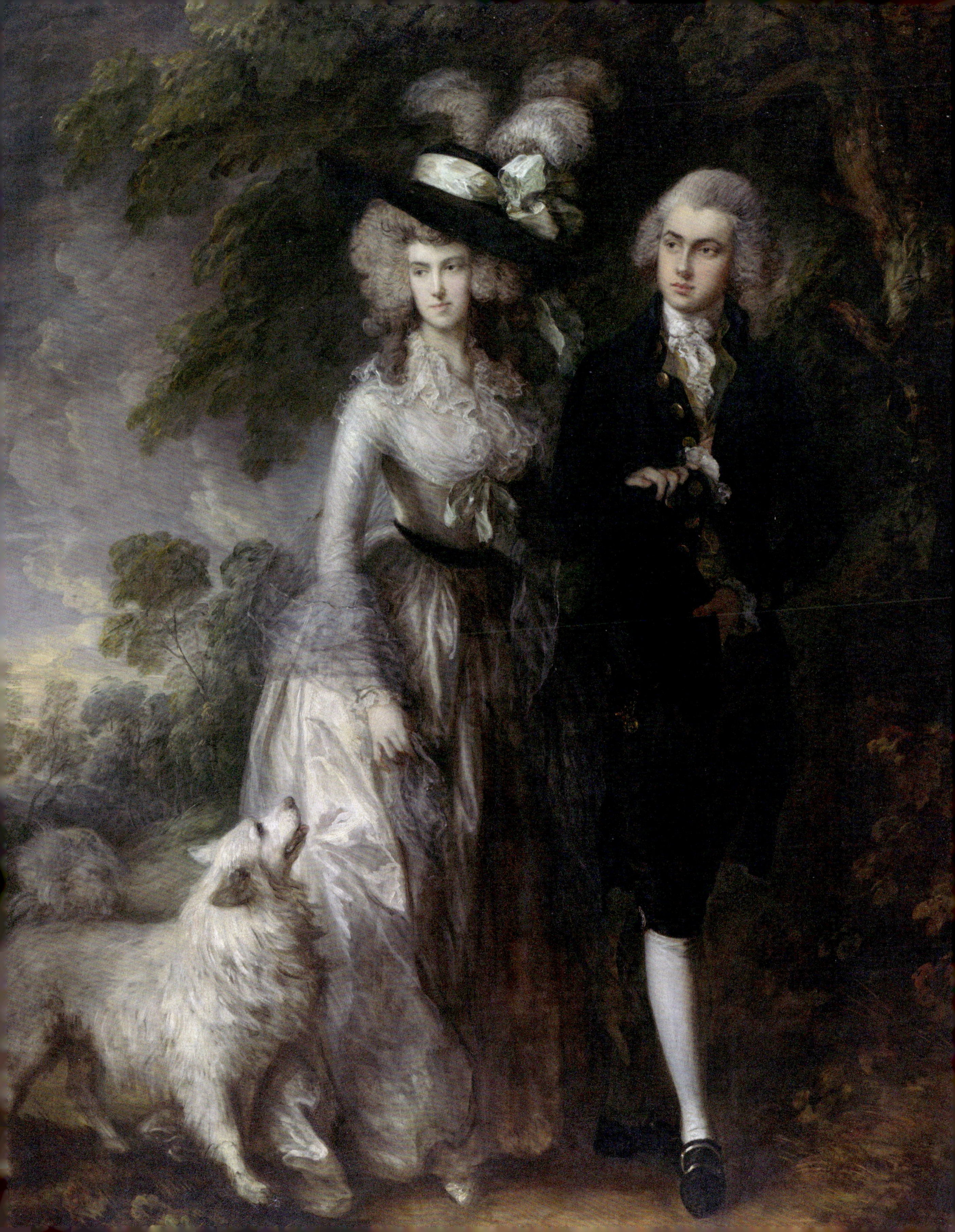

FOUR

Recorded for Posterity

The Portrait Painter's Studio

I'm sick of Portraits and wish very much to take up my Viol da Gamba and walk off to some sweet Village where I can paint Landskips and enjoy the fag End of Life in quietness and ease.
Sir Thomas Gainsborough, letter to William Jackson, 1768[1]

THIRTY YEARS LATER SIR THOMAS LAWRENCE was to echo Gainsborough's despairing view of his profession as a portrait painter: 'I begin to be really uneasy at finding myself so harnessed and shackled into this dry mill-horse business.' George Romney, too, complained of being tied to 'this cursed portrait-painting', while John Hopner invented the term 'potboiler' to describe his routine production of portraits.[2]

Why were these successful eighteenth-century portrait painters so disparaging about a profession that provided them with a healthy income, brought the aristocracy to their door and raised their status within society? The answer lies in the hierarchy of genres, which ranked portraiture well below history painting – considered the noblest form of art as it required the painter to employ the intellect and imagination to tell a story taken from history, mythology or the Bible. Portrait painting had a whiff of being 'in trade' about it and therefore not a profession for a gentleman.

Portraits had long been symbols of power and privilege. From the fifteenth century onwards, not only royalty, princes and prelates and aristocrats, but members of other social groups – from merchants to bankers – sat for their portraits. They were keeping themselves, quite literally, in the public eye. Portraits could also be a statement of social success: a family 'on the make' could advertise its arrival on the social scene by having its members painted by a fashionable artist. They were a form of social currency: numerous copies were made and distributed

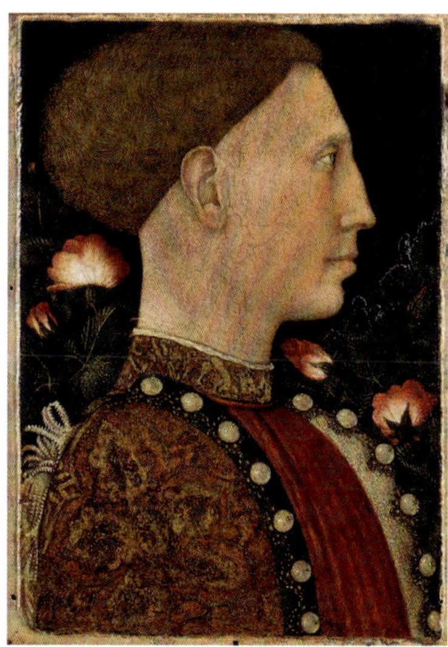

52. Antonio Pisanello, *Portrait of Leonello d'Este, Marquess of Ferrara*, *c.* 1441

Pisanello's few remaining painted portraits reflect the medals for which he was best known. He was also an exquisite draughtsman and watercolourist; his animals and birds accurate and hauntingly alive.

OPPOSITE: 53. Thomas Gainsborough, *The Morning Walk*, 1785

This superb portrait, typical of the artist's flickering, impressionistic style, is often seen as the epitome of English portraiture.

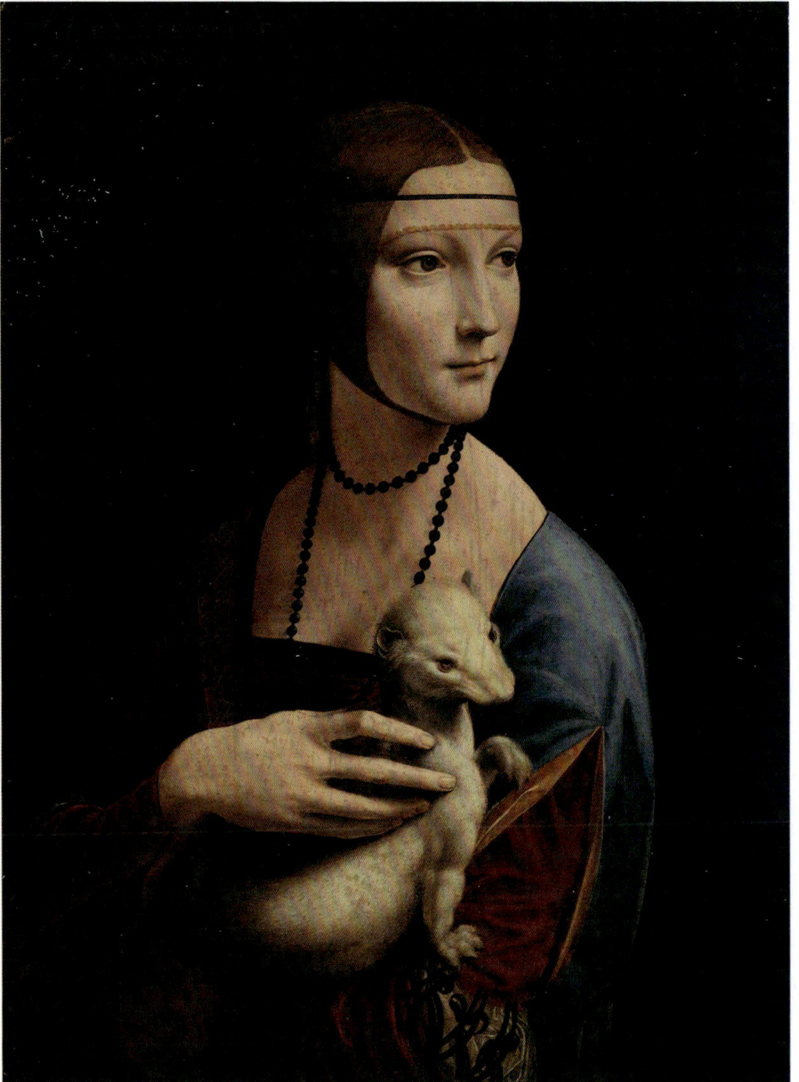

throughout the family; presented as gifts to friends, lovers or admirers. Members of royal or aristocratic families required numerous extra copies so they could be distributed between the various houses and palaces.

This desire by individuals to have their features recorded for posterity goes back to the ancient Romans, whose profiles on busts and coins greatly influenced the revival of personal portraits during the Renaissance.[4] The pure profile portrait gradually evolved first into three-quarter profiles, with the eyes averted, and then the face gradually turned directly towards the viewer – as in Jan van Eyck's mesmerising *Portrait of a Man with a Red Turban* (see page 12).

Leonardo's *Portrait of Cecilia Gallerani* has been acclaimed by art historians to be 'the first modern portrait' because of the way in which

'Cecilia's *contrapposto* pose and gently vivid facial expression conveys the motions of her mind and her soul.'[5] The portrait was painted in the studio that Leonardo established in Milan in the late 1480s. The studio would have been similar to Andrea del Verrocchio's workshop in Florence where Leonardo had trained. Some of the workshop's products, like Cecilia's portrait, were almost entirely his own work, but others would have been mainly painted by pupils or assistants working under his supervision.[6]

Some forty years after Leonardo painted the portrait of Cecilia Gallerani, one of the towering figures of portraiture, the German-Swiss painter Hans Holbein the Younger was appointed court painter to Henry VIII. Until his life was cut short by the plague eleven years later, Holbein painted gloriously vivid portraits of the Tudor court and created the iconic image of a swaggering, formidable and ruthless king.

Little is known about where Holbein lived in London but he is thought to have taken up residence in Aldgate, a prosperous area popular with London's German community, which consisted of a series of buildings around courtyards. This is where he would have worked up the sketches he made of Charles de Solier, Sieur de Morette, the French ambassador.

Much more is known about the abode of another superlative sixteenth-century portraitist: Titian (active *c*. 1506–76). A Venetian to his fingertips, he lived in a house near the Fondamento Nuove on the northern shore of the city, looking over the lagoon. Commissioned to paint portraits of members of Europe's ruling families, he had travelled extensively, including to Spain to paint Emperor Charles V who became his most prominent patron. Charles was so enamoured of Titian's portraits that he declared that henceforth he would be painted by no one else. The artist's reputation soared to new heights: everyone wanted to be painted by him and the list of his sitters reading like a sixteenth-century *Who's Who*.[8] One of his most touching portraits depicts the twelve-year old Ranuccio Farnese, son of the illegitimate son of Pope Paul III.

An assistant who helped the ageing Titian in his studio describes how he built up a composition, then 'turned the picture to the wall and left it for months without looking at it, until he returned to it and stared critically at it, as if it were a mortal enemy ... If he found something that displeased him, he went to work like a surgeon.'[9]

Despite the continual disparagement of portraiture by art theory at the time, the genre experienced an exceptional blossoming during the seventeenth century in the person of Anthony van Dyck.[10] Having been a star pupil in Rubens's workshop in Antwerp, he pursued an independent career around Europe before establishing himself in London in 1632. For the last seven years of his life – he died at the age of

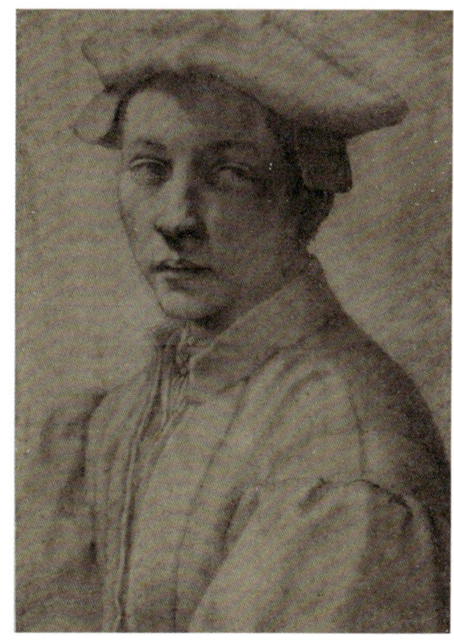

55. Michelangelo, *Portrait of Andrea Quaratesi*, 1528–31

Michelangelo's portraits were rare. According to Vasari, the artist 'hated drawing any living subject unless it were of exceptional beauty'.[7]

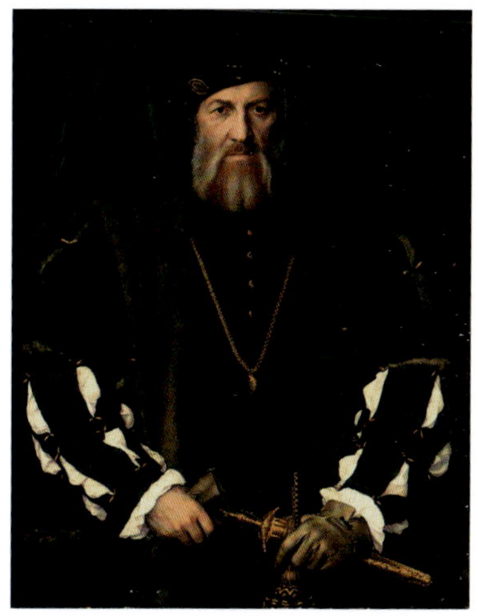

56. Hans Holbein the Younger, *Charles de Solier, Sieur de Morette, c.* 1534

De Solier was France's ambassador to the court of Henry VIII. By filling the entire frame with de Solier head on, his eyes looking directly at the viewer, Holbein creates an impression of a man of wealth and power.

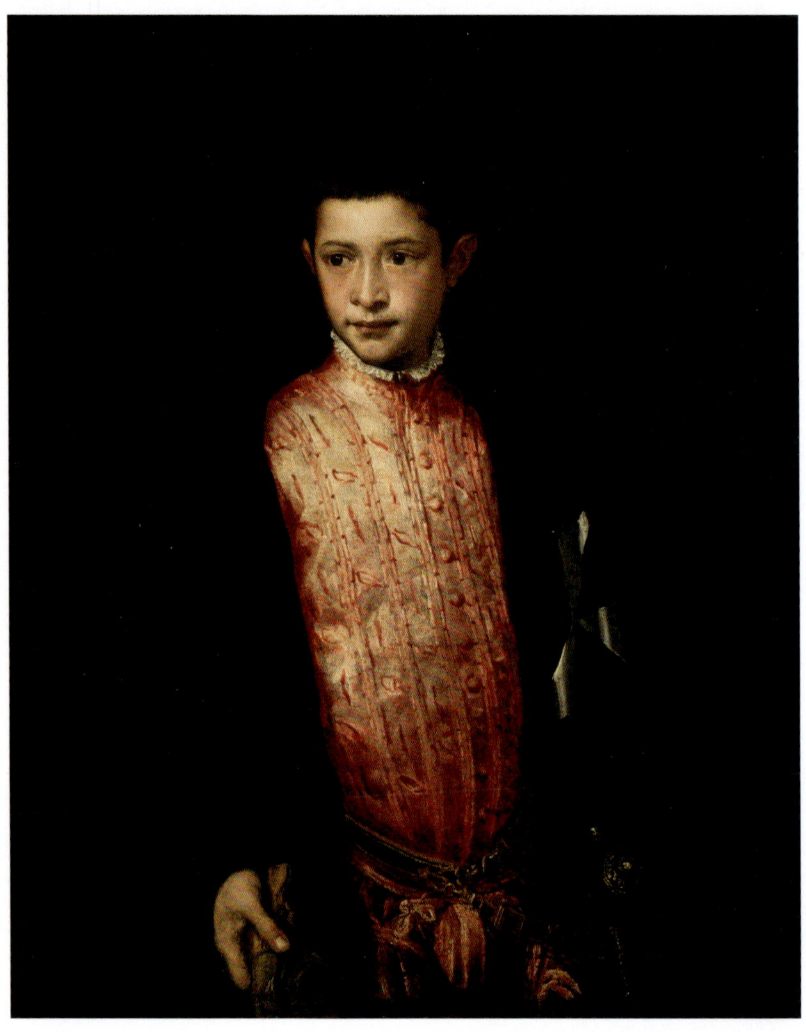

The boy wears the uniform of the
Order of the Knights of Malta as he
had just been created a prior of the
Order. At fourteen, he was made a
cardinal. Titian painted the portrait
when Ranuccio was passing through
Venice on his way to school in
Padua.

forty-two – he was court painter to Charles I and his wife, the French-
born Henrietta Maria.

Charles provided him with a house and garden on the Thames
at Puddle Dock in St Andrew-by-the-Wardrobe, next to Blackfriars.
It was easily reached by boat from Whitehall, especially when a new
causeway and stairs were built to enable Charles to alight there 'to goe
to Sr Anthony Vandikes howse there to see his Paintings ...'[11] Here he
lived in some splendour, the house full of servants, musicians, singers
and jesters and his studio staffed by a team of assistants. There is
evidence to suggest that he got into 'a fast set' at Court and was living
beyond his means. But his aristocratic sitters, King Charles among
them, were not famous for the prompt payment of their debts and he
was often owed 'severall great summes of monie'.[12]

In his book of essays, *Nothing if Not Critical* (1987), Robert Hughes

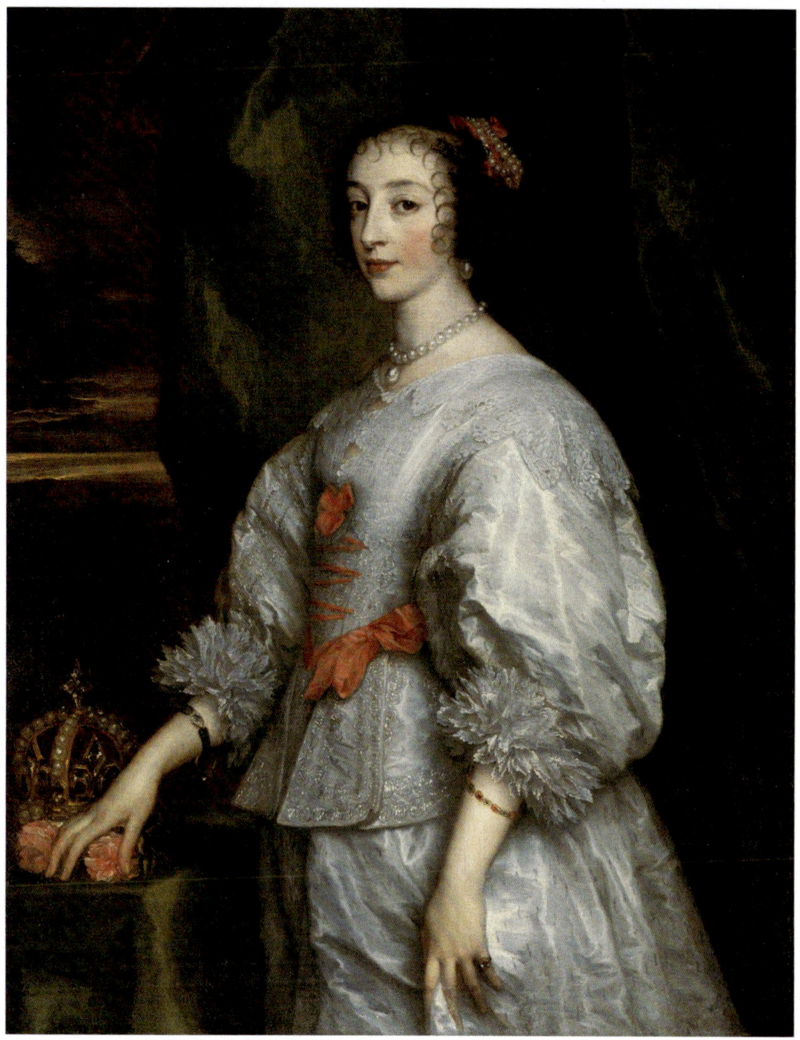

wrote that Van Dyck's great achievement 'was to have invented the English gentleman – not the mild, knobbly creature one sees beneath its bowler in the street, but the now vanishing archetype of aristocracy, calm and straight as a Purdey gun barrel, with the look of arrogant security guaranteed to paralyse all lesser breeds from Calais to Peshawar'.[13]

In order to achieve these dazzling images, Van Dyck was occasionally obliged to resort to some skilful flattery. One of Prince Rupert's sisters, who knew Henrietta Maria only through her portraits by Van Dyck, was dismayed to meet 'a short woman with crooked shoulders, spindly arms, and teeth that stuck out of her mouth "like guns from a fort"', and not the fragile beauty she was expecting.[14]

Although the eighteenth century continued to rank portraiture well behind history painting, in England it was a golden age, largely

58. Anthony van Dyck, *Queen Henrietta Maria*, 1632

One of the unwritten laws of portraiture was that sitters should never be painted smiling. At this date, few of them possessed a mouthful of healthy teeth. Obeying this rule, the Queen has kept her mouth firmly shut.

due to the brilliance of two artists, Sir Joshua Reynolds and Thomas Gainsborough. Together they not only made England one of the most important centres of portraiture but evolved an independent tradition of painting, freed at last from the overpowering influence of continental artists like Holbein and Van Dyck. Due to extensive research, a great deal is now known about their portrait practices and their studios.

According to the Swiss miniature painter, Jean André Rouquet, in his book *The Present State of the Arts in England* (1755), a portrait painter 'makes his fortune in a very extraordinary manner. As soon as he has attained a certain degree of reputation, he hires a house fit for a person of distinction. His aim is then not so much to paint well, as to paint a great deal; his design is to be in vogue.'[15] In short, who you painted was more important than how you painted them.

Reynolds was definitely 'in vogue', as he owned a house in Leicester Fields (now Leicester Square), a stone's throw from the West End with its elegant squares and grand houses inhabited by potential clients. It was also close to Soho and Covent Garden, home to many of the artisans and craftsmen who were essential to the conduct of an artist's profession.

When Reynolds bought the house, he added painting rooms (studios) for himself and his assistants, and a gallery for the exhibition of his works where prospective clients could appraise his style and select the pose they preferred. Such galleries were often littered with portraits that had been left on the artist's hands for a variety of reasons: the sitter's death, a family quarrel or a client's inability to pay. Discarded mistresses were another hazard for a portraitist: once all passion was spent, the client was reluctant to pay.

Reynolds's Leicester Fields studio was an octagonal room, measuring about 60 x 48 m and lit by only one small window set high in the wall.[16] There was a sitter's chair, raised on a dais which turned round on castors. A vital component for any studio was a stove, not just for the artist's comfort but to keep the client warm or to prevent a naked model from freezing to death while posing. Stoves frequently feature in images of artists' studios, their long black flues extending upwards until they disappear through a hole in the wall. (Some artists, Cézanne and Delacroix among them, even painted 'portraits' of their stoves; see page 96.) They were also safer than open fires, due to the flammability of artists' materials. Reynolds once caused a blaze in his studio by carelessly flinging spirits of turpentine into the fireplace, which required a very expensive visit from the local 'fire engine'.

Artists themselves usually arranged the sittings, rather than leaving it to an assistant: a fashionable portraitist was not dealing with a class of people who suffered mistakes or cancellations kindly, thus a sitters'

OPPOSITE: **59.** Joshua Reynolds, *Portrait of Jane Fleming*, 1778

Reynolds created a new type of portraiture. He endowed his clients with dignity and refinement by depicting them in spectacular 'swagger' portraits. Jane Fleming's toga-like dress and outstretched arm is intended to remind the viewer of the Apollo Belvedere.

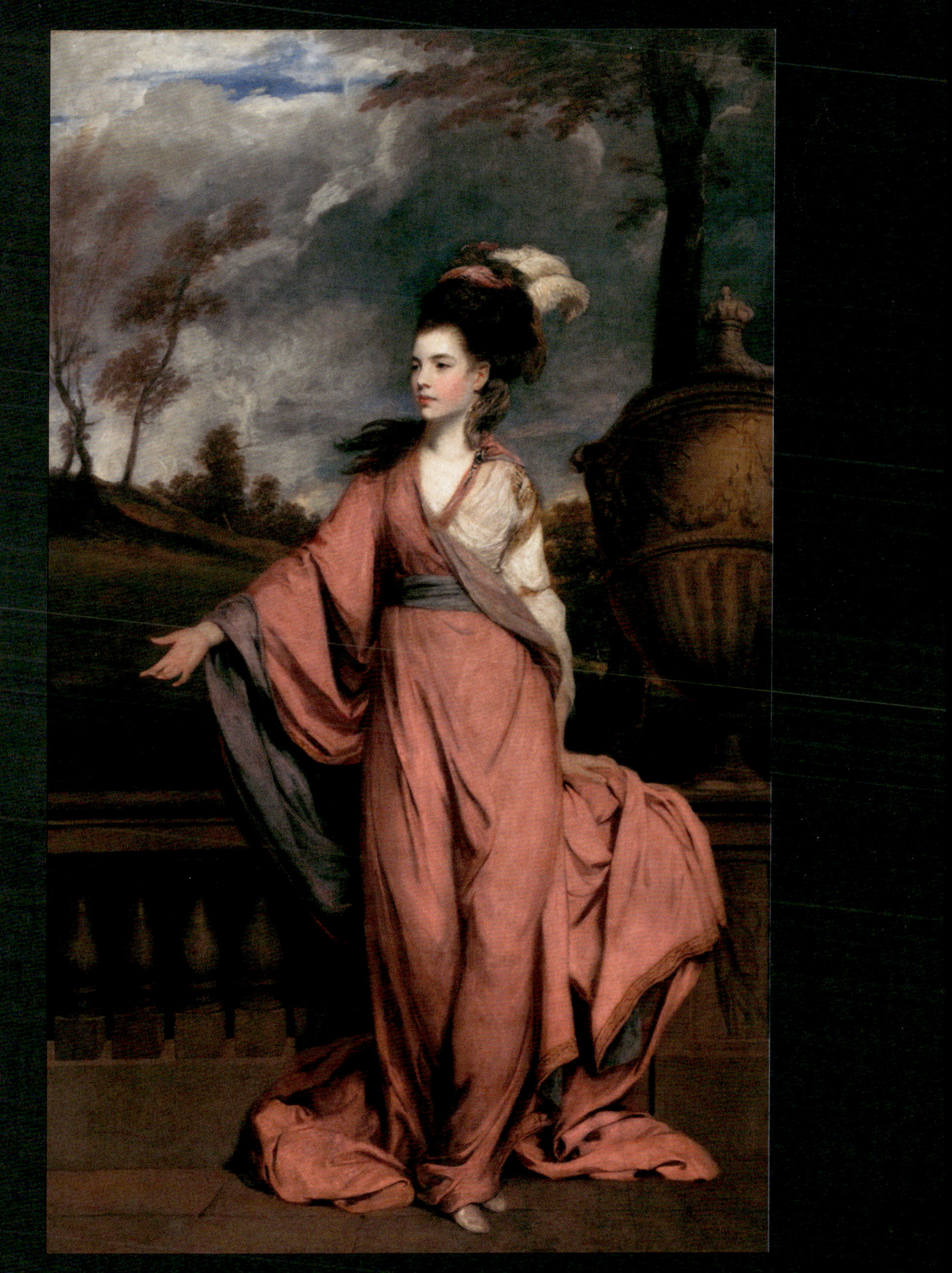

Due to the writings of Jean-Jacques Rousseau, the cult of the happy family was very strong in the late eighteenth century, and Reynolds has depicted Lady Cockburn as an adoring mother. The macaw is probably Reynolds's own bird, the one that hated his cook.

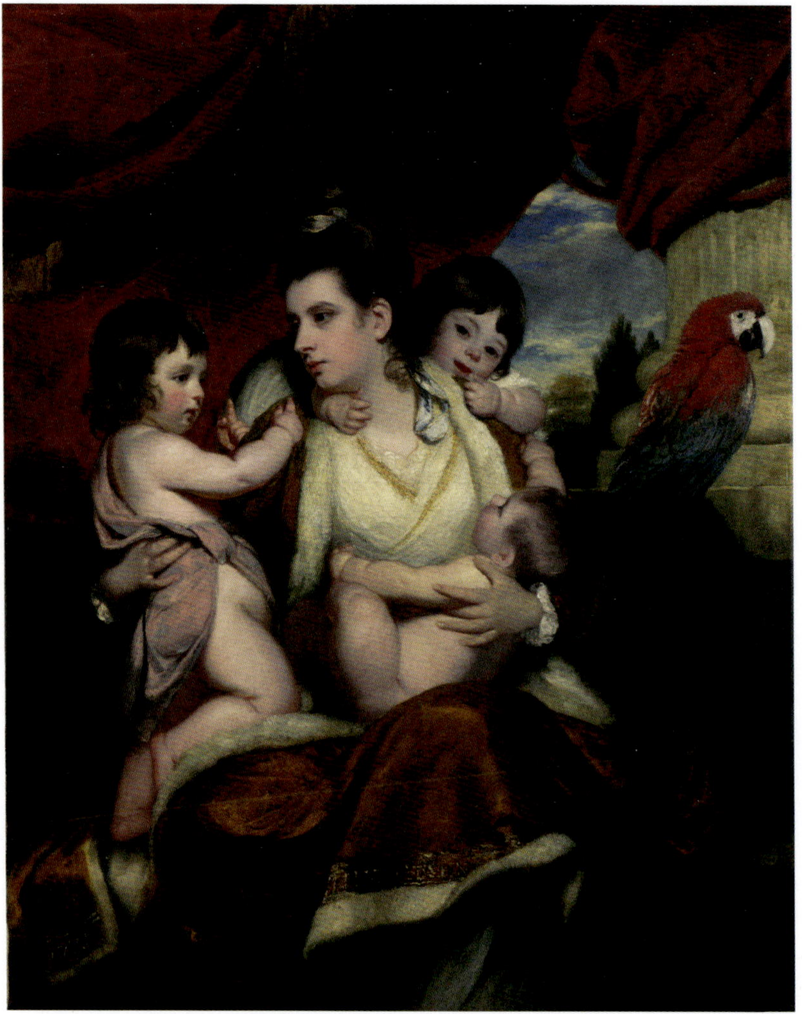

book was vital. As no contracts appear to have been drawn up between artist and client, it was the artist's only proof in the event of a dispute. Reynolds was as meticulous about his sitters' book as he was about every other aspect of running his studio. Had it not been for his ability to conduct his business efficiently, it is doubtful that his skill alone would have been enough to keep him at the very peak of his profession, especially in the latter half of the eighteenth century when competition in London was at its fiercest. A page from his pocketbook of 1761 shows that he worked every day but Sunday and was receiving four or five sitters a day – and earning a fortune.

A portraitist's studio often included a 'props' cupboard containing an assortment of garments, pieces of fabric, hats, a sword, perhaps a guitar or a broken violin. One of Reynolds's props was a pet macaw which flew freely about the house. This bird hated the cook, who had 'ill-used it'. When Reynolds's assistant, James Northcote, painted the cook's portrait, the bird 'flew over to it with the utmost fury and bit at the hands and face [and] when he found he could not get hold of it he looked so very cunning, and went to the side and back to examine it.'[17]

These props came in useful when a sitter wished to be portrayed with an 'attribute' that denoted their literary or musical interests, such as a particular book or a sheet of music. The sitter's pose was also part of the 'language' of portraiture. A military man might adopt a heroic stance in imitation of an antique Roman sculpture. Reynolds tended to swathe his female sitters in yards of rich drapery and to assume a somewhat contorted Classical pose – as in his portrait of Jane Fleming. There were certain poses, however, which were not considered appropriate: a portrait by Gainsborough of the musician Ann Ford raised eyebrows because she was shown with her legs crossed *above* the knee.

The shrewd portraitist ensured that his studio was in a fashionable area and was furnished in such a manner that clients felt at ease in their surroundings and not as if they were slumming it. The miniature painter Ozias Humphry, determined to prove himself a man of taste and substance, spent an enormous sum decorating his studio in blue and white, with fine French furniture, expensive carpet and curtains, and no less than three mirrors.

Mirrors were a useful studio tool as they enabled artists to see a reversed version of their composition – a 'fresh' eye, as it were. Reynolds's octagonal studio was furnished with a mahogany swing mirror 1.2m tall.[18] Vigée Le Brun advised her niece: 'You should also have a mirror positioned behind you so that you can see both the model and your painting at the same time ... it is the best guide and will show up faults clearly.'[19] It also enabled the sitter to watch the portrait's progress.

Most successful portrait painters employed one or more assistants, young men who were taken on to learn from the master but also to carry out the many tasks associated with the running of a busy studio. These tasks included replenishing the stock of artist's materials, returning a sitter's clothes that had been borrowed for copying, and arranging the frequent comings and goings of the finished portrait – to the engraver, the gilder, the framer – and finally ensuring that it was safely delivered to the client. For a particularly important commission, the finished portrait would be crated up and sent by coach, accompanied by a chaperone or minder.

For a female portraitist, employing assistants was problematic: having young men in her studio would have been thought improper, while trained girls were hard to find. The Venetian pastellist, Rosalba Carriera, avoided gossip by training her sister Giovanna to run her studio, to paint drapery and to make copies of the finished portraits. The seventeenth-century artist, Mary Beale, was lucky enough to have

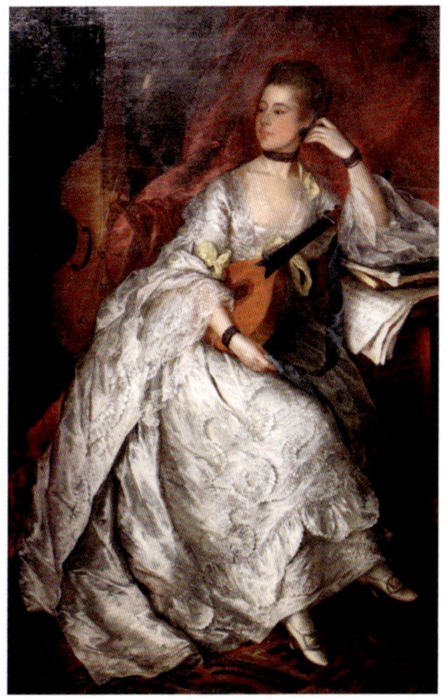

61. Thomas Gainsborough, *Ann Ford, Mrs Philip Thicknesse*, 1760

Eighteenth-century portraitists had to take care that a sitter's pose did not send the wrong message. This portrait was criticised for showing Ann Ford seated in a manner that was considered by polite society to be masculine and immodest.

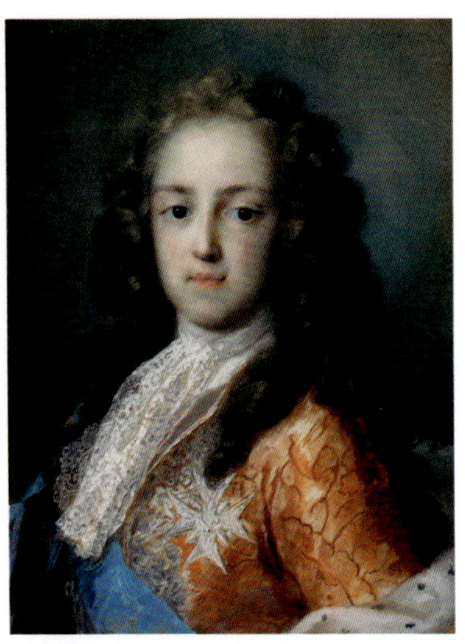

62. Rosalba Carriera, *Louis XV as a Boy*, 1720–21

Louis succeeded his great-grandfather Louis XIV at the age of five. Carriera was invited by a rich banker to leave her native Venice and spend a year in Paris. Her consummate skill as a pastellist has captured the creamy intricacies of the boy's lace jabot and his haughty expression.

a husband who ran her studio for her, leaving her free to paint the portraits that earned the family's income.

Rouquet's comment that the aim of English portraitists was 'not so much to paint well, as to paint a great deal' is borne out by the sheer number of portraits an artist had to produce to make a living. Romney, for instance, received a total number of 593 sittings in a single year, 1783, but for the son of a Lancashire builder and cabinet maker, this enormous output had been his route to fame and fortune.[20] Working under such pressure, it is no wonder that artists resorted to taking short cuts. Hands and feet disappeared behind drapery, and backgrounds became hazy landscapes as they were simpler to paint than a detailed interior. But the principal short cut was to delegate the painting of the client's clothes – the most elaborate and time-consuming part of a portrait – either to a studio assistant or to a specialised drapery painter. The portraitist then had only the face and hands to paint.

If an artist eschewed a drapery painter, a useful aid to the painting of a sitter's clothes was a lay-figure, or mannequin, on which the garments selected by the sitter were arranged. These figures could be life-sized, with flexible, jointed limbs. Michelangelo is recorded as having used lay figures in his work in the Sistine Chapel 'to help him register light, shadow and dramatic effects of foreshortening'.[21] In the following centuries these lay-figures became standard pieces of studio equipment. Careful examination of images of artists' studios often reveal one of these figures lurking in the background, a painter's silent and unacknowledged partner. Reynolds once famously painted 'a fierce cocked hat' on one of his sitters, dispatched the picture to the drapery-painter who later returned it having painted a standard posture which included a second hat under the sitter's arm.[22]

Thomas Gainsborough never used drapery painters, but he did use lay figures, although judging by an account by fellow artist Ozias Humphry of Gainsborough's working practice, it is a wonder that he could see to paint at all: 'These Pictures ... were often wrought by Candle Light, and generally with great force and likeness. But his Painting Room even by Day (a kind of darkened twilight) had scarcely any Light; and our young Friend [the landscape designer Uvedale Price] has seen him, whilst his Subjects have been sitting to him, when neither they nor the pictures were scarcely discernible.'[23]

Many artists preferred to paint by candlelight as it was far more stable than the shifting moods of natural light, but good beeswax candles were expensive, while the cheaper tallow ones guttered and smoked and smelt horrible. Candlelight also enhanced the shimmer of silk and satin, enriched the folds in velvet and gave to gold a spectacular radiance.

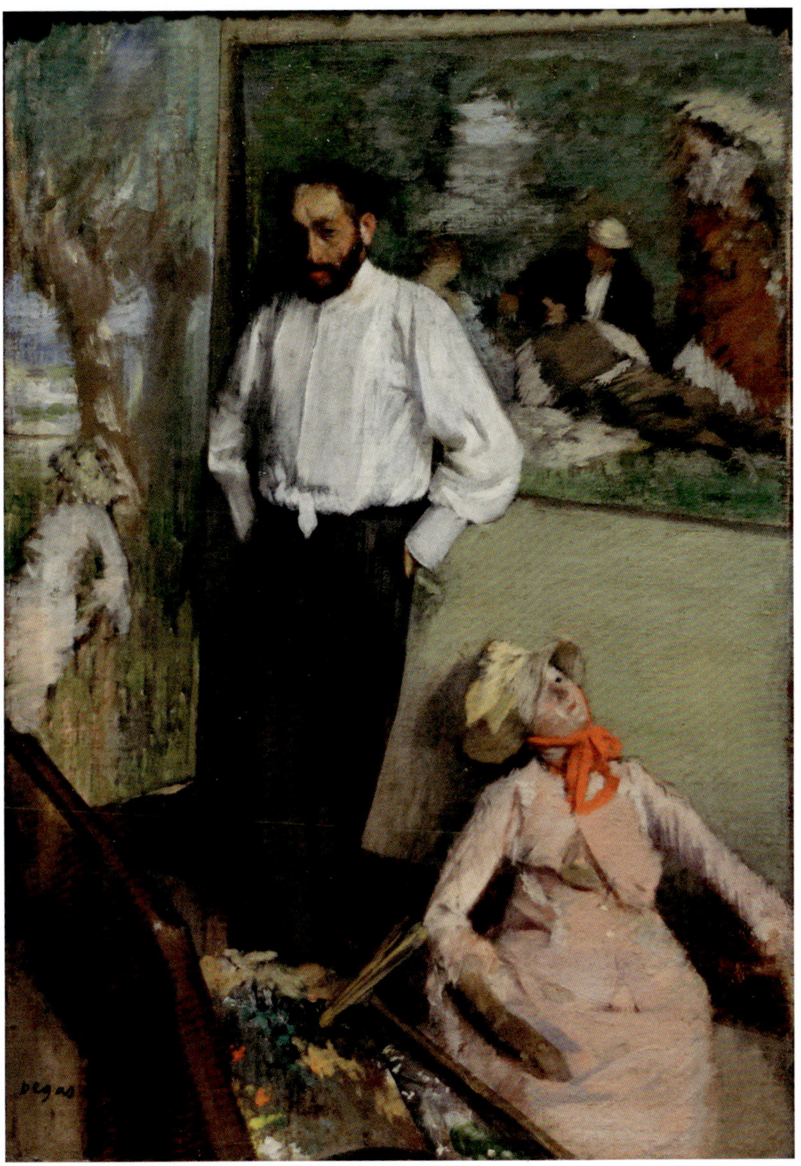

When painting a large portrait, Gainsborough preferred to have the canvas loose enough to be flapping. 'In effect he was painting on a ship's sail, rigged perhaps like a small yacht, the canvas prone to bellying with every move he made.'[24] Using six-feet-long brushes, he would step back from the canvas, then forward again – a restless process for both artist and sitter.

After a long and successful period in Bath, in 1774 Gainsborough moved into the west wing of Schomberg House in Pall Mall. He immediately added a new painting room and gallery on to the rear, looking over St James's Park. 'There must also have been a set of high doors in the extension to take frames in and out … The ceiling must

63. Edgar Degas, *Portrait of Henri Michel-Lévy*, 1878

Artists were often very discreet about using mannequins or lay figures as an aid to painting drapery, but Degas does not hesitate to show one in this portrait of his friend, although the crumpled pink figure, with hat askew, has an air of abandonment, as if the artist wished to be disassociated from it.

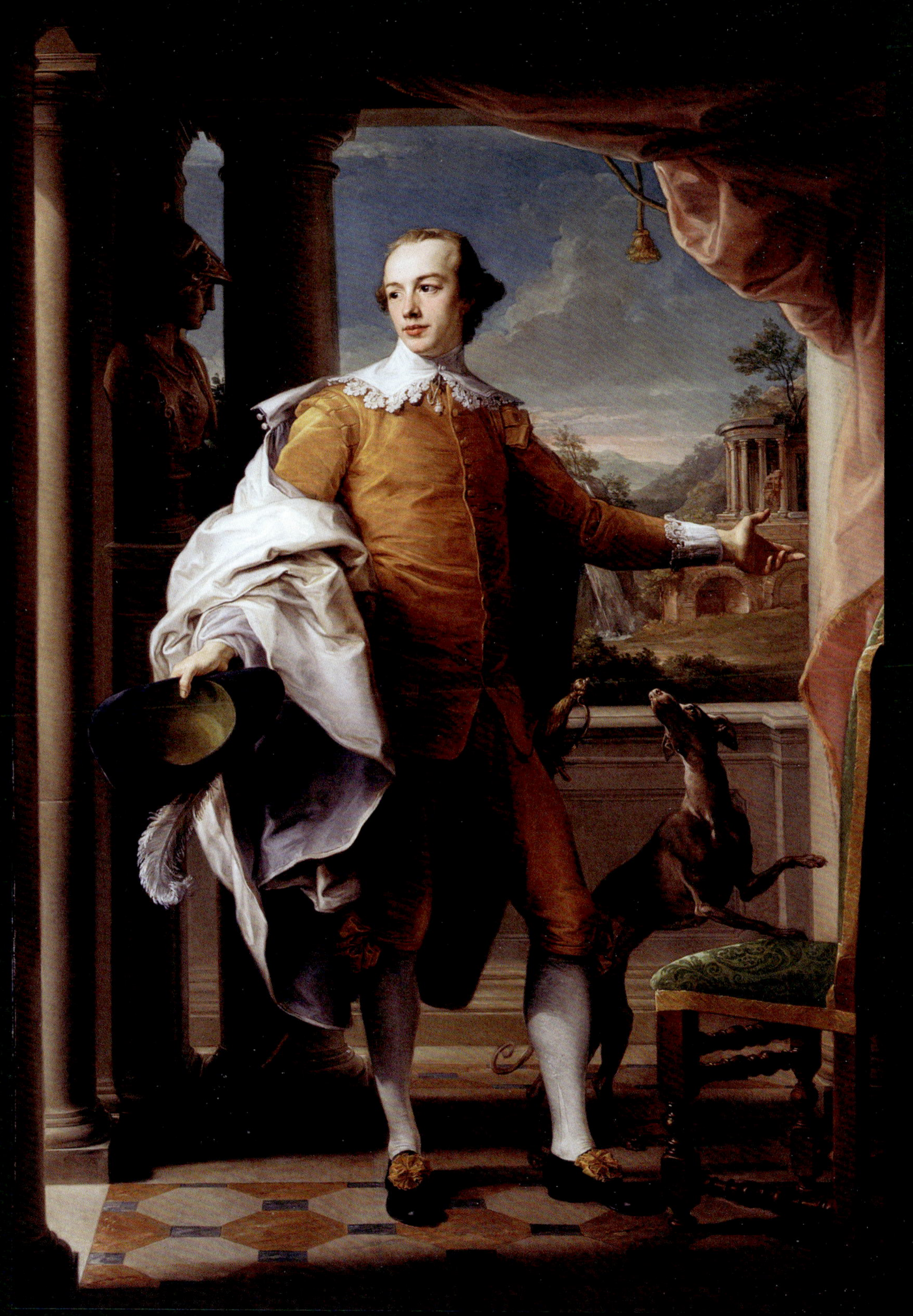

have been at least fifteen feet [5m] high because it was here that he painted his largest canvases.'[25] It was also at Schomberg House that he painted the sublime double portrait, *The Morning Walk* (see page 60). The recently married and discreetly elegant Mr and Mrs Hallett and their devoted dog stroll through a hazy landscape of dappled light and shade, an example of eighteenth-century English portraiture at its finest.

In London at that date a portrait painter's studio played a distinctive role in society as one of the few places where people of a different class could meet on equal terms; friends and relations could while away an idle hour; lovers could make illicit assignations; and as a haven for those who had become *persona non grata* in society.

Reynolds's visitors to his house in Leicester Fields were greeted with great ceremony by a liveried footman. The essayist and critic William Hazlitt delights in describing their comings and goings: 'What a rustling of silks! What a fluttering of flounces and brocades! What a cloud of powder and perfumes! What a flow of periwigs! What an exchange of civilities and of titles! What a recognition of old friendships, and an introduction of new acquaintances and sitters.'[26]

Depictions of the British upper classes were not limited to British artists: the Italian artist Pompeo Batoni (1708–87) was among the most celebrated portraitists in Europe, his clients ranging from kings, emperors and popes to Catherine the Great. His main clients, however, were the British *milordi*, sent on the Grand Tour to broaden their minds and keep them out of mischief until they were mature enough to be useful, responsible citizens – a sort of aristocratic Gap Year, although some tours lasted much longer. More than 200 wealthy gentlemen and noblemen beat a well-trodden path to Batoni's large house in Bocca di Leone in Rome where they were portrayed in poses of casual elegance, often sporting their splendid new outfits made for them by Roman tailors at a fraction of the cost charged by their English counterparts.

Grand Tourists were prone to taking their dogs with them on their travels, as illustrated by the whippet that is looking adoringly at its master in Batoni's portrait of Sir Wyndham. However, they often came to a sticky end. The Earl of Carlisle's dog, Rover, was due to be painted by Batoni but had suffered a broken leg in Florence. He was later run over by a coach in Paris. Horace Walpole's King Charles spaniel, Tory – which, according to Horace was 'the sweetest, fattest, dearest creature' – met an even worse fate: when crossing the wild and mountainous Mont Cenis pass, Horace let the dog out of the chaise for an airing, whereupon he was seized by a young wolf and carried off. 'It was shocking to see anything one loved run away with to so horrid a death,' Walpole lamented.[27]

OPPOSITE: **64.** Pompeo Batoni, *Sir Wyndham Knatchbull-Wyndham, 6th Bt*, 1758–59

Batoni has depicted Sir Wyndham in Van Dyck dress, with the Temple of Vesta at Tivoli in the background and a bust of the goddess Minerva peering out of the shadows. His debonair stance evokes the famous statue of the Apollo Belvedere.

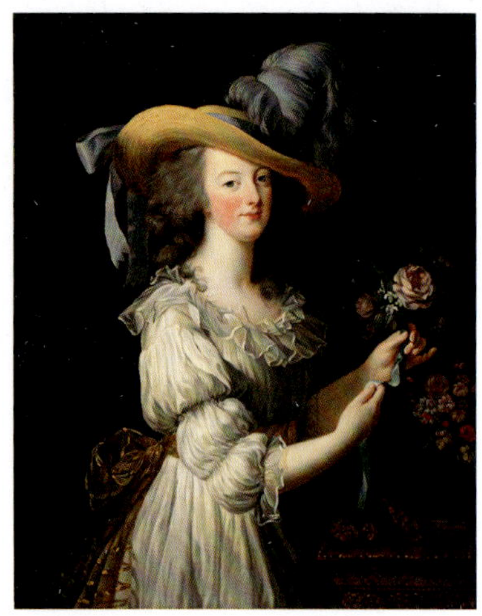

65. Élisabeth Vigée Le Brun,
Marie Antoinette en Gaulle, 1783

The Queen spent enormous sums
on her clothes and this portrait
of her wearing a simple sheath of
muslin may have been an attempt
to convince people that she was not
bankrupting France. Despite the
disapproval of the establishment,
it earned the artist great celebrity.

OPPOSITE: 66. Diego Velázquez,
Las Meninas, c. 1656

This is the only known self-portrait
of the artist. The red cross on his
doublet signifies his subsequent
knighthood and was added to the
painting later. The king and his wife
appear in the mirror on the rear wall.
The colours on the artist's palette
accurately reflect those he is using
in the picture.

For women artists, portraiture was the natural choice. Compared
to history painting, it was relatively small scale and far less dependent
on mastery of the human figure. However, its practice was not without
its risks or its detractors: Boswell reported that Dr Johnson thought
'portrait painting an improper employment for a woman'. 'Publick
practice of any art,' he observed, 'and staring in men's faces, is very
indelicate in a female.'[28] Despite this widely held view, the eighteenth
century saw an increasing number of women becoming successful
portrait painters.

One woman who overcame every obstacle to become the most
sought-after female society portraitist, not just in her native France
but throughout Europe and Russia, was Élisabeth Vigée Le Brun.
Unlike Batoni and Reynolds, who liked to paint their sitters in the
Grand Manner, she preferred them to look as natural as possible, even
boasting that she had changed fashion by encouraging them to adopt
softer, simpler styles and to leave their hair unpowdered. When she
was appointed Painter to Queen Marie Antoinette, for one portrait she
persuaded her to wear a dress of ruffled white muslin and an enormous
straw hat. When the portrait was exhibited at the Salon in 1783, it
caused a furore. Vigée Le Brun was accused of portraying the Queen in
'her underwear', and the portrait had to be withdrawn.

To paint the Queen and other members of the royal family, Vigée
Le Brun would have made the journey to the palace at Versailles. In
her *Souvenirs*, she recalls one occasion when she had missed a sitting
because of illness during her pregnancy, but was greatly relieved when
the Queen offered her another sitting: 'I remember that in my haste to
respond to this favour, I seized my box of colours with such vivacity that
it tipped over: my brushes fell on to the parquet ...' She was overcome
when the Queen, remarking that Vigée Le Brun was 'too far advanced'
in her pregnancy to bend down, picked them up herself.[29]

Vigée Le Brun, who painted fast and with fierce concentration,
disliked having visitors to her studio, even begging her clients 'not to
bring their friends to the sitting, for they all want to give advice and will
spoil everything'.[30] This was wishful thinking, however, as artists' studios
had always attracted visitors. One such relates how he found Rubens
'in his atelier, listening to a recitation of Tacitus, giving dictation, and
entertaining guests, even while working on a painting'.[31] Vasari records
that when Leonardo completed his *Virgin and Child with Saint Anne and
the Infant Saint John*, for the two days it was on show, the room was filled
with 'a crowd of men and women, young and old, who flocked there
as if they were attending a great festival, to gaze in amazement'.[32] In his
biography of Michelangelo, Martin Gayford comments on this event:
'This is an extraordinary moment. For the first time since, perhaps,

     FOUR / RECORDED FOR POSTERITY

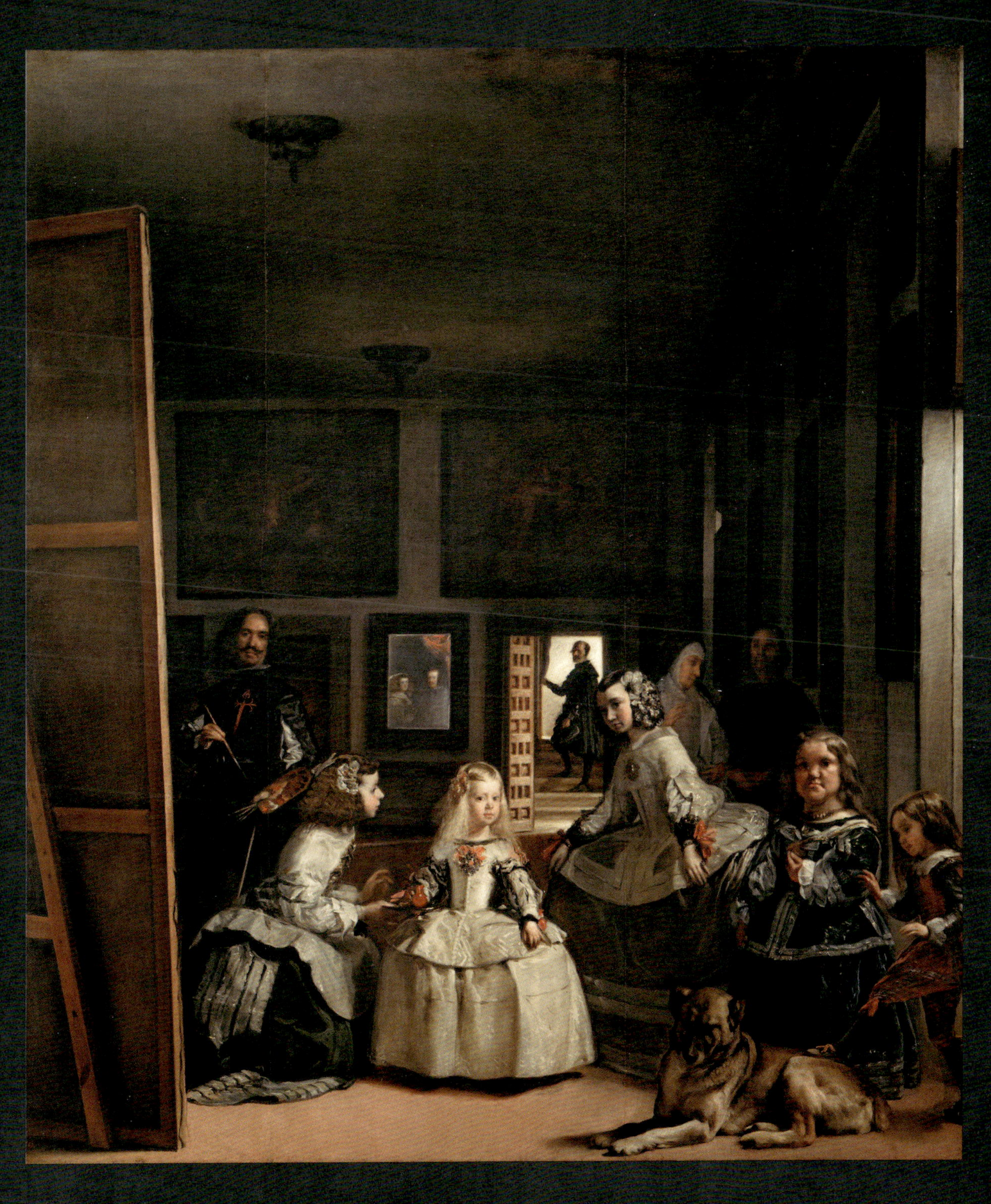

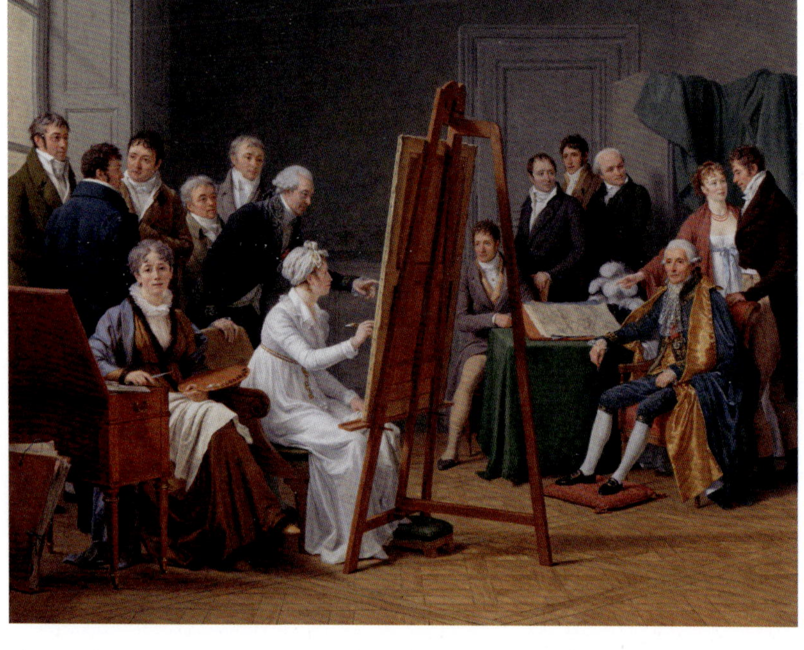

67. Marie-Gabrielle Capet, *Studio Interior*, 1808

A fashionable portraitist's studio was not just a working space but acted as a rendezvous for friends and relatives. It was also one of the few places where people of a different class could meet on equal terms to while away an idle hour.

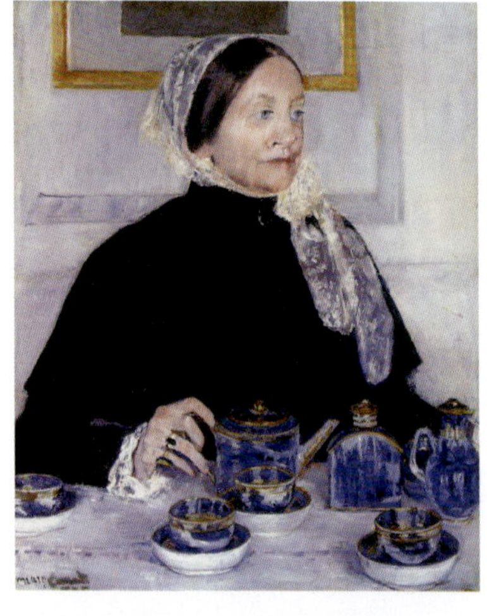

68. Mary Cassatt, *Lady at the Tea Table (Portrait of Mary Dickinson Riddle)*, 1883–85

Cassatt painted Mrs Riddle to thank her for the gift of the blue porcelain tea set on the table before her. Once celebrated as a great beauty, Mrs Riddle rejected the portrait because her daughter thought her mother's nose was too large.

classical antiquity, an audience assembled to admire a work of art not because of what it represented but for its own sake, as a "marvel".[33]

There are countless other examples of artists receiving important visitors: Michelangelo was visited by Pope Julius II; Emperor Charles V visited Titian's studio and allegedly retrieved the artist's brush when he dropped it; Charles I enjoyed watching Van Dyck painting in his studio by the Thames; Christina, the former Queen of Sweden, visited the sculptor Bernini in his Rome studio. But the most famous painting to depict a royal visit is *Las Meninas* by Diego Velázquez (1599–1660).

This painting shows Velázquez in the studio in the palace at Madrid that the Spanish king, Philip IV, gave him when he became Court Painter in 1623. Velázquez, splendidly dressed in a silk doublet, is standing before an enormous canvas. In the centre of the painting is the little Infanta Margarita, flanked by two *meninas* (maids of honour), her tutors, page, dwarf and a huge, slumbering hound. A mirror on the rear wall shows the king, accompanied by his wife, caught in the act of visiting the artist. Or are they? Whether it actually reflects them visiting, or posing for their portrait, remains a mystery to this day.

Throughout the nineteenth century the majority of the art that sold well remained academic and traditional. The sands, however, were shifting. Émile Zola expressed what many had come to feel: that the way art was taught at the École des Beaux-Arts had slowly drilled out of its students 'all sparks of originality and spontaneity', crushing them 'beneath the dead hand of tradition that was now reduced to over-taught formulae.'[34] In effect, Zola was encouraging artists to devise a new way of communicating in paint what they saw before them.

When the first Impressionist exhibition was held in Paris in 1874 – to be greeted with cries of horror – it was clear that a new breed of artists was at last making itself felt, one that disdained the almost photographic realism of the past and instead sought to capture the fleeting effects of reflected light, the 'sensation' produced by a landscape or a street scene, rather than a dutiful, detailed rendering of the subject. Landscape and genre painters were urged to make a more direct connection with their subjects by painting *en plein air*, out of doors. Although artists had been sketching outside for centuries, the nineteenth century witnessed its increasing popularity, and it became one of the central tenets of the Impressionist movement.

Portraiture, too, was affected by this new freedom. With the advent of photography, artists no longer felt the need to paint every hair and wrinkle, or load the image with symbolic 'attributes'. Nor was the sitter asked to assume some tortured pose in the studio against a confected background of temples and Roman pillars, but was portrayed in the sitter's home, garden or even in the theatre. The marvellous image of Mrs Dickinson Riddle by the American artist Mary Cassatt (1844–1926) is a perfect example of this new naturalism. It reflects, too, the desire by the wealthy bourgeoisie to signal its rise to economic and political power, a desire illustrated by the veritable flood of portraits of the middle classes in the Paris Salon exhibitions during this period.

Mary Cassatt, one of the most popular portraitists of her day, brought a new intimacy to images of her family, friends and their offspring. Her particular talent was in depicting children as they really are and not the trussed up little 'adults' so dear to the Victorians.

When the art critic Edmond Duranty wrote the following in his 1876 pamphlet 'The New Painting', it was with Edgar Degas' images of ballet dancers and washerwomen very much in mind: 'The idea, the very first idea, was to eliminate the partition separating the artist's studio from everyday life, and to introduce the reality of the street ... It was necessary to make the painter come out of his sky-lighted cell, his cloister, where his sole communication was with the sky – and to bring him back among men, out into the real world.'[35]

Degas certainly came out of his 'cloister' to make *Six Friends at Dieppe*, an informal portrait of his companions, but he would then have worked it up in the studio. For Degas, his studio was a world apart; few were allowed to enter, let alone watch him at work. But on this occasion, he had – unusually for him – set up his easel on the beach. Portraiture had come a long way from the days of embroidered waistcoats, billowing satin and the elite posing with ramrods up their backs.

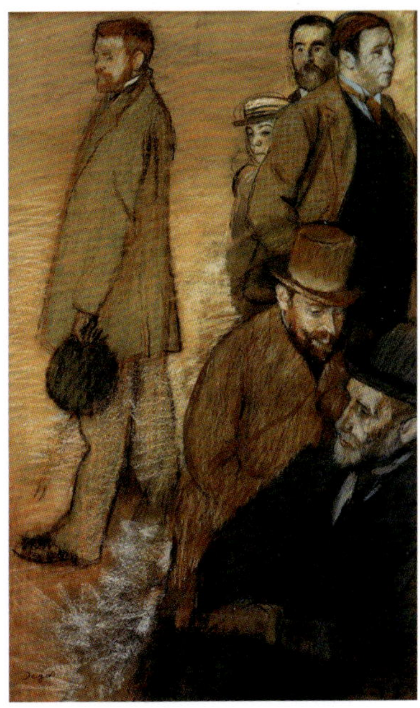

69. Edgar Degas, *Six Friends at Dieppe*, 1885

For this sketch, Degas would require a box containing his pastels, a collapsible easel, a stool and an umbrella with which to direct the sun's rays and protect him while he worked. All but two of the group gathered on the sands are painters. Walter Sickert is on the left.

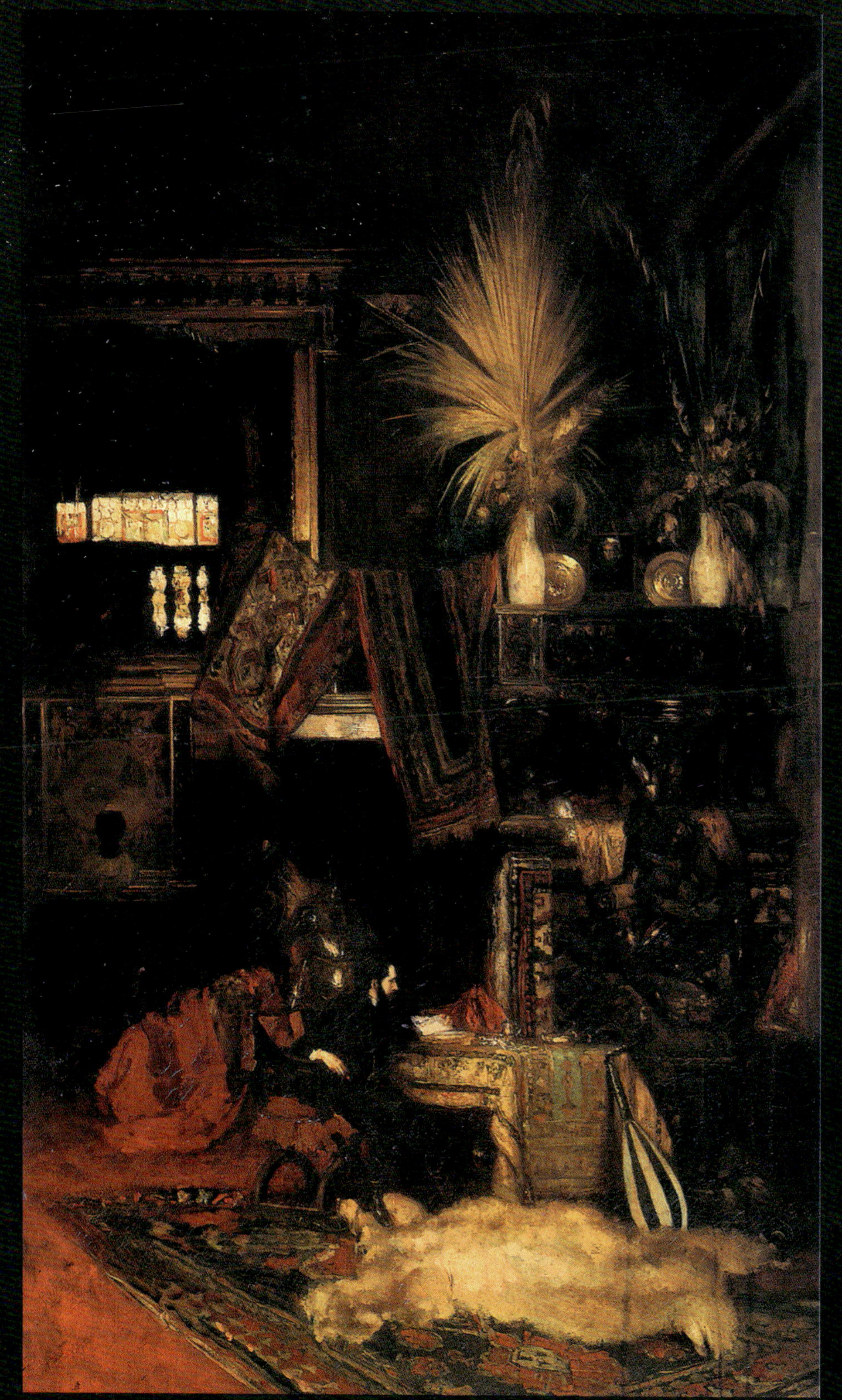

FIVE

A Sumptuous Life
The Celebrity Studio

*In our epoch the painter is no longer the labouring artisan who locks
himself away in his studio behind a closed door living in a dream.
He has thrust his head foremost into the bustle of the world and
participates in the elegant Paris; he has his day when his studio is
transformed into a salon where he receives the elite of polite society.*
Albert Wolff in *La Capital de l'Art,* 1886[1]

THE CELEBRITY ARTISTS OF THE NINETEENTH CENTURY were
a phenomenon created by an era of social fluidity, increasing wealth, a
rising middle class and an avid market for 'fashionable' art, fuelled by the
vast fortunes amassed by industrialists and speculators, both in Europe
and in America. In this febrile atmosphere, certain artists, who captured
the tastes and appetites of the day, became immensely wealthy. They
could afford to buy or build grand houses, with magnificent integrated
studios that became showcases for their art and the hub of both social
and cultural life.

The studios of these society darlings resembled stage sets designed
by Visconti for a Puccini opera. Buried among the rich velvet curtains,
tapestries, exotic rugs, gilt-framed paintings, Turkish hookahs, bric-a-
brac and the ubiquitous potted palm, the artists themselves seemed
dwarfed by the splendour of their surroundings. There is often little sign
of an easel, or the mess created by an artist at work, because these were
showplaces designed to amaze and impress, and to entice visitors to
buy their paintings. The Austrian artist Hans Makart (1840–84), seated
at a table in his studio, is so hung about with opulent furnishings, his
feet warmed by a lion skin, that he is difficult to pick out of the gloom.
And this was just one small corner of his studio in Vienna. Pull back,
and its full glory is revealed. With its soaring ceiling, acres of oriental
carpet and sumptuous furnishings, it was a monument to the artist's
wealth and ambition.

70. Eduard Charlemont, *Hans
Makart in his Studio in Vienna, c.* 1875

The splendour of Makart's studio is
typical of the studios of a handful
of artists whose work was so
fashionable that they became rich
and famous. Visitors to Makart's
studio were impressed by its
sheer scale, its countless grottoes,
fountains, palm trees, elaborate
furnishings and exotic pets.

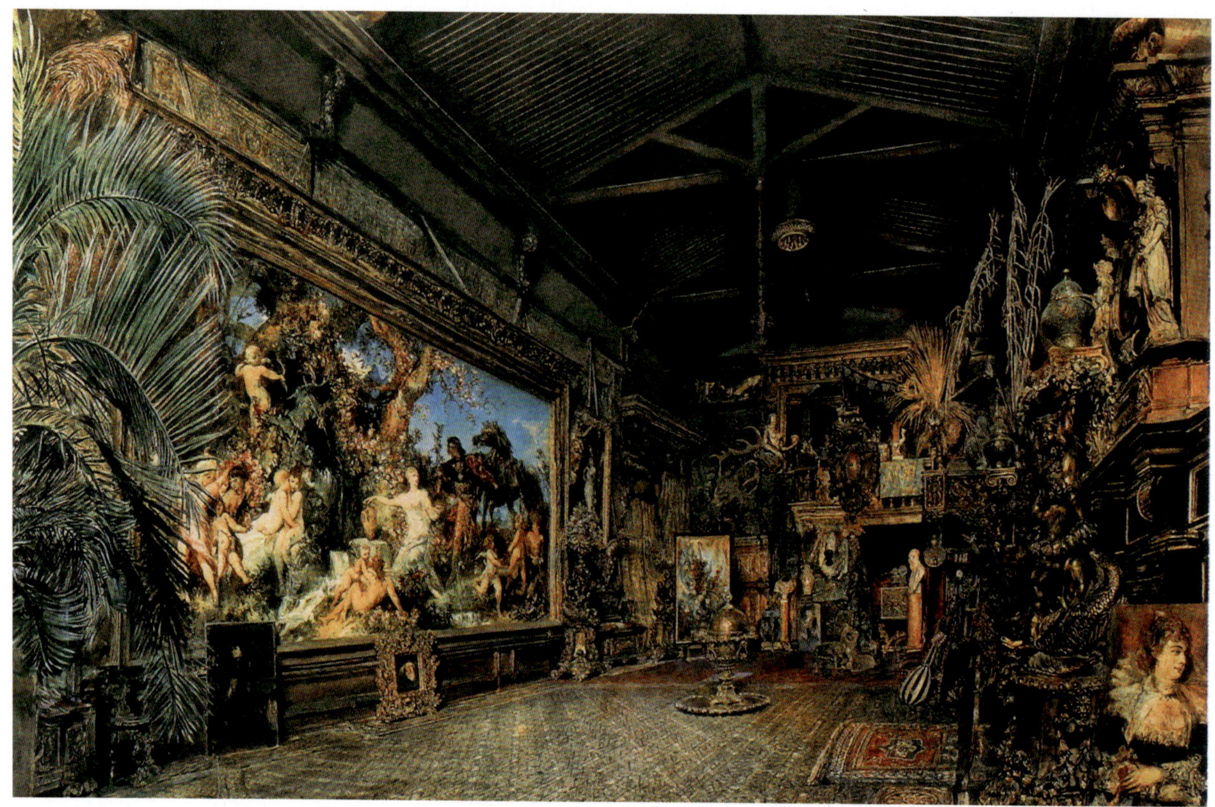

71. Rudolf von Alt, *Hans Makart's Studio in Vienna*, 1885

The huge painting, entitled *Spring,* that fills the studio's left-hand wall, is representative of Makart's subject matter, its vibrant colours showing the influence of his great hero Peter Paul Rubens. There is not an easel or paint rag in sight.

Many of Makart's allegorical and history paintings are invested with female nudes who float about with no apparent purpose other than to expose their graceful contours and substantial backsides – even when the painting depicts the entrance of Charles V into Antwerp in 1520. Makart's visit to Egypt produced more nudes, including Cleopatra with marble breasts and brandishing her asp. But the public loved these *grandes machines*, as this type of painting was called, and Makart made a fortune. He was also highly successful as a costume designer. His decoration of the interior of many of Vienna's public buildings engendered the term 'Makartstil' or 'Makart style' which came to define cultural life in the city and had a marked influence on other artists, notably Gustav Klimt.

Makart was just one of a handful of nineteenth-century artists whose paintings –and the reproduction rights they sold to engravers – became so fashionable and sought after that the artists could afford to live on a grand scale. But fashion is a fickle mistress, and within one hundred years the majority had been forgotten, their work engulfed by the tidal wave of Impressionism and the Avant-Garde.

Germany also had its Makart: Franz von Lenbach (1836–1904). Lenbach had started out as a journeyman mason in Bavaria, but then studied at the Academy of Fine Arts in Munich and became a portraitist

     FIVE / A SUMPTUOUS LIFE

of renown. He was helped on his way to prosperity by Makart – a friend from student days – and by the end of his life he had married into the aristocracy and lived in style in a magnificent neo-Renaissance villa built for him in Munich. (The villa was so large and splendid that it now houses Munich's Stadtische Galerie.) He won international acclaim through his portraits of a remarkable range of prominent personalities that included William Gladstone, Richard Wagner, Emperor Franz-Joseph, Pope Leo XIII, Clara Schumann and the cabaret singer Yvette Guilbert. He is perhaps best known for some one hundred portraits of Otto von Bismarck. Lenbach's paintings were very popular as gifts among the Nazi leaders. One of the Bismarck portraits was given as a birthday present to Hitler by Göring. Goebbels also gave him a Lenbach, noting in his diary, '[Hitler] is very touched and takes the greatest joy in my Lenbach.'[2]

Lenbach devised a new method of portrait painting which he felt avoided his sitters falling into such 'stereotypical poses' that it was impossible to capture their characters. He would begin by making sketches of his sitters. The second stage was to have them photographed – which was now a simpler process owing to the recent introduction of dry plates and the box camera. He would then paste a series of photographs on to a piece of cardboard. Seeing them in sequence gave him a sense of the range of the sitter's expressions. Once he had selected the one he thought was most characteristic, he copied it on to his canvas.

Although the new medium of photography was widely used by artists, they tended to be very discreet about it. A work of art was supposed to be unique, a product of the artist's imagination and creativity, but a photograph was – at that date – a copy of whatever was in front of the camera. The sitter may have felt the artist was cheating – taking a short cut. But Lenbach was aware of this attitude, and was both diplomatic and shrewd in the way he dealt with it: when he had sensitive sitters, he simply hid the camera behind curtains. In the case of clients like Bismarck, who was accustomed to being endlessly photographed, he made no attempt to disguise his technique.[3]

Photography had affected artists in different ways. Despite the widespread fear that this new invention had 'dealt a death blow to art', photographs proved a useful tool to some. For his *Execution of Emperor Maximilian,* Manet had taken the likeness of the Emperor from photographs in the French newspapers (see page 54); Delacroix had photographs made of his models, arranging the pose and supervising the lighting himself.[4] For others, the effect was more profound: they strove to replicate the accuracy and realism that a camera could achieve and their obsessively accurate paintings proved enduringly popular with buyers.

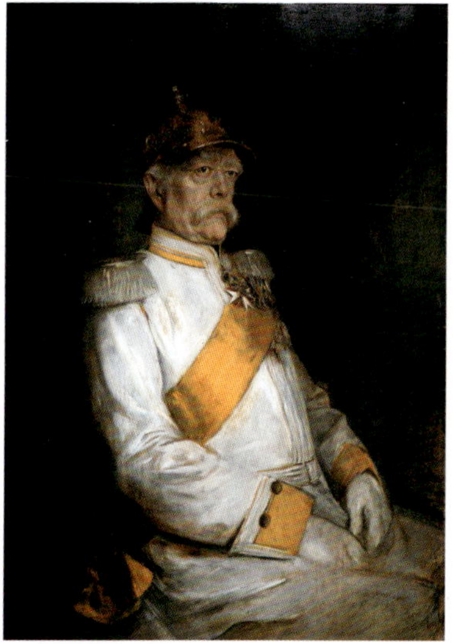

72. Franz von Lenbach, *Portrait of Otto von Bismarck,* 1871

Painted in his seventy-fifth year and shortly after his resignation as Germany's Chancellor, Bismarck looks old and tired. As well he might: the Prussians had just won the Franco-Prussian War, followed by Bismarck's completion of the unification of most of the German states to form the German Empire.

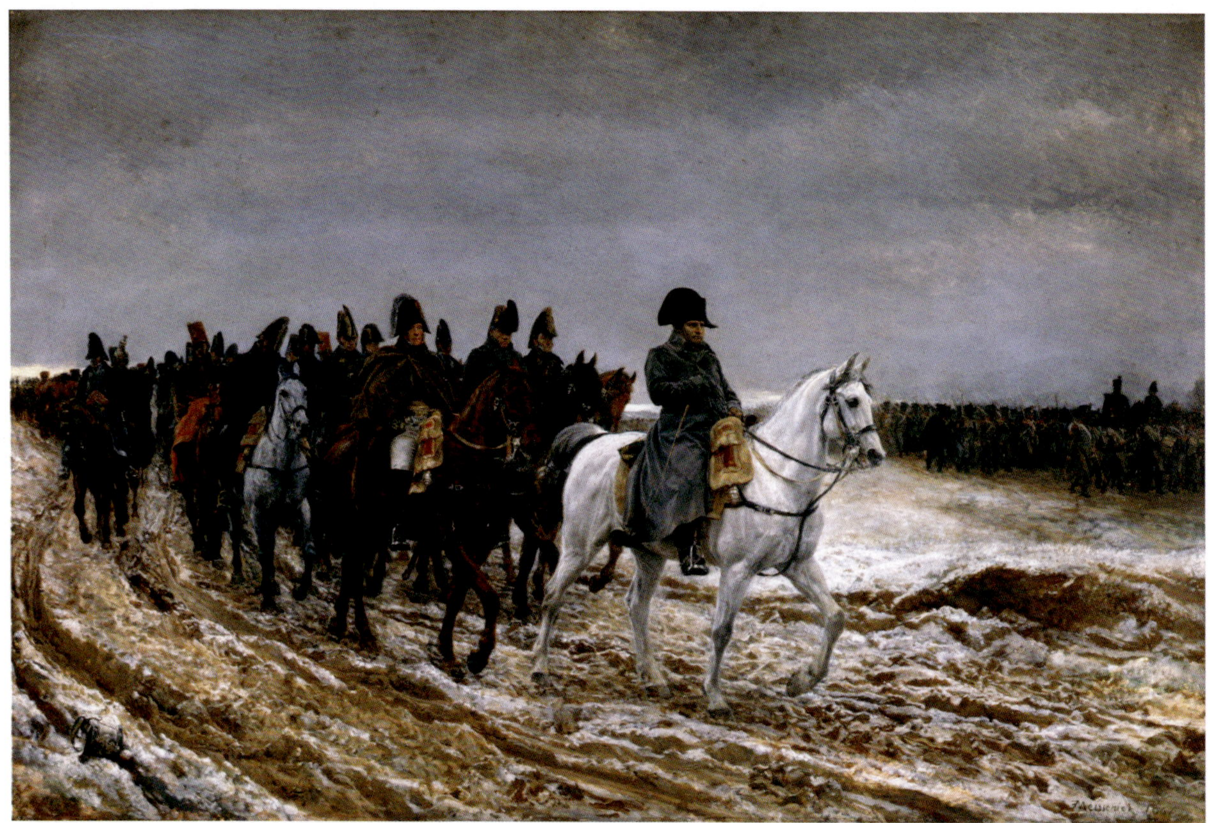

73. Jean-Louis-Ernest Meissonier, *Napoleon on Campaign, 1814,* 1864

For this painting – often wrongly thought to show Napoleon's retreat from Moscow – the artist carried out detailed research and questioned numerous eyewitnesses. He even tried unsuccessfully to borrow the grey coat the Emperor is wearing in the painting.

The French artist Jean-Léon Gérôme (1824–1904), was an influential and very popular teacher at the École des Beaux-Arts for nearly forty years. One of Gérôme's students, visiting his tutor's studio on the top floor of his house in boulevard de Clichy, 'stood dazed in the middle of the splendid room, with its great sculptures and paintings, some still unfinished, and a famous collection of barbaric arms and costumes. A beautiful model was posing on a rug.'[5]

Gérôme had also taken the advent of photography seriously. He considered that 'Photography is an art. It forces artists to discard their old routine and forget their old formulas. It has opened our eyes and forced us to see that which previously we have not seen; a great and inexpressible service for Art.'[6] His minutely detailed paintings of the Middle East and Egypt bear witness to his obsessive quest for reality. When he died, he left twenty-eight large volumes of photographs which he had used as reference for his work.[7]

The military painter Ernest Meissonier (1815–91) was another artist fanatically obsessive about accuracy, producing genre pictures and battle scenes painted with a Hollywood type of 'historical correctness' which were snapped up by eager buyers, Americans and the *nouveaux-riches* in particular. Although his pictures were often exceedingly small (some measured less than 10cm square), he painted so slowly and in such detail that demand far outstripped supply and consequently they were very expensive. 'The prices of his works,' noted the critic Albert Wolff, 'have attained formidable proportions, never before known.'[8] Meissonier made so much money that he was able to build himself a mock-Renaissance villa on the place Malesherbes in Paris, which boasted a spiral staircase and an inner courtyard, complete with cloisters. There, in his vast studio, hung with a forest of draperies, tapestries, arms and armour of every description, he made endless sketches for each tiny painting. His meticulousness sometimes went to absurd lengths: having worked on one of his famous paintings, *1807*, for fourteen years, he was about to send it to the Salon when he realised he had painted the wrong number of dragoons. So he painted all of them again. For another picture, he waited for snow to fall in Paris, then instructed his servants to stamp about in it to give it a churned-up appearance. He then set up his easel in the bitter cold and sketched the scene.[9] He kept a stable of horses and studied them *ad infinitum*. He was so sure of the way they moved that when he first saw Eadweard Muybridge's photographic studies of horses galloping he accused the camera of falsification.[10] By the end of his life, Meissonier had received every medal possible, including the Grand Cross of the Légion d'Honneur, and was a member of the French Institute. Today he is a figure of obscurity.

So too is Émile Carolus-Duran (1837–1917). Good-looking, highly cultured and the epitome of charm, he not only ran one of the most sought-after private academies in Paris but was also a famous portraitist who numbered among his clients Mrs William Astor and other society luminaries. He was an accomplished musician, playing both the organ and the guitar, a fine swordsman, horseman and had read everything worth reading. The French novelist and art critic Gabriel Mourey thought Carolus-Duran had been born out of his time: 'He would have delighted to live in an age when kings picked up their painter's brushes, when artists were sent as ambassadors to neighbouring states. Thus he is an ardent admirer of Velásquez and of Rubens, as much for the sumptuous life they led as for the works they created.'[11]

A visit to Carolus-Duran's luxurious studio in Montparnasse, hung from floor to ceiling with gilt-framed paintings, was an event for Parisian society. This was his showroom and the world flocked to his door. Open day was on Thursday from 9am to 11am. This was something of a challenge for the *haute-monde* as 'a Parisian woman', according to Wolff, 'never rises before midday except on Thursdays to visit Carolus-Duran'.[12] While painting the portrait of some fashionable lady, his studio crowded with her friends and relatives, he would liven up proceedings by 'fencing' with his paintbrush, dashing in a tiny detail with a flourish,

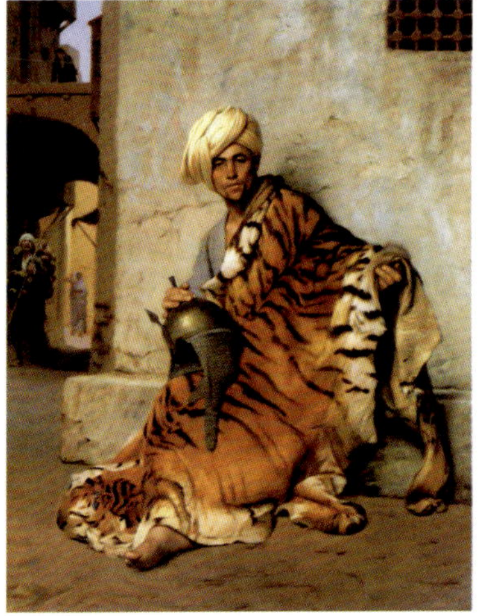

74. Jean-Léon Gérôme, *The Pelt Merchant, Cairo*, 1869

Fascinated by the 'Orient', Gérôme made six trips to Turkey and Egypt, returning with photographs, sketches, costumes, arms, furniture and ceramics. Equipped with this aide-mémoire, he was able to paint scenes with great accuracy.

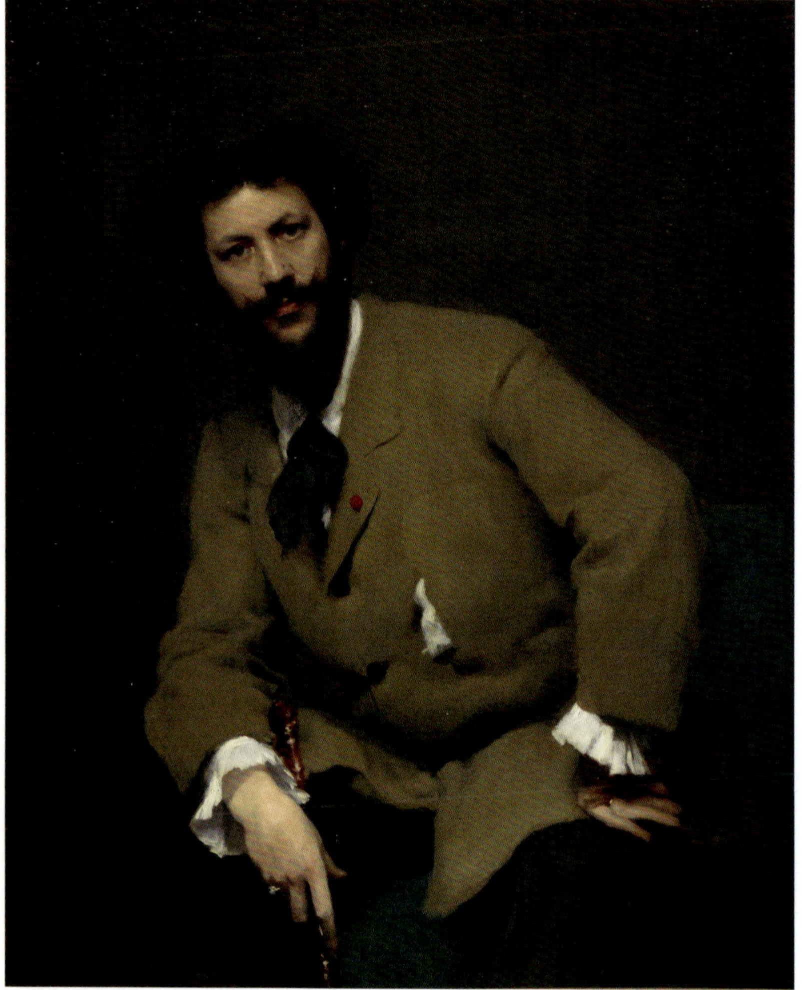

dancing back to judge the effect, then leaping forward again.[13] However, he did not receive much praise from some of his fellow artists, who were perhaps jealous of his success. Degas once remarked that 'Manet is in despair because he cannot paint atrocious pictures like Duran, and not be fêted and decorated ...'[14]

It might seem odd to include the great *tragedienne* Sarah Bernhardt (1844–1923) among these celebrity artists, but as well as her spectacular and tumultuous career on stage, she was a passionately enthusiastic amateur sculptor with a studio easily as grand as theirs. Her original studio was in Montmartre but she then moved into a grand building – all neo-Renaissance knobs and turrets – on the corner of the fashionable avenue de Villiers and rue Fortuny. She decorated it with spears, antlers, leopard skins, rare flowers, bouquets of roses and enormous palms that rivalled in size those in the Palm House at Kew. 'She had a ménage of lovers and a menagerie of animals.'[15] There seems

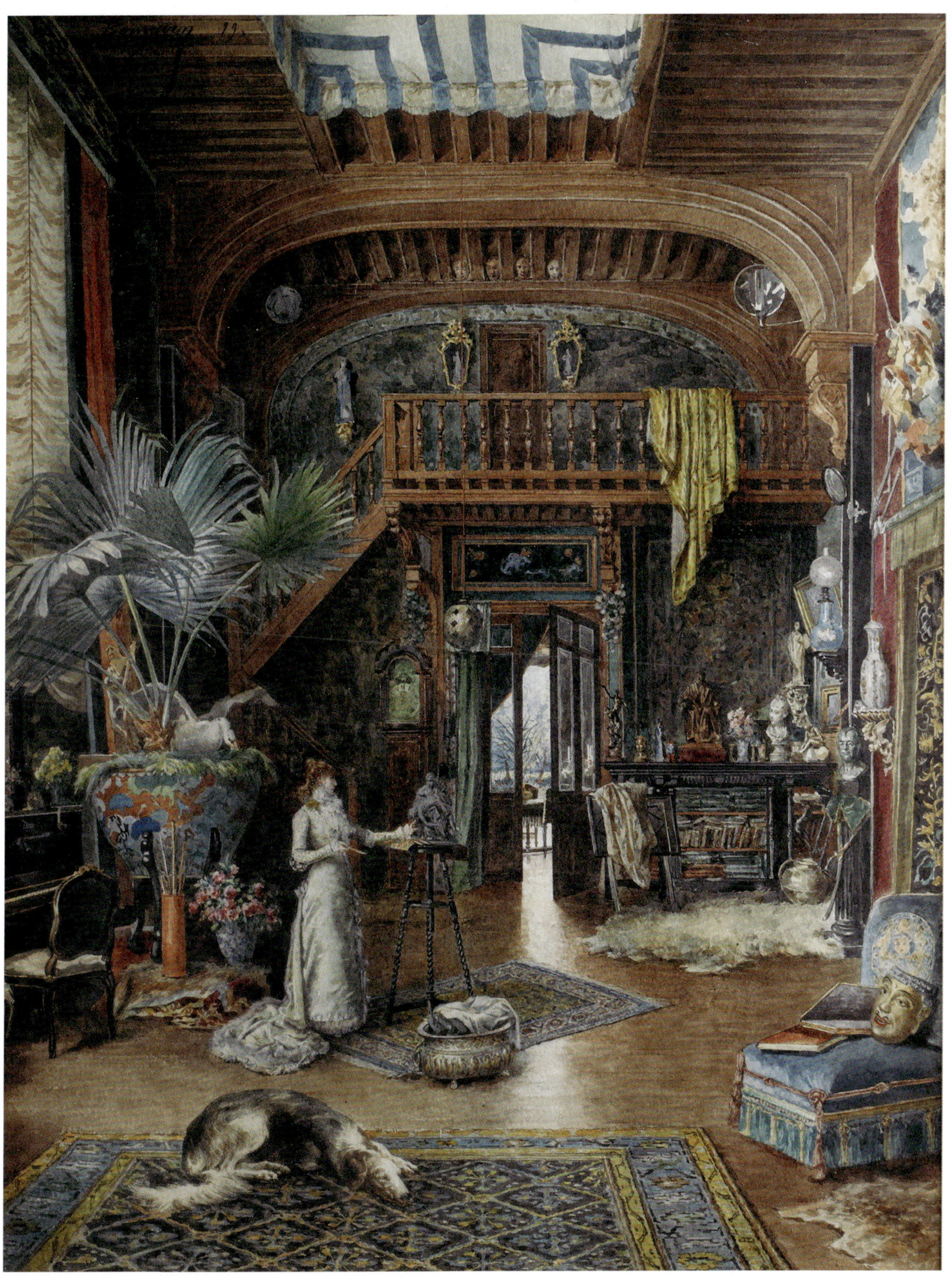

to be some confusion in the biographies about which animals she kept where, but they included a cheetah, seven chameleons, Darwin the monkey and two dogs called Cassis and Vermouth. She kept a lion cub (some sources say there were two) in a cage in the Salon, but it had to be removed because of its offensive smell. 'In New Orleans she bought an alligator which reacted to its French diet of milk and champagne by dying. She also had a boa constrictor which ate sofa cushions and had to be shot – by Sarah herself.'[16] According to a visiting journalist, her last studio – in boulevard Pereire – had some added curiosities: 'swarms of Buddhas were scattered about on settees ...' and the oriental carpets were thickly strewn with skins, the heads of jackals and hyenas and the paws of panthers.[17] Her studio was her stage when she was not on stage. She would receive her numerous guests – her 'court' – dressed in her sculptor's mode: a white silk trouser suit, designed by Worth. Whatever she did provided endless fodder for journalists, which she was very far from discouraging. As Henry James put it, 'She is a celebrity because, apparently, she desires with an intensity that has rarely been equalled to be one ...'[18]

Rodin dismissed her sculptures as 'old-fashioned tripe', but they were good enough to be shown in the 1893 Columbia Exposition in Chicago and at the 1900 Exposition Universelle. She was also attacked in the press for 'pursuing an activity inappropriate for an actress'. She was defended by Émile Zola, who wrote, 'How droll! Not content with finding her thin, or declaring her mad, they want to regulate her daily activities ... Let a law be passed immediately to prevent the accumulation of talent!'[19]

In 1915, her leg was amputated almost to the hip – it had never recovered from a previous injury to the knee – but she continued to act either sitting down or balancing on the remaining leg. She even went on a farewell tour of America and visited the First World War battlefields where she performed for soldiers who had just returned or were about to go into battle. When she died in 1923, thirty thousand mourners attended her funeral in Paris.

The United States also had its celebrity artists. Rising from humble beginnings, William Merritt Chase became one of the foremost artists and teachers of his generation. He had been aided in his ascent by America entering what was known as the Gilded Age when industrial expansion led to an accumulation of enormous fortunes and the almost frenzied amassing of goods and art to fill the palatial homes that those fortunes had built.[20] With the increasing focus on American art and the proliferation of galleries, auction houses and exhibitions, the period was pivotal in establishing New York in the international art market.

Chase had trained in New York and Munich and travelled widely

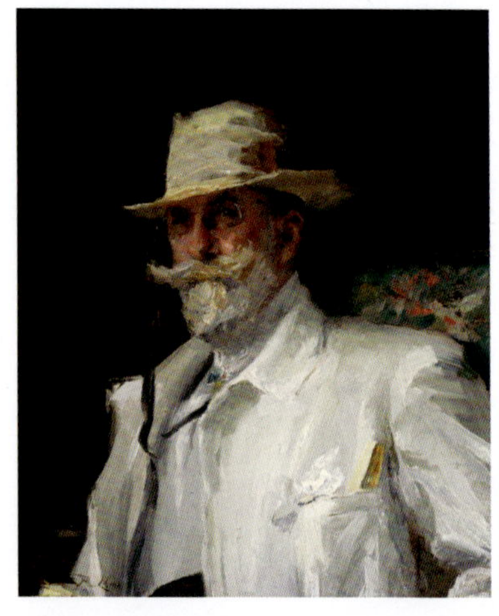

77. Annie Traquair Lang, *William Merritt Chase*, 1910

Chase was an inspiring teacher and Lang was among his many talented pupils. She painted several portraits of him. He was always immaculately dressed, his students recalling how he painted in a white flannel suit without getting a spot of paint on his clothes.

FIVE / A SUMPTUOUS LIFE

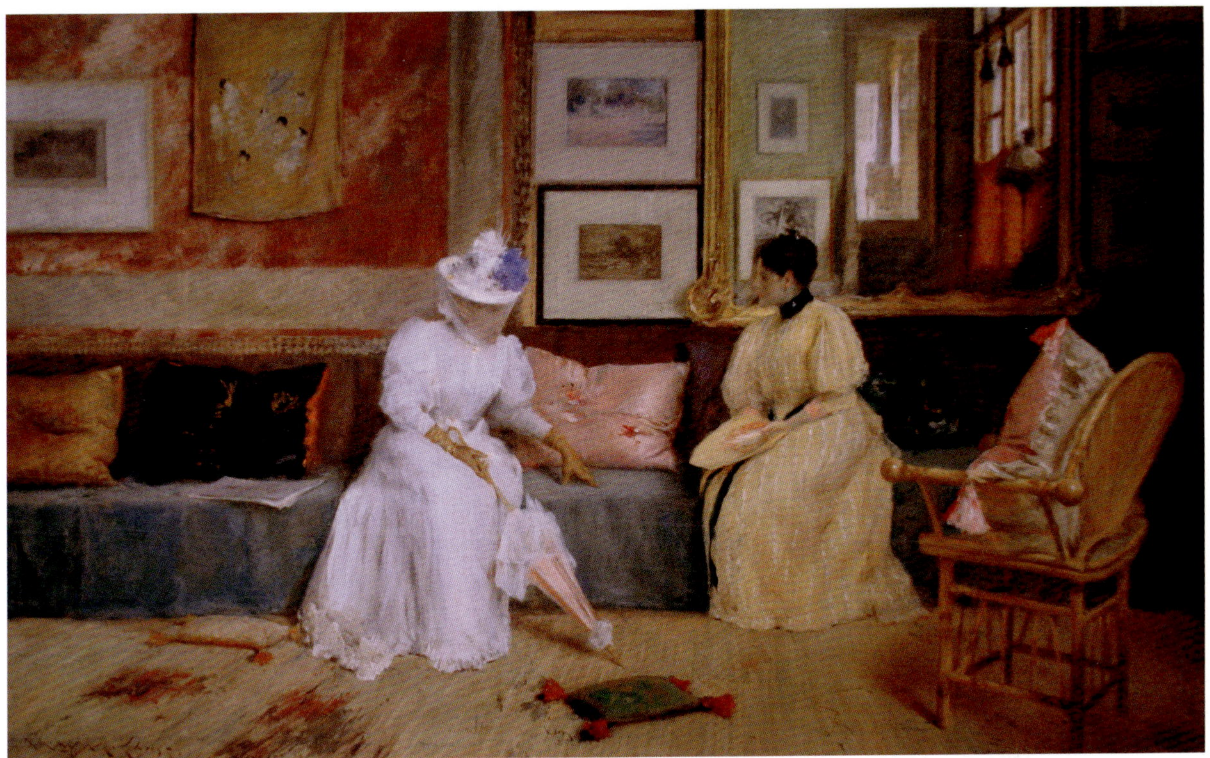

in Europe, including frequent visits to Paris. He had so thoroughly assimilated French ways that he was described as 'being more French than the Latin Quarter' and was a key figure in introducing French Impressionism to the American public.[21] He could be seen about town sporting a top hat, white spats and a three-piece suit with a carnation in his buttonhole. His students used to marvel at his ability to work in a white flannel suit without getting a spot of paint on his clothes. With his charm and elegant attire, he was very much the gentleman artist. His magnificent studio in the Tenth Street Studio Building, with its impressive collection of *objets d'art*, dogs, parrots, pet monkeys and a serving man wearing a fez, was a focal point for the sophisticated and fashionable members of the New York City art world of the late nineteenth century.

Chase was an inspiring and benevolent teacher. The students who enrolled in his classes in New York, Brooklyn, Philadelphia and the Shinnecock School on Long Island numbered in their thousands. Georgia O'Keeffe, who studied under him in New York in 1907, noted: 'There was something fresh and energetic and fierce and exciting about him that made him fun.'[22] After seventeen years, however, the cost of maintaining the Tenth Street studio as well as his other residences, and of bringing up his large family of eight children, forced Chase to close it and to auction the contents.

78. William Merritt Chase, *A Friendly Call*, 1895

Chase was adept at capturing the genteel, privileged life of polite society in the 1890s. This scene is set in Chase's elegant summer house at Shinnecock Hills, Long Island, where he ran extremely popular art classes, including one for women. The artist's wife, Alice, on the right, listens attentively to her visitor.

Sir Frederic Leighton (1830–96), handsome, charming, widely travelled, highly cultured, fluent in five languages, an extremely effective President of the Royal Academy, the owner of a magnificent house and studio in London and a friend to many, was most definitely a celebrity. His paintings depicted historical, biblical and classical subjects, produced in a glossy, historically correct, academic style. They were enormously popular and sold for high prices. His house too, was a work of art (it is now a museum.) Built to Leighton's design, it contained one of the grandest studios ever built. Situated on the upper floor, the huge room was lit by a vast north-facing bay window which looked out over the extensive garden. At one end was a minstrels' gallery, built to accommodate Leighton's tallest canvases. He later added a Winter Studio – effectively, a glass house supported on cast iron columns – to alleviate the problem of the lack of natural light during the winter months.

As Leighton's reputation grew, so did the demands on his time. He never married but he had a host of friends and was devoted to numerous causes. His Sunday afternoon 'At Homes' were well attended,

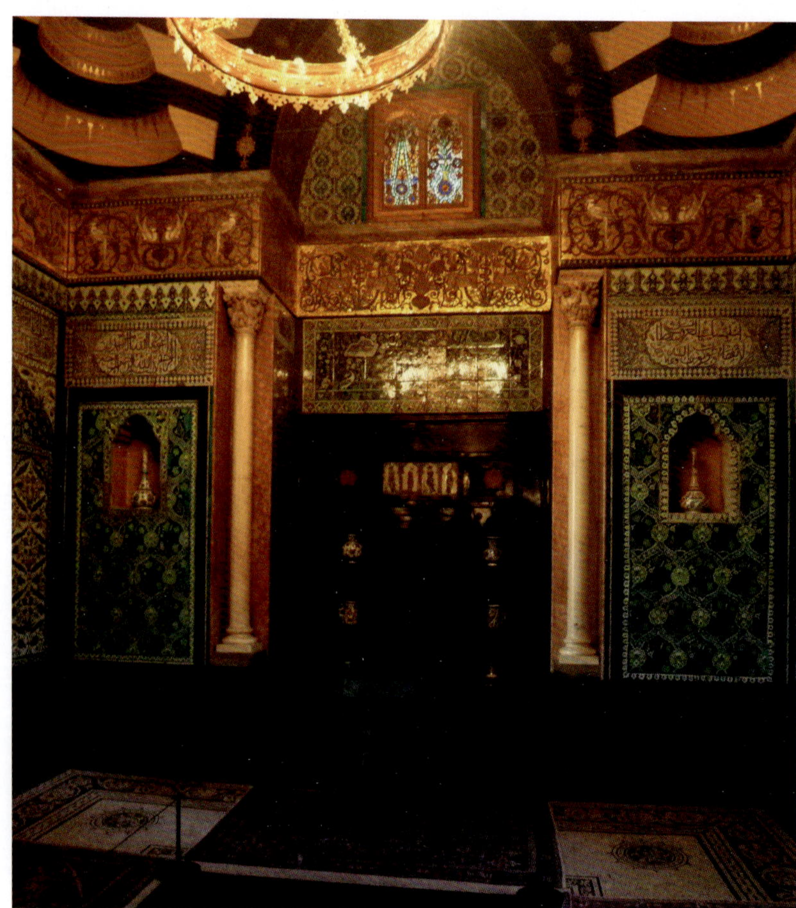

79. The Arab Hall, Leighton House, London

Leighton satisfied his passion for Islamic tiles by creating a perfect setting for them when he added the Arab Hall to the original house. The tiles, garnered from the Middle East, and the gold mosaic frieze designed by Walter Crane, create a sumptuously coloured magic kingdom in the heart of Kensington.

but it was his annual Show Sunday, usually held in the spring, which was a major social event. Walter Crane recalled how the street was thronged with carriages and 'the courteous and princely way' in which Leighton received his visitors. He also held an annual musical evening that was regarded by those fortunate enough to be invited as 'one of the real treats of the year'.[23] His painting, however, always came first. 'He made a mosaic of his days,' wrote his architect George Aitchison, 'in which every hour was set down, with its appointed task, and he allowed nothing to interfere with that part which related to his work.'[24] He was the only British artist ever to be raised to the peerage.

At the outer edges of north London lay a picturesque, semi-rural enclave of widely-spaced villas in spacious well-wooded gardens. St John's Wood had become a haven for successful professional men, including numerous artists, James Tissot (1836–1902) among them.

Tissot was born in Nantes but trained in Paris, where he became friends with Degas, Manet and Whistler. Having fought in the Franco-Prussian War, in 1871 he left France for England to escape the Paris Commune. By then he was already a successful artist and could afford to buy the lease of a large villa and garden at 17 (now 44) Grove End Road in St John's Wood. His genre scenes depicting the daily lives of beautiful, elegantly dressed women were snapped up, especially by rich industrialists. His painting *In the Conservatory (Rivals)* shows the type of image at which he excelled (its title is confusing as the studio is in the foreground and the conservatory beyond.) The exotic plants, oriental and eighteenth-century *objets d'art*, and the young women in their pleated muslin gowns all indicate the world in which Tissot lived and worked. Edmond de Goncourt joked that Tissot had a manservant who wore silk stockings, was always polishing the leaves of his plants and kept chilled champagne available at all times for studio visitors.[25]

In about 1876 Tissot met the love of his life. Irish-born Kathleen Newton was divorced with two young children. Officially, she and the children lived with her sister just down the road. In reality, she lived with Tissot and only saw her children at teatime each day. Kathleen became more than a lover: she was Tissot's beloved muse, her graceful form and pale, distinctive face appearing frequently in his paintings. As she was consumptive, several of the paintings show her lying quietly on a chaise longue, often in the garden. Within six years of their meeting she was dead. Five days after her death, a grief-stricken Tissot returned to France where he went through a mystical crisis and spent much of the rest of his life painting scenes from the Old Testament.

Tissot's villa was bought by yet another celebrity artist: Dutch-born Lawrence Alma-Tadema (1836–1912), who had settled in England in 1870. Victorian society's penchant for images depicting life in ancient

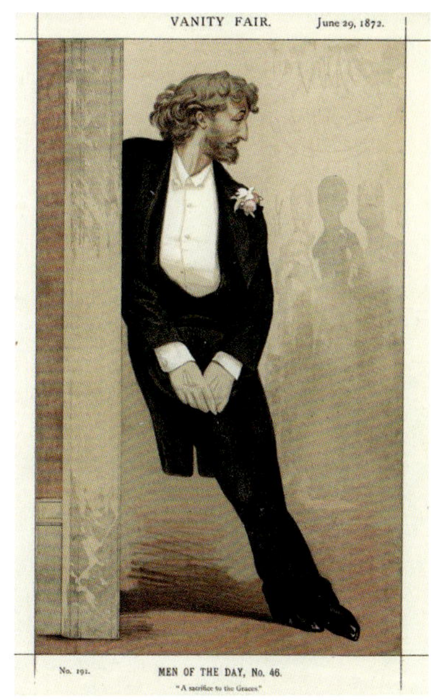

80. James Tissot, *Caricature of Frederic Leighton*, 1872

Tissot's caricature, which appeared in *Vanity Fair*, depicts Leighton as a languid man of fashion. While he was extremely gregarious and a generous host, Leighton's private life remains elusive, although he is rumoured to have had a tender regard for the opera singer Adelaide Sartoris.

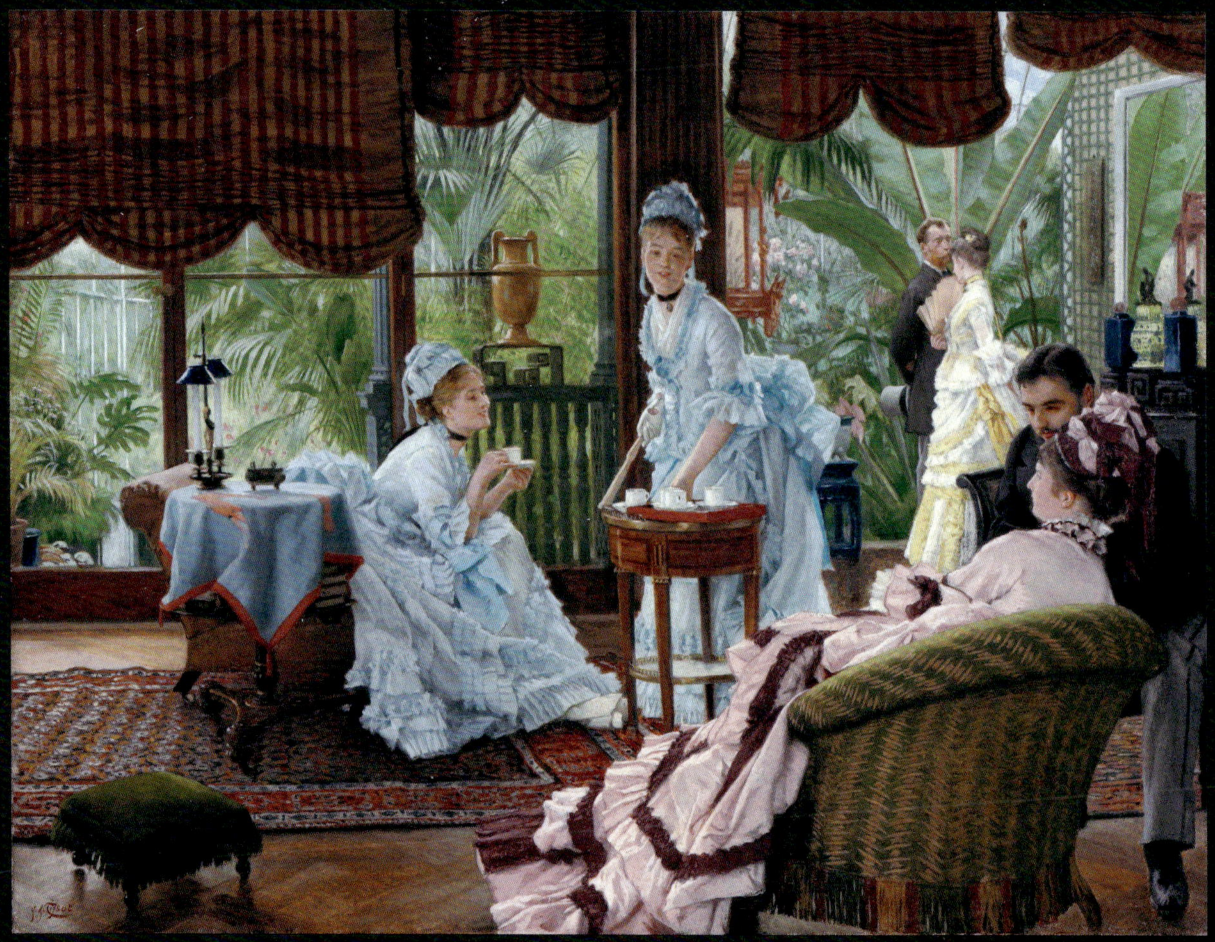

81. James Tissot, *In the Conservatory (Rivals)*, n.d.

Tissot was a master storyteller, planting tantalising clues in his paintings which challenge the viewer to interpret them. Why is the man on the right not interacting with the woman in pink? And is the woman with the fan flirting with the man with a ginger moustache?

Greece, Rome and Egypt, painted with meticulous veracity, made him a rich man. His paintings were so accurate in every tiny detail that they inspired Hollywood directors: Cecil B. DeMille used them as reference for *The Ten Commandments, Cleopatra* and *Ben Hur.* 'If you want to know what those Greeks and Romans looked like,' Alma-Tadema asserted, 'come to me. For I can show not only what I think, but what I know.'[26]

Once he had purchased Tissot's house, he set about enlarging and beautifying what was once a Queen Anne villa into a resplendent mansion. His vast studio had a domed ceiling fitted with amber glass, the walls were panelled with green Siena marble and the apse and dome were covered in aluminium leaf. With marble floors, an atrium, fountains, and doors modelled on those he had seen at Pompeii, the house came to be known as Casa Tadema. He had built a slice of ancient Rome in St John's Wood. This remodelling was said to have cost £2m (in today's money), a sum that illustrates his very substantial wealth at the height of his career.

A devoted husband and family man, Alma-Tadema was portly, fun-loving, popular, extremely hard-working, ambitious and a shrewd businessman. He and his wife Laura entertained royally, giving lavish dinners and concerts for friends such as the Prince and Princess of Wales, Tchaikovsky, Rodin, Sarah Bernhardt, Leighton and Winston Churchill.

The last years of Alma-Tadema's life saw the rise of Post-Impressionism and all the 'isms that came after. His paintings, which had sold for thousands of pounds were now worth hundreds. By the late 1960s, however, the interest in Victorian art revived – and continued to do so. In 2010, one of Alma-Tadema's paintings was sold at Sotheby's New York for nearly $36m.

One artist became a celebrity not because of the success of his work but because one of his paintings had deeply offended the British art establishment: James Abbott McNeill Whistler. When he moved from Paris to London in 1859, Whistler lived on Cheyne Walk, facing on to the River Thames. He was fascinated by the great river, producing atmospheric images in which insubstantial objects – lights, boats, bridges, cranes – loom in and out of the fog. The two Greaves brothers, who lived nearby, recalled how they often stayed up with him all night, rowing him about on the river. 'When he came to a view which interested him, he would stop and sketch it with white chalk on brown paper ...'[27]

The painting that made him a celebrity, although a dubious one, is *Nocturne: Black and Gold – The Falling Rocket*. It was painted in his small, severely simple studio at 96 Cheyne Walk, a positively modest affair when compared to the studios of other artists in this chapter. There

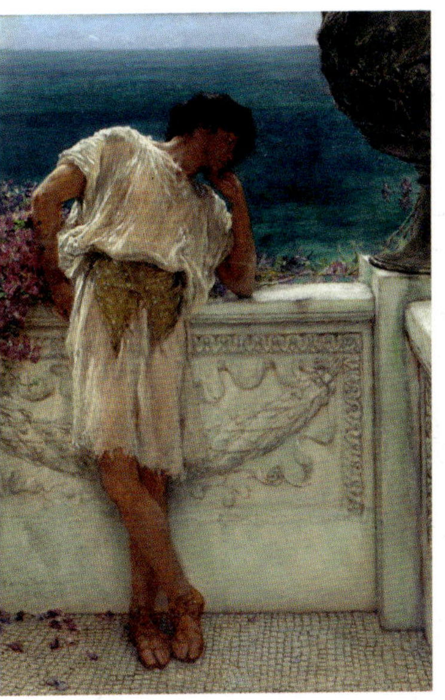

82. Lawrence Alma-Tadema, *The Poet Gallus Dreaming*, 1892

This is a perfect example of the style and subject which made Alma-Tadema a rich man. Banished from Rome, the unhappy poet is dreaming about his beloved mistress. Alma-Tadema was so skilled at depicting marble – which appears frequently in his paintings – that he was dubbed 'the marbellous painter'.

were no soaring palms, bric-a-brac, Grecian urns, large dogs or lion cubs. (Whistler's near neighbour, Dante Gabriel Rossetti, however, kept a small zoo of exotic animals, including a wombat, a racoon, an armadillo and numerous peacocks which made such a din that subsequent occupiers of the house were prohibited from keeping them.)

When *The Falling Rocket* – which had shattered the boundaries of conventional painting – was exhibited at the Grosvenor Gallery in 1877, John Ruskin accused Whistler of asking '200 guineas for flinging a pot of paint in the public's face'. Whistler was so enraged that he sued Ruskin for libel. The case became a *cause célèbre*. Everyone took sides. Ruskin was on the verge of a nervous breakdown and was too ill to attend the trial in person. At one stage in the proceedings, Sir John Holker, representing Ruskin, asked Whistler how long it had taken

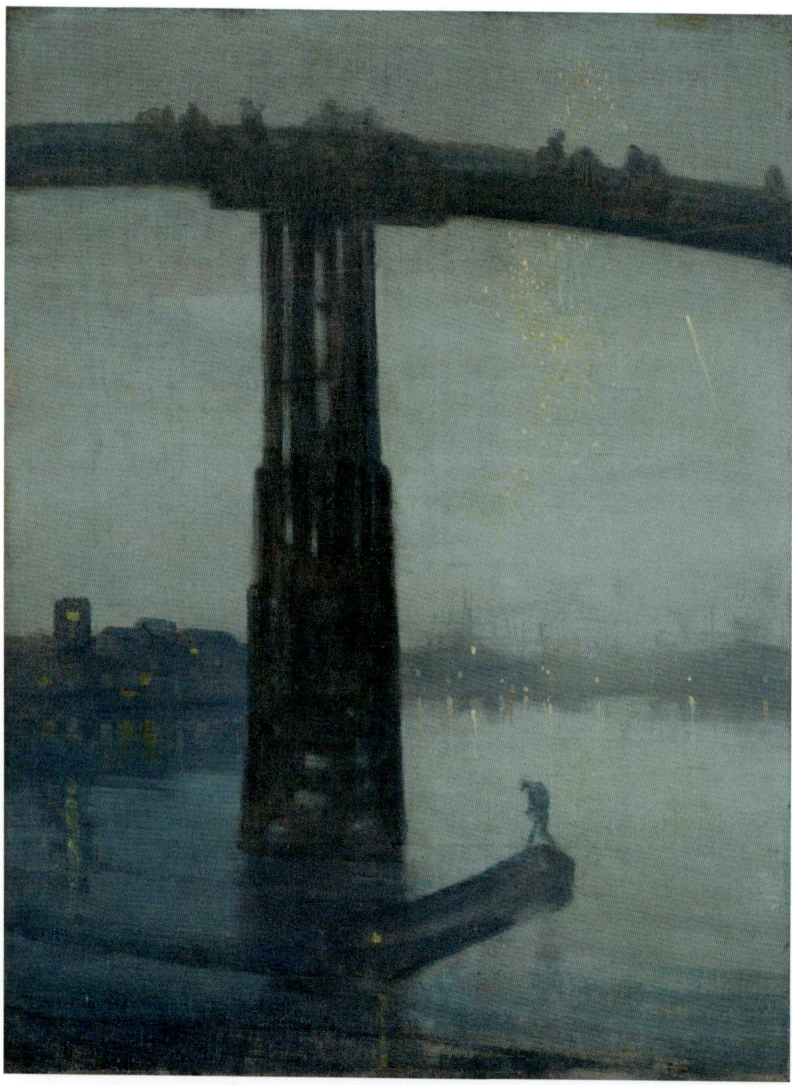

83. James Abbott McNeill Whistler, *Nocturne: Blue and Gold – Old Battersea Bridge, c.* 1872–75

This is one of Whistler's most controversial works and was produced as 'evidence' in the famous Whistler-Ruskin trial of 1878. It is the fifth in a series of Nocturnes, produced during the 1870s. Whistler's aim in these works was to convey a sense of the beauty and tranquility of the Thames by night.

him to 'knock off' the painting. Whistler replied: 'I knocked it off in a couple of days.' 'And for the *labour of two days* you asked 200 guineas?' 'No,' Whistler responded, 'It was for the knowledge gained through a lifetime.'[28] It was a brilliant response and the courtroom burst into applause.

During the trial, another of Whistler's most controversial paintings – *Nocturne: Blue and Gold – Old Battersea Bridge* – was challenged for the accuracy of its depiction of the bridge. Whistler responded: 'I didn't intend it to be a portrait of the bridge. It is a moonlight scene, a harmony of colour.'[29] Whistler won the case but was awarded only token damages of a farthing. But the costs contributed to his bankruptcy and he lost his house, his studio contents and his prized collection of oriental blue-and-white porcelain. Hoping to recoup his losses, Whistler went to Venice where he produced a series of superb etchings and pastels – not of the city's 'sights', but of its nooks and crannies.

The studios of these 'society darlings' – with the exception of Whistler – may seem unnecessarily opulent and grandiose, their trappings a pretentious display of wealth, but these artists had reached the peak of their profession by dint of their unremitting labour. If luck came into the equation, it was that the subjects they painted and the manner in which they painted them struck the right note at the time. Fortunately, most of them had died before their work became unfashionable, nor did they know that their names were destined to become mere footnotes in art histories. They had, however, triumphantly avoided the grinding poverty and thwarted hopes that beset so many struggling artists.

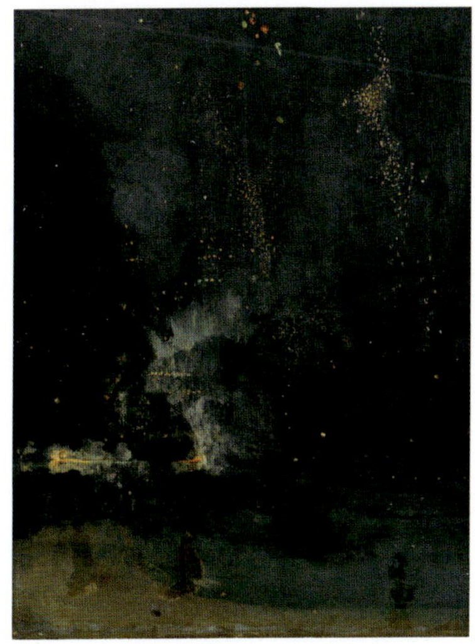

84. James Abbott McNeill Whistler, *Nocturne: Black and Gold – The Falling Rocket, c.* 1875

The pleasure gardens at Cremorne, which could accommodate 1,500 people, were a short distance from Whistler's house in Cheyne Walk and he liked to stroll there, especially after dark to watch the nightly firework displays.

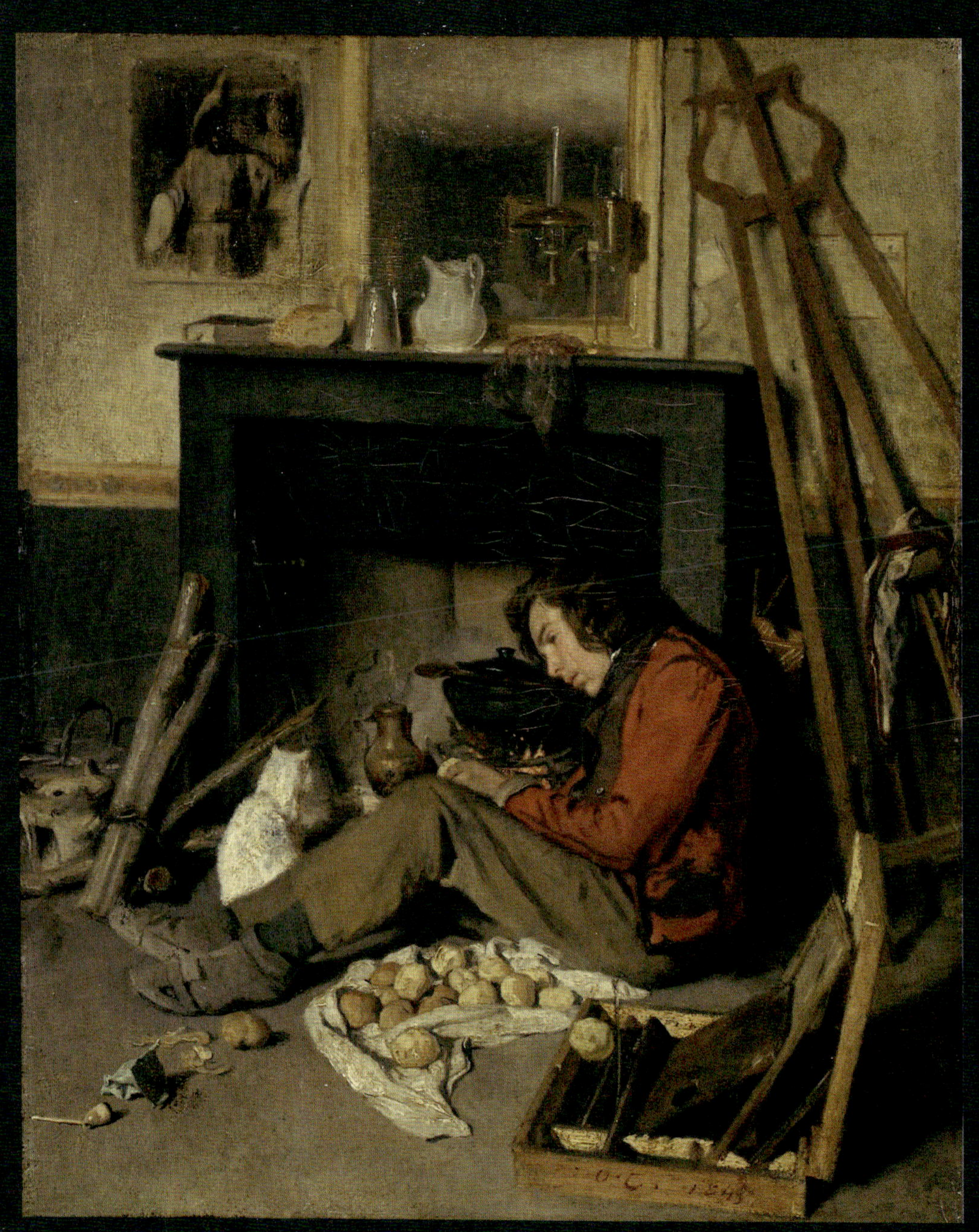

SIX

On the Fringes of Society

The Artist's Garret

They [bohemians] are the race of obstinate dreamers for whom art has remained a faith and not a profession … They live … on the outskirts of life, in isolation and inertia … They die, for the most part, decimated by that disease to which science does not dare give its real name, want. Henri Murger, *Scènes de la Vie de Bohème*, 1851[1]

HUDDLED BEFORE THE FEEBLE EMBERS of the fire, the forlorn young man in Tassaert's *Interior of a Studio* encapsulates the potent myth of the impoverished painter starving in his garret for the sake of his art. Octave Tassaert (1800–74) painted it in 1845, the same year that the first instalment of novelist and poet Henri Murger's *Scènes de la Vie de Bohème* appeared in Paris (it was published in book form in 1851.) Based on his personal experiences, Murger's romanticised, often humorous descriptions of the lives of his fellow writers, musicians and artists and the various ruses they employed to keep body and soul together, were wildly popular. Their popularity increased when they were turned into a sensationally successful musical play in 1849, which became in turn the source of Puccini's opera *La Bohème*.

The bearded and moustached bohemians of Paris's Latin Quarter, with their bizarre garb of pointed felt hats, tailcoats, enormous floppy cravats and puffing on their ubiquitous pipes, lived on the fringes of society. They rebelled against everything remotely bourgeois. They roosted in garrets up six flights of stairs; water had to be carried from an iron pump in the courtyard; sanitation was primitive and smelly; and their lives were ruled by their *concièrges*. A student recalled that the majority of these 'were gossiping, mischief-making hussies who struck terror into the soul of the unfortunate individual who was not ready to the very moment with his rent'.[2] They played ingenious practical jokes on each other and 'dallied' with the *lorettes* (women of easy virtue), their

OPPOSITE: **85.** Octave Tassaert, *Interior of a Studio*, 1845

This is an image of an artist who has abandoned all hope. He has sacrificed all to his art, but to no avail. The tiny flame under the cooking pot will neither warm his wretched garret nor cook the potatoes. Even his paintbox is empty.

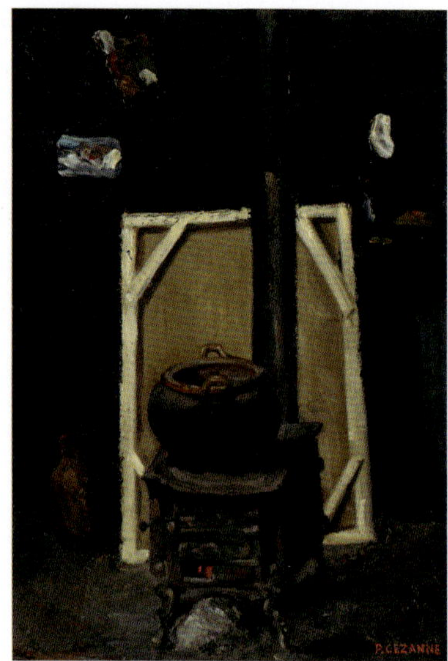

86. Paul Cézanne, *The Stove in the Studio*, 1865–70

After an artist's materials, the stove was the most vital object in a studio. Together with the cooking pot, the two helped to sustain life. This stove was a gift from Cézanne's childhood friend and supporter, Émile Zola. But Zola's anti-bohemian novel, *The Masterpiece*, caused a rupture in their friendship.

models and the local shop girls. Their social life centred on the cafés – such as the Nouvelle Athènes and Café Guerbois – where they drank more than they ate and held heated discussions about their favourite topics: art and politics.

This all sounds very merry, but there was a dark side too: not only did they die of want, but they froze (the studio stove became a symbol of endurance during the winter months) and their carefree promiscuity too often led to venereal diseases. Syphilis, a lingering and painful death, killed Manet at the age of fifty-one, Bohemia's most gifted poet Charles Baudelaire at forty-six and Henri Murger himself at thirty-nine. (Renoir once lamented that he could not be a true genius because he alone among his friends had not caught it.) Writers and art critics, Edmond and Jules de Goncourt, left a terrible description of a visit to Murger as he succumbed to the disease 'which results in a man dying in shreds … without enough strength left in him to suffer, and complaining of only one thing, the smell of rotten meat in his bedroom – the smell of his own body'.[3] Many sought inspiration – or oblivion – by taking drugs. A few, like Tassaert, who specialised in genre paintings of the poor and wretched, finally gave up the struggle and committed suicide.

Needless to say, Paris did not have a monopoly on misery: artists had been starving in garrets for centuries. Although not all Dutch painters were paupers, depictions of poverty-stricken artists in dilapidated studios seem to be particularly numerous in the Netherlands. One of the best-known images is by Adriaen van Ostade (1610–85) an artist who specialised in small, brilliantly painted interior scenes of peasants behaving badly: chamber pots usually sit ostentatiously in his foregrounds and drunken peasants throw up in front of their friends. The buying public loved them. The etching made from this painting went through as many as twelve versions.

Rembrandt's *The Artist in his Studio* was painted when he was only twenty-three and living in Leiden. He painted himself in a bare studio, empty of an artist's usual paraphernalia, contemplating a large canvas set firmly on an easel. The room shows signs of decay: the damp has eaten its way into the plaster beneath the easel, exposing a triangle of rosy brick that he has painted with infinite care. The wall above the door also shows signs of crumbling. The coarse-grained planking of the floor and the bare plastered walls give little feeling of warmth and comfort. The whole scene shows how precariously many artists lived, particularly in seventeenth-century Holland where the traditional forms of patronage – royalty and the Church – had ceased and commissions were hard to come by.

The arresting self-portrait by James Barry (1741–1806) gives no hint of the travails that were to beset him. Painted during the years he was

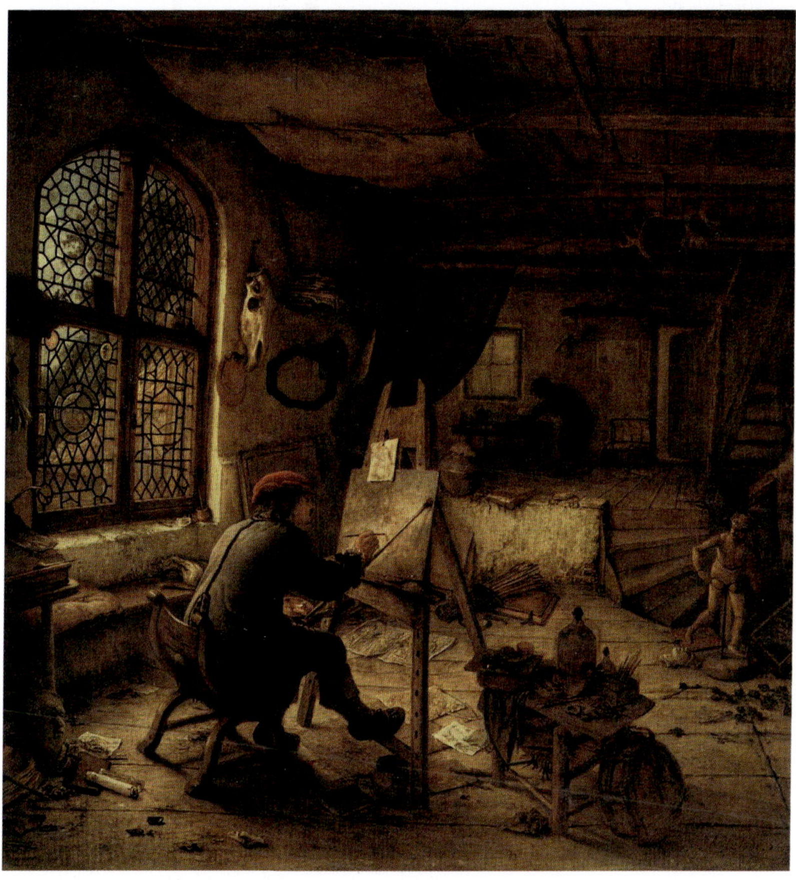

studying in Rome – paid for by his fellow Irishman Edmund Burke – he presents a bright and quizzical face to the world. Soon after his return to England, Barry was elected a member of the Royal Academy and in 1782 he became its Professor of Painting. During these years he executed what proved to be his masterpiece: six vast paintings (two are nearly 13m long) representing *The Progress of Human Culture* for the Great Room of the Society of Arts in London. Thus, by his early forties he was undeniably doing well. But his character was against him. He saw persecution everywhere and responded by going on the attack, using his lectures as Professor as 'vehicles of invective and satire against the principal Academicians, and most pointedly against Sir Joshua [Reynolds, President of the Academy] who was reduced by it to so awkward a situation ... that he was obliged at last either to appear to be asleep or to absent himself from the place'.[4] Understandably, Barry's relationship with the Academy deteriorated beyond recall and he became the first of only two Academicians ever to be expelled.

In his final years Barry lived in increasingly paranoid isolation, estranged from friends and colleagues. His house, situated in a smart terrace just north of Oxford Street, appeared to be uninhabited.

87. Adriaen van Ostade, *The Painter in his Studio*, 1663

Van Ostade always contrives to make his interiors look messy. Here, the bare boards are littered with his painting materials. In the background, either grinding colours or cooking lunch, the artist's wife is bent double at her task. Note the wooden lay figure on the right.

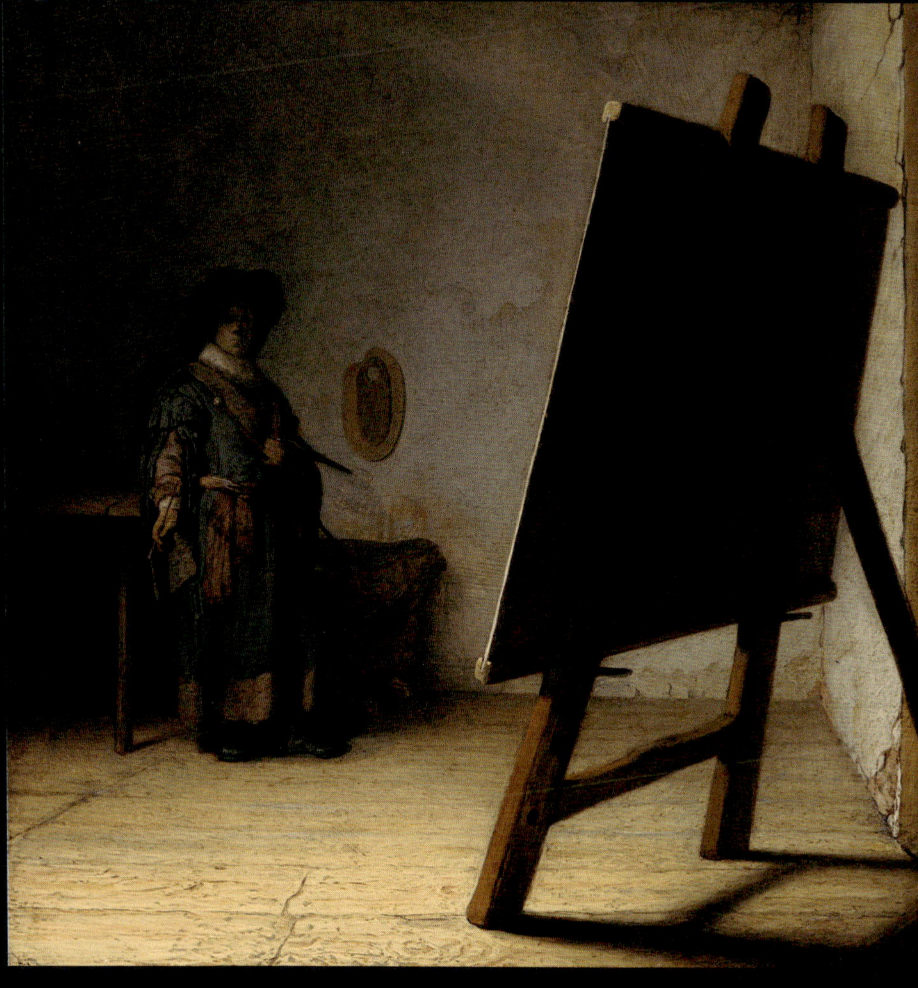

88. Rembrandt van Rijn, *The Artist in his Studio*, 1629

Rembrandt is bundled up against the cold in ordinary clothes, since 'artistic' dress was not introduced until the nineteenth century. A spare palette hangs on the wall behind him and he holds a paintbrush in one hand and a palette and mahlstick in the other.

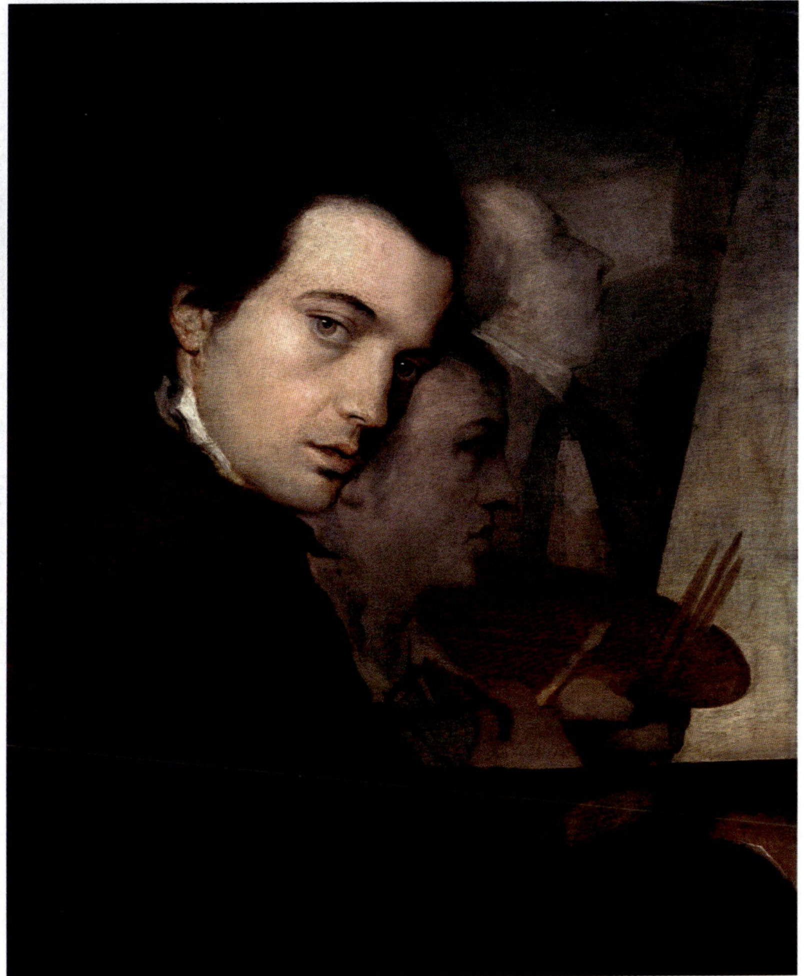

A visitor reported that the 'glass of the lower windows was broken, the shutters closed, and the door and the walls strewed with mud' thrown by street urchins who believed the house 'was occupied by an old wizard or necromancer'.[5] The yard was littered with the skeletons of cats and dogs, marrow bones and wastepaper. A dead cat lay putrefying on the windowsill. Barry slept on 'a bedstead with no other furniture than a blanket nailed on the one side'.[6] In his studio on the ground floor he laboured on his historical paintings and copper-plate prints, the epitome of the Romantic hero relentlessly driven by his creative urge and sacrificing every worldly comfort to his art. Ironically, when he died in 1806, Barry was given a grand funeral and was laid to rest in St Paul's Cathedral beside his old adversary, Reynolds. If only he had been able to enjoy this reversal of fortune!

In 1851, another artist was given a grand funeral: J.M.W. Turner. The mourners in the procession filled eleven official coaches and eight private carriages. In his account of the day's events, the artist

89. James Barry, *Self-Portrait with Dominique Lefèvre and James Paine the Younger, c.* 1767

This is an image within an image. Barry has shown himself painting a picture in which his friend Paine is depicted painting a fragment of the famous *Belvedere Torso* while, beyond, Lefèvre gazes at the sculpture with rapture. Barry turns to the viewer with a quizzical air, as though he has been interrupted in his work.

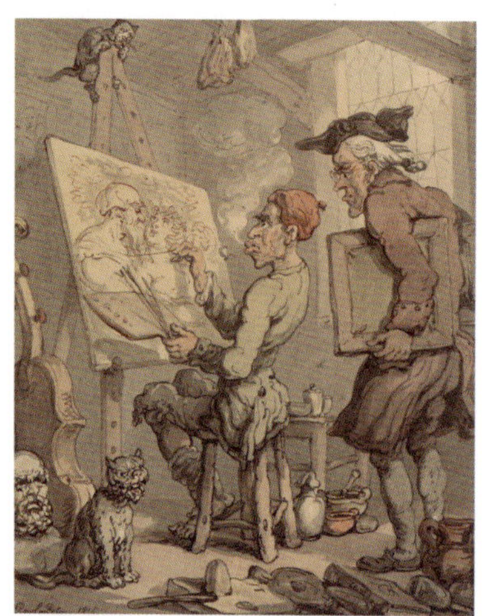

90. Thomas Rowlandson, *The Artist's Studio*, 1814

Rowlandson can always be relied on to poke fun at any subject his fecund imagination lighted upon. He produced numerous caricatures of painters and sculptors ogling their sitters. Here the threadbare artist, puffing away at his clay pipe, is hoping to sell his portrait of an amorous couple to a picture dealer.

Richard Redgrave, wrote: 'Strange that one who lived so penuriously, and made so little ostentatious display in his lifetime, should desire so splendid a memorial at his death.'[7] Stranger still was the fact that he left a fortune of nearly £140,000 (nearly 4.5m today), yet he lived like Scrooge in his various squalid dwellings. 'That Turner the man could have been a character invented by Dickens is borne out repeatedly by contemporary descriptions of his various houses and his strange, secretive comings and goings.'[8] But the conditions under which he painted were immaterial to Turner. Once, while painting in the open air, he was asked how he worked under such conditions. He replied that 'light and a room were absurdities, and that a picture could be painted anywhere'.[9]

Turner's principal house was in Queen Anne Street in Marylebone. As a contemporary noted, the house from the outside 'presented the appearance of a place in which some great crime has been committed'.[10] Obsessive about his privacy, few people were allowed inside it, although his colleagues tried various schemes to engineer an invitation. The house was looked after by a Mrs Danby 'who had lived with him for many years. She had some fearful cancerous malady which obliged her to conceal her face, which did not add to the charms of the domicile' – yet another character seemingly created by Dickens.[11]

One person, however, obtained permission to visit the house in Turner's absence. He said that he had 'felt a strange lonely feeling' come over him as he looked about before going into the gallery, where he was shocked by the dilapidated state of the pictures. Many of the panes

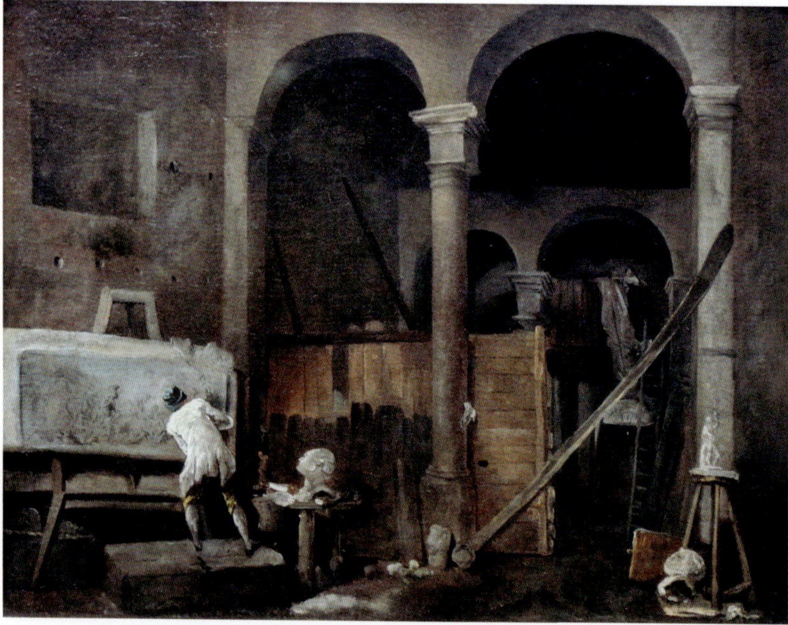

91. Hubert Robert, *The Artist's Studio*, 1760

Unable to afford a studio, this young artist has improvised one in the corner of an abandoned building in Rome. Robert was known for his landscapes and his semi-fictitious picturesque depictions of ruins.

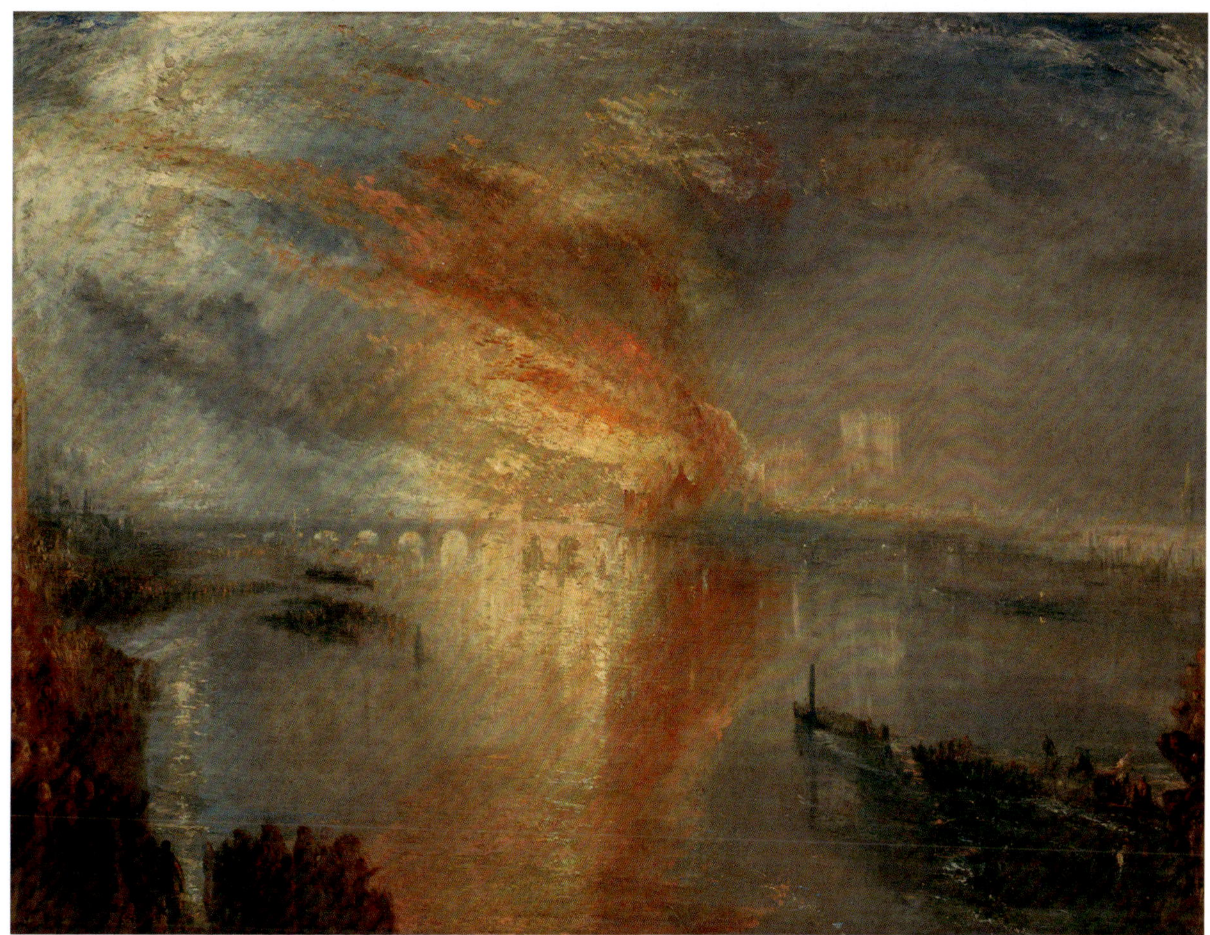

of glass in the skylights were missing 'and all the time I was there …
I had to keep my umbrella open over my head. The whole place looked
wretched.'¹² He was also thoroughly unnerved by Turner's colony of
Manx cats, which pursued him round the house, glaring at him from
the shadows.

During his last years Turner more or less abandoned Queen Anne
Street in favour of a small, waterfront cottage in what is now Cheyne
Walk, where he lived with a widow, Mrs Booth – described as 'exactly
like a fat cook' – under the name of Mr Booth. 'The house had but three
windows in front, but possessed a magnificent prospect both up and
down the river. With this exception, the abode was miserable in every
respect … The rooms were very poorly furnished, all and everything
looking as though it was the abode of a very poor man.'¹³

Whereas Turner chose to live as he did, for Vincent van Gogh
(1853–90) there was no such option. During his brief, self-destructive
and tragic life he was constantly on the move. Before he realised that
he wanted to be an artist, he had various jobs, but his eccentric and

92. J.M.W. Turner, *The Burning of the
House of Lords and Commons*, 1835

Turner is known to have watched
the fire from a boat on the Thames.
On the left, people can be seen
gazing in awe at the horrifying
spectacle. The ghostly towers of
Westminster Abbey are just visible
through the smoke. The flames are
enhanced by Turner's liberal use of
Indian Yellow, a staple of his palette.

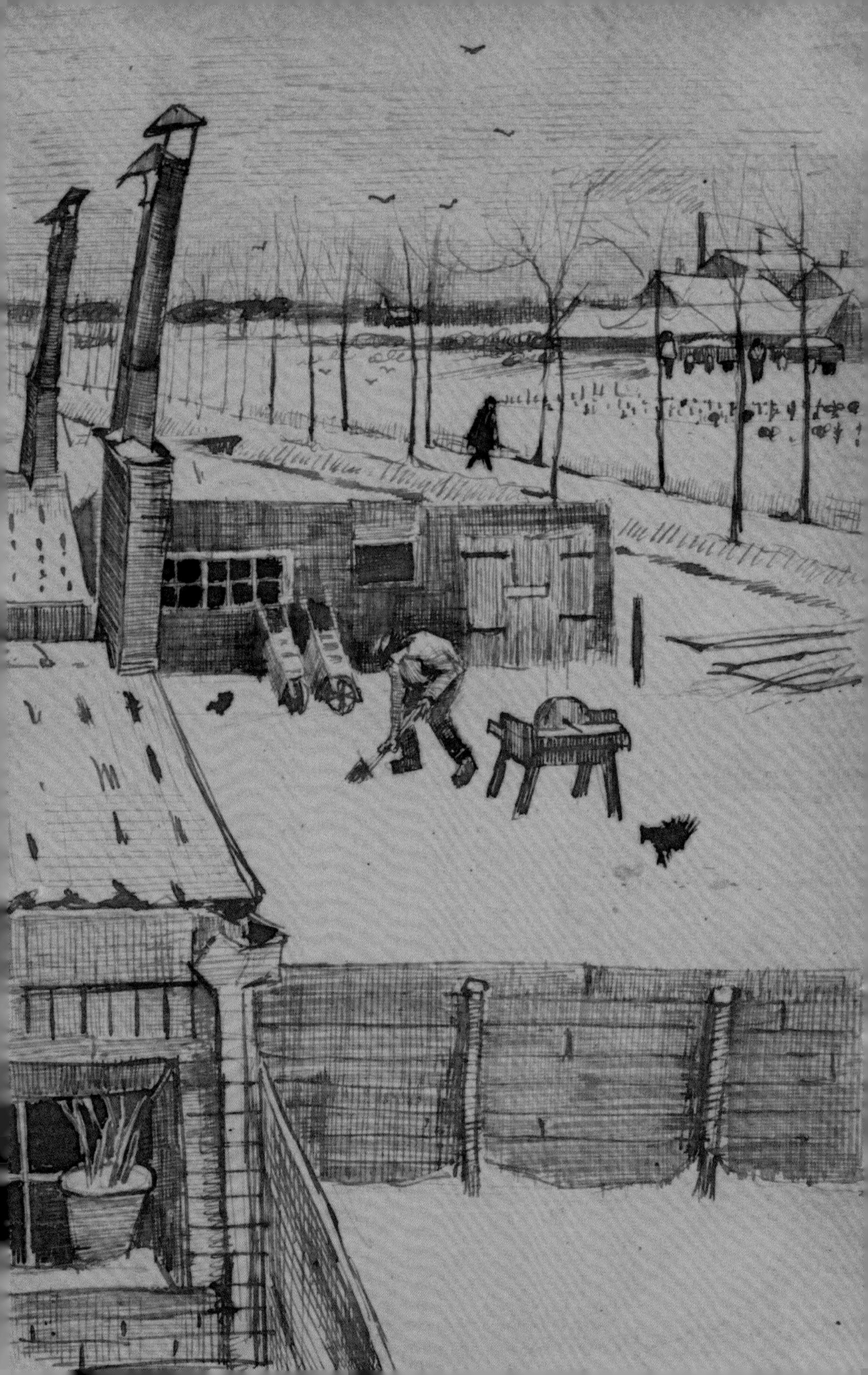

belligerent behaviour made him virtually unemployable. He fought with everyone, the trail of broken relationships lengthening throughout his tempestuous existence.

In 1881, following a failed attempt to marry a cousin and a blazing row with his father, he fled to The Hague. Thanks to another cousin, Anton Mauve, who was a successful artist, he at last obtained his first ever studio on Schenkweg on the edge of the city. Mauve also lent Van Gogh money for the rent to add to his monthly allowance from his younger brother Theo in Paris. Once installed, he described his new abode to Theo: 'A room and alcove, the light is bright enough, for the window is large … and it's more or less facing south. I've bought furniture … (I have real kitchen chairs, for example, and a really sturdy kitchen table.) …. But now, old chap, I have a real studio of my own and am terribly pleased with it.'[14] He bought other luxuries such as books and prints, and a prodigious supply of artist's materials. He also employed a steady stream of vagrants and prostitutes as models. To pay for everything he demanded more money from Theo, threatening that he would 'break down' if he failed to send it. His spending went beyond simple profligacy: he had come to believe that he *deserved* to be supported in order to pursue his 'noble purpose' as an artist.[15] Yet he refused to follow Theo's constantly reiterated advice to give up his endless production of black-and-white figure drawings of the poor and wretched and instead concentrate on landscape and colour – that is, on *painting* – which would at least make his work more saleable.

Van Gogh's relationship with Mauve, who had added lessons on the use of watercolours and oil paints to his financial assistance, inevitably foundered. With his unerring ability to make life difficult for himself, Van Gogh now gave sanctuary to Sien, a pregnant prostitute, her small child, Sien's sister and mother. While his family saw Sien as a vulgar, alcoholic whore who was deceiving him to gain a roof over her head, he saw her as 'an angel' and believed that he at last had a family of his own. Without a word to Theo, he rented the apartment next door, filling it with furniture and a cradle for the coming baby, demanding more money to pay for it all.

By the summer of 1883, his situation was becoming untenable. People began to shun him and his sordid Schenkweg household, and he was increasingly isolated. Relations with his long-suffering brother were reaching a crisis point. Forced to choose between reconciliation with his family and continuing his liaison with Sien, he chose the family. His dream of having his own studio had become a nightmare. He paid some of his debts, bade a tearful farewell to Sien and her dependants and escaped to a desolate part of northern Holland. Although he had at last begun to paint with oils – though only briefly – he was soon

OPPOSITE: **93.** Vincent van Gogh, *View from the Window of Vincent's Studio*, 1883

Whenever he arrived in a new place, Vincent recorded the view from the window. From his second-floor vantage point, he shows the carpenter in his yard shovelling snow, and the flat meadows beyond. It was while he occupied this studio that he made his first attempts at painting with oils.

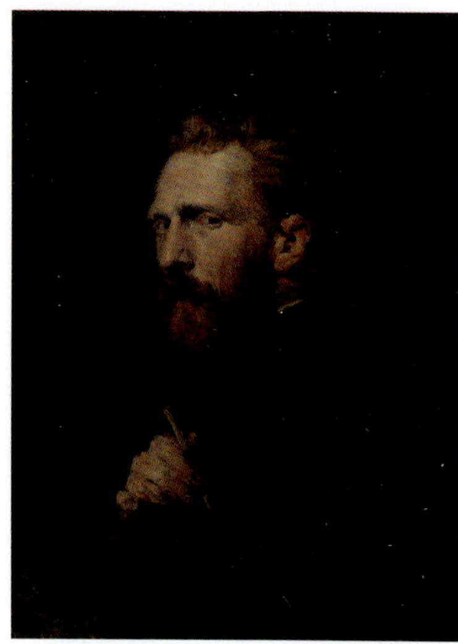

94. John Peter Russell, *Vincent van Gogh*, 1886

This is the first ever portrait of the artist. Russell was an Australian impressionist painter, born and raised in Sydney. In his late teenage years he attended an art school in Paris where he met and became a lifelong friend of Van Gogh, one of his fellow students.

driven by loneliness to take refuge with his parents. He stayed two years; years full of recrimination, desperation and furious abuse of his father, whom he blamed for everything that had gone wrong in his life. When his father had a massive stroke and died, people said that Van Gogh's rages had killed him. A spell in Antwerp followed, before, in 1886, he suddenly decided that he had to be in Paris and descended on Theo. Two years later he went south, into the sun and vivid colours of Provence.

For Gwen John (1876–1939), Paris was where she craved to be, and she settled there for good in 1904. When she had joined her ultra-bohemian brother Augustus at the Slade School of Art in London, they had shared rooms together, living, like monkeys, on a diet of fruit and nuts.[16] At one point, Gwen had rented a basement flat in Fitzrovia which, according to Augustus, was 'a kind of dungeon, into which no ray of sunlight could ever penetrate'.[17] Although no stranger to squalor himself, Augustus worried about his sister's policy of self-neglect, fearing that she starved herself (she always looks painfully thin in her self-portraits.) It was a concern also voiced by Auguste Rodin when Gwen became his model and lover. He kept insisting that she ate properly and took exercise. When he expressed his disgust at the slovenly state in which she lived, she became instead obsessed by cleanliness. Her paintings of her series of small apartments in Paris show chaste, spartan interiors, her models – nearly always female – often seated in the wicker chair that appears in several views she painted of her rooms.

Her passionate and secretive affair with Rodin lasted some ten years, but Rodin began to tire of her intensity and neediness and only visited her sporadically. Gwen was now very much alone. 'I am nothing,' she wrote, 'but a piece of suffering and desire.'[18] To feel closer to him, she moved to Meudon, a village just outside Paris, where Rodin had established a studio at the Villa des Brillants. Her last home was a simple wooden shack on stilts in the village where she lived a solitary existence surrounded by her beloved cats, a withdrawal from a clamorous world that she had always sought.

Another artist who gravitated to Paris was Pablo Picasso. Arriving from Barcelona in 1903, he found a studio in the Bateau Lavoir. Named after the laundry boats that worked the Seine, it was a crazy, wooden conglomeration of shacks which tumbled downhill from the heights of Montmartre. Like a rabbit warren inside, with twisting staircases, narrow unlit passages and mysterious cul-de-sacs, the place was an oven in summer, icy and leaking from every pore in winter. It reeked of unwashed humanity, oil paint, tom cats and drains. There was one tap for some thirty tenants. Next to the tap was a dark and filthy hole – the lavatory – with an unlockable door that banged in the wind. There was

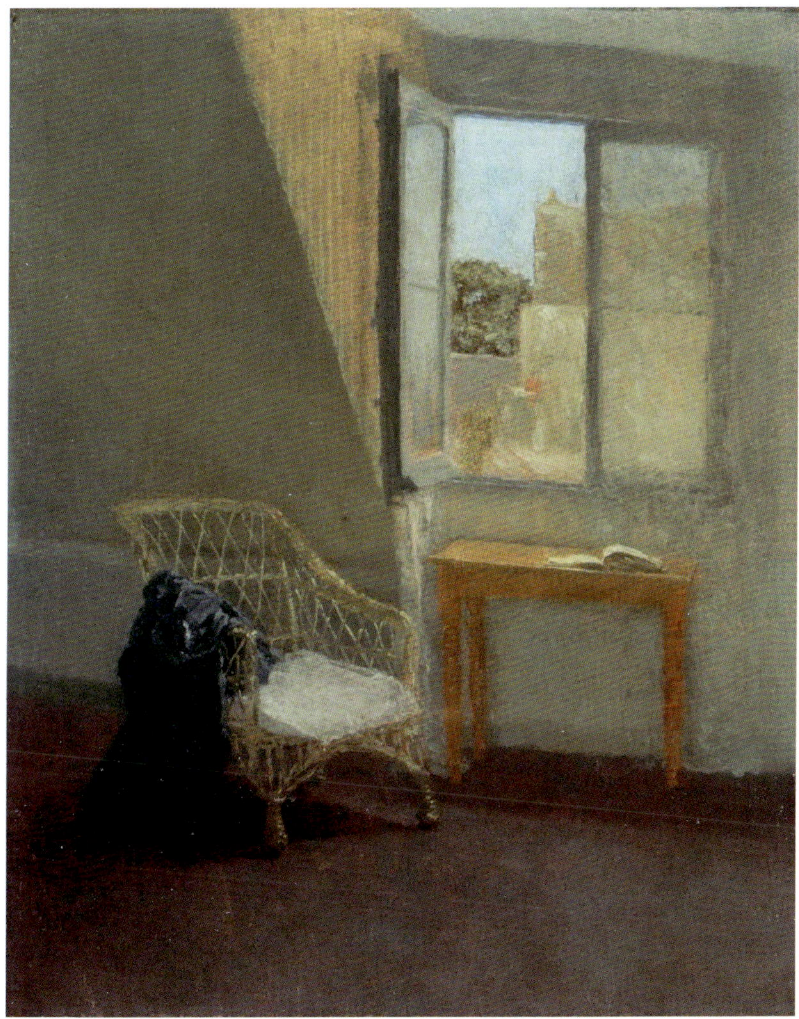

95. Gwen John, *A Corner of the Artist's Room in Paris*, 1907–09

This was just one of a series of cheap two-room apartments John rented in Paris. One of the rooms had to double as her studio. They were always sparsely furnished, the wicker chair a recurring feature. The painting conveys much about her life, a sense of controlled passion, of order, quiet and absolute calm.

no gas or electricity, and the walls were so thin that every creak and cry was audible.

The Bateau Lavoir's great charm for impoverished artists was that the rents were wonderfully cheap. This was not only because of what the building was, but for where it was. Montmartre was notorious for its whores, anarchists, writers, artists, students, dancers and vagrants who lived among its narrow winding streets, ate and got drunk in its numerous dives and bistros.

Yet Picasso was to look back on the years that he lived in this insalubrious dump as some of the happiest of his life. He was young and without commitments, and he and his Spanish gang of friends – known as the *bande à Picasso* – were free to live as they pleased. He also began to make exciting new friends like the writers Max Jacob, André Salmon and Guillaume Apollinaire. Painters like Kees van Dongen, Juan Gris and, briefly, Amedeo Modigliani were fellow tenants. Henri

Matisse, André Derain and Constantin Brâncuşi were just some of the regular visitors.

Early in his time at the Bateau Lavoir, Picasso met Fernande Olivier, a languorous, auburn-haired model with green, almond-shaped eyes who became his muse and first great love. When they met, she was living with a sculptor and also having an affair with a Spanish painter, but within a year she moved in with Picasso. In her explosive memoir, *Picasso and His Friends,* she described her first reaction to his rooms: 'Huge, unfinished canvases stood all over the studios, and everything suggested work: but, my God, in what chaos!' But at least there was a bed – a mattress on four legs. (It was said that the reason many of the Bateau Lavoir's tenants 'used *L'Intransigeant* as a mattress was that it had six more pages than other newspapers'.[19]) Apart from the bed, there was a little rusty iron stove and, for washing, a yellow earthenware bowl, a towel and a minute stub of soap. The only other furniture was a table, a cane chair and a little, black-painted trunk which 'made a pretty uncomfortable seat'. 'Easels, canvases of every size and tubes of paint were scattered all over the floor.'[20] One visitor described the studio as 'filled to a respectable height with food tins'.[21]

Because the studio was so hot in summer, Fernande recalled that 'it was not unusual for Picasso and his friends to ... receive visitors half-naked, if not totally so ...' In winter, it was 'so cold that the dregs of tea left in cups overnight were frozen by morning'.[22] When not semi-nude, Picasso usually wore black jacket and trousers with 'a broad, pink girdle wrapped round his waist in the pure toreador style'. What impressed people when they met him were his eyes, which 'were very black and shone with an extraordinary brilliance'.[23]

Picasso loved animals. He could never live without a dog. He had a mongrel called Gat, given to him by Maurice Utrillo, and as soon as he settled in the Bateau Lavoir he acquired two more, Feo and Frika. Fernande remembers him having three cats, a little monkey and, in the drawer of the table in his studio, 'was a pet white mouse which Picasso tenderly cared for and showed to everybody'.[24]

Picasso and his circle were permanently broke. The key to survival was to live on credit, an art they had perfected. They were aided by the local shopkeepers and café owners who were trusting and prepared to open accounts. They would also accept a painting in lieu of money. Picasso and his gang often returned at night drunk and raised hell, which included firing shots – Picasso always carried a Browning revolver – proof that they were able to buy alcohol on credit. They also regularly smoked opium, although this habit came to an abrupt end when a fellow opium user committed suicide. Picasso had been shocked by his discovery of the hanged body.

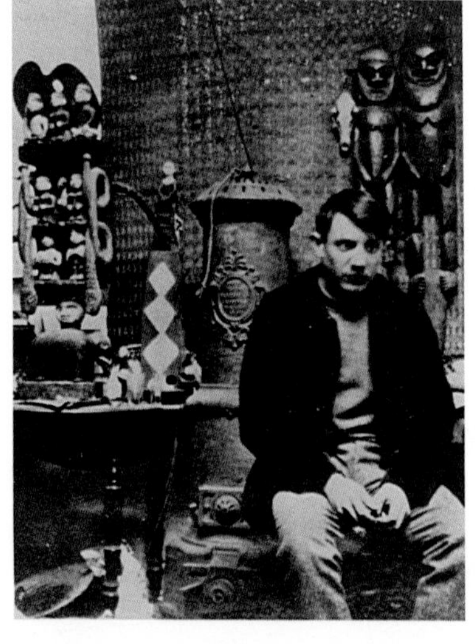

96. Picasso in his studio at Bateau Lavoir, 1908

In her descriptions of Picasso's studio, his lover Fernande Olivier describes the rusted cast-iron stove which looms behind him. The African masks are said to have influenced Picasso when he was working on his shocking and revolutionary painting *Les Demoiselles d'Avignon* in this studio.

SIX / ON THE FRINGES OF SOCIETY

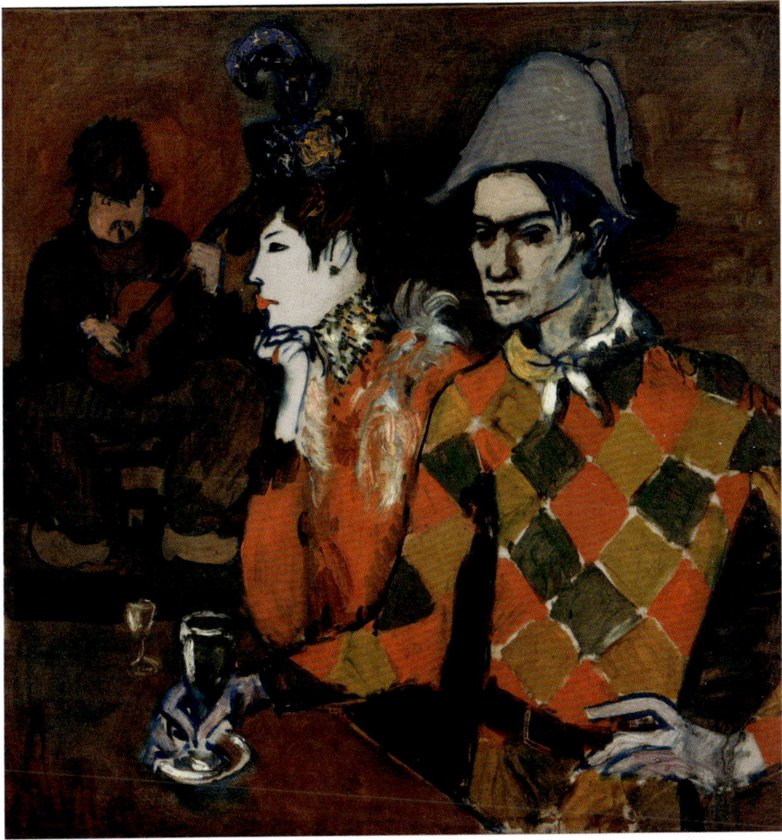

97. Pablo Picasso, *Au Lapin Agile*, 1905

Picasso and his friends frequented this café, particularly after an evening at the circus. Picasso would sit on the rustic terrace with his dogs. The harlequin is a self-portrait; the girl is Germaine Pichot, Picasso's part-time girlfriend. The man playing the guitar is Frédé, the café's proprietor.

In his great biography of Picasso, John Richardson contends that the artist's use of opium should not be over emphasised, that he 'regarded his work as sacrosanct and always kept his physical and mental energies tuned to the highest pitch. Work, sex and tobacco were his only addictions.'[25] Despite the poverty and the struggle just to stay alive, Picasso never ceased painting, preferring to work at night when he knew he would not be disturbed.

Picasso's arrival at the Bateau Lavoir had signalled a transition from the gaunt misery of his Blue Period to the images of *saltimbanques* (acrobats) and circus performers of the Rose Period. Art dealers were taking an interest in his work and patrons like Gertrude Stein were now buying it. His ramshackle home was to become the scene of one of western art's great innovations: Cubism. When Picasso finally showed *Les Demoiselles d'Avignon* to his friends and patrons, they were shocked (Matisse was said to have been actually angered by it). They viewed the painting, with its simplified forms and bold, unflinching stares – based on ancient African and Iberian masks – as an aberration. It had taken Picasso some 800 preparatory sketches and nine months of working through the night in a studio lit by a highly impractical, dangerous oil lamp, to produce the huge painting nearly 2.5m square.

Kenneth Clark in *The Nude* wrote of *Les Demoiselles*: 'Starting from a brothel theme … it developed into an enraged protest at everything involved in the conventional notion of beauty.'[26] Virtually the only person who at once understood Picasso's great leap into the unknown was the young art dealer, Daniel-Henry Kahnweiler. His perspicacity was to pay off, as he became Picasso's dealer for the next sixty years.

By 1909 Picasso could afford a less incommodious home. He found one just south of Montmartre on boulevard de Clichy, with a large, airy studio facing north. Although not far from the Bateau Lavoir, the change in his circumstances was stark. He now ate his meals in a dining-room, served by a maid in a white apron. He slept in a proper bed 'with heavy, square, brass ends', and there was a well-furnished drawing-room. Picasso had become respectable. The studio, however, was the usual dust-covered, chaotic mess, the floor carpeted with cigarette butts.[27]

In the early twentieth century Montparnasse, at the southernmost edge of Paris, was a thriving artistic and literary centre. Picasso's great friend, the poet Guillaume Apollinaire, wrote: 'Here is the Montparnasse which has become, for the painters and poets, what Montmartre was for them fifteen years ago: a haven of fine, free simplicity.'[28] Centred on the Vaugirard abattoir, with its early morning bellowing of cattle being led to the slaughter, was another dilapidated edifice housing a community of artists. Situated in the Passage Dantzig, this extraordinary three-storey, circular, twelve-sided building was known as La Ruche (literally, 'the beehive'). Left over from the Great Exposition of 1900, it had been dismantled and subsequently re-erected to form wedge-shaped studios – like slices of Brie cheese. The entrance was surprisingly impressive: two caryatids – more leftovers from the Exposition – flanking the door. As the demand for studios grew, odd structures had mushroomed around the main building until their number reached some 200.

As in the Bateau Lavoir, there was no gas, water or electricity. There were sewers, but they leaked. The halls were dark, with rubbish heaped in the corners, home to fleas, flies and mosquitoes. Each studio had a raised platform at the pointed end, which served as the sleeping quarters, reached by a ladder which must have been difficult to negotiate when inebriated. Sculptors tended to occupy the ground floor studios so that they were relieved of humping their work up the rickety stairs to the upper floors.

The list of La Ruche's residents reads like a roll call of some of the century's best-known artists: Fernand Léger, Amedeo Modigliani, Constantin Brâncuși, Diego Rivera and Robert Delaunay all occupied a studio at various times. The extremely low rents attracted penniless immigrants from Russia and central Europe, including numerous Jews who were fleeing anti-Semitism and the rules that dictated that

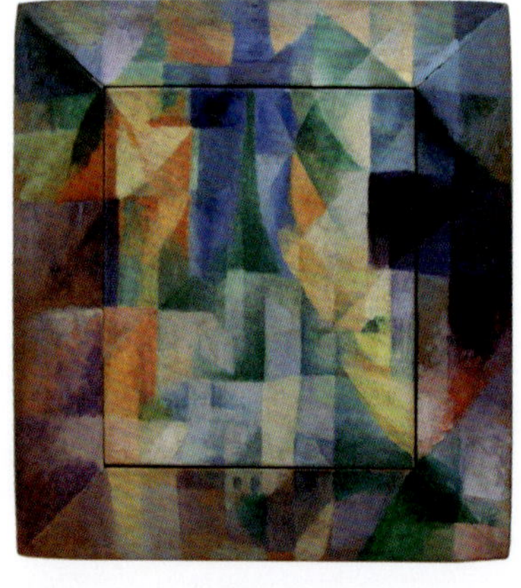

98. Robert Delaunay, *Simultaneous Windows on the City*, 1912

Delaunay was one of the artists who rented a studio in the infamous, odiferous and rubbish-strewn La Ruche in Paris. So many of its impoverished tenants later became so well-known that their work today sells for astronomical prices.

SIX / ON THE FRINGES OF SOCIETY

all art must be religious: Chaïm Soutine, who sang in Yiddish while
he painted; Léon Bakst, who in 1909 designed the sets for *Cleopatra,*
the first of Diaghilev's Ballets Russes productions; Marc Chagall, who
painted in the nude and took life and work intensely seriously. The
Russian painter Pinchus Kremegne arrived at the Gare de l'Est with
three roubles in his pocket and knowing only two words in French,
'Passage Dantzig' – the address of La Ruche – but they were all he
needed to get him there. 'In those studios,' wrote Chagall, 'lived the
artistic Bohemia of every land.'[29]

Everyone was desperately poor. Unable to afford an easel, Chagall
simply pinned his canvas to the wall. He recalls that on the floor of his
studio 'lay the remains of a herring which I used to cut in two – the
head end for one day, the tail end for the day after'.[30] He bought the
herrings from a Jewish merchant with a long, black beard who set up his
handcart at the La Ruche gates.[31] Léger described a meal of cat sauteed
in vodka which he shared with a group of 'nihilist' Russians. Modigliani
and Soutine briefly shared a studio and a friend recalled finding them
'lying next to each other on mattresses, with water splashed all around
their little island to discourage the bedbugs'.[32] (Soutine, who never
washed, was once found to have a nest of bedbugs in his ear.[33])

The poverty of most of these artists is undeniable, but some of
them seem to have deliberately chosen to live in squalor. Artists such as
Michelangelo and Francis Bacon made the same choice, the former so
possessed by his desire to create that he seldom changed his boots and
complained that he did not even have time to eat. For the bohemians,
setting themselves apart from the common herd – the bourgeoisie,
whose conventional lives they despised – enforced their sense of
'otherness', that they occupied an exotic realm that was not concerned
with the mundanities of life, such as personal hygiene. These feelings
were reinforced when they associated with fellow artists who had
chosen the same path.

Despite their early years of struggle and destitution, some of
the artists featured in this chapter became rich and famous in their
lifetimes. Picasso could look back on the deprivations of his years in
the Bateau Lavoir as a first step in a phenomenal career. Yet Rembrandt,
who rose to greatness ended as a bankrupt and Turner, although he
achieved fame and fortune, chose to live like a pauper. Any work by
Van Gogh, who sold only one painting before he died, now sells for
astronomical prices.

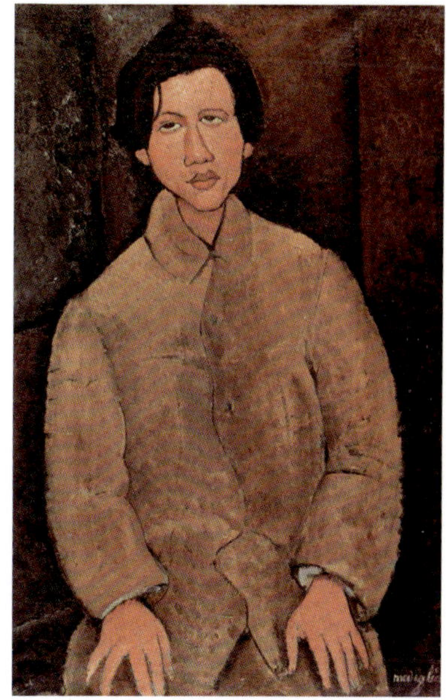

99. Amedeo Modigliani, *Portrait of
Chaïm Soutine,* 1916 or 1917

The intimate friendship between the
handsome, cultured and charismatic
Modigliani and the coarse, ugly and
tormented Soutine surprised all who
knew them. Of the four portraits
that Modigliani painted of his friend,
this one captures his mournful,
suspicious attitude to life.

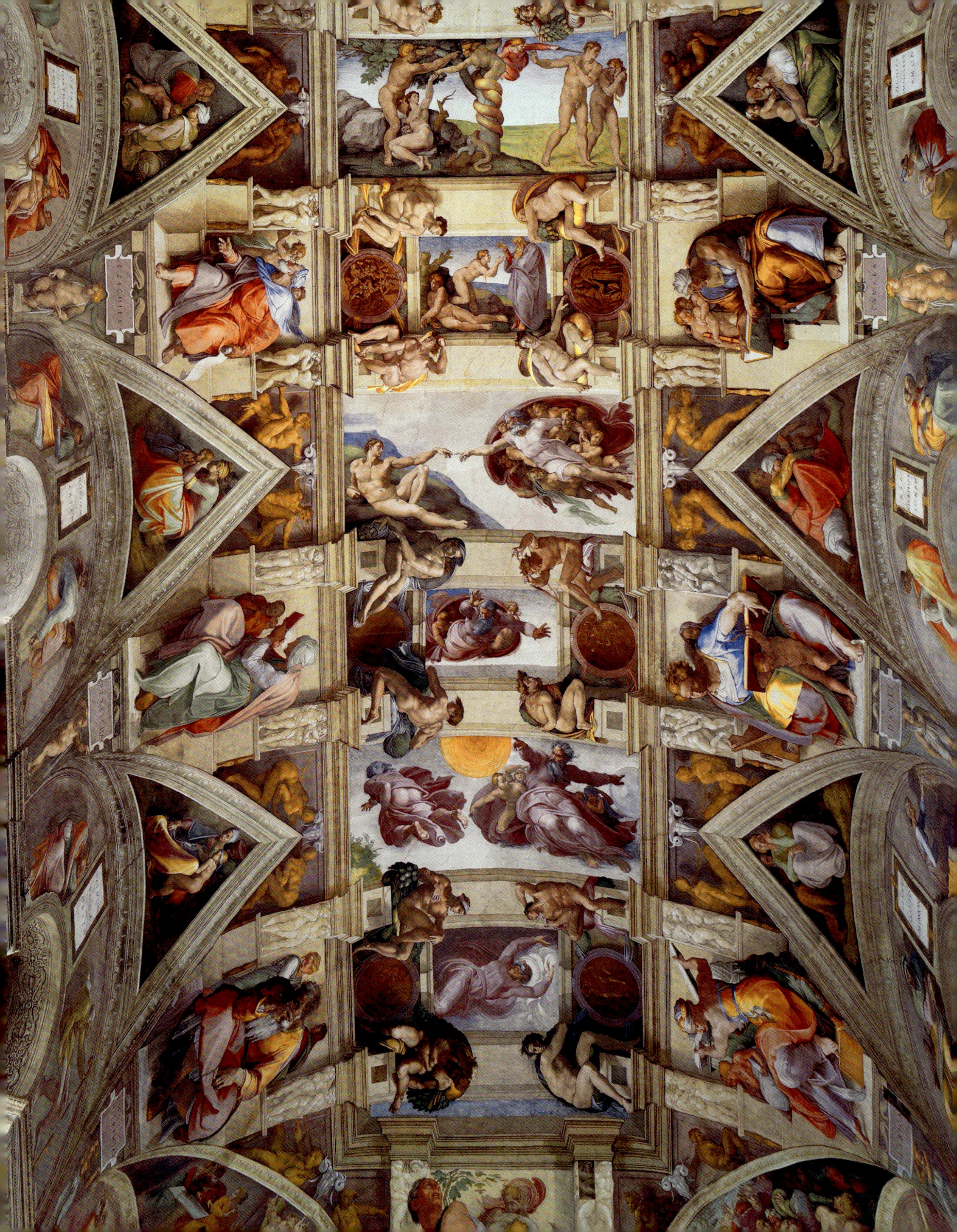

SEVEN

Improvisation and Spontaniety

The Temporary Studio

SOME OF THE GREATEST WORKS OF ART have been created not in a studio but *in situ.* Artists who accepted commissions requiring them to leave the convenience of their studios were then faced with circumstances which could involve impressive feats of planning and logistics. Even the freedom of painting *en plein air* came at a price: easels and equipment had to be humped to inaccessible locations; the weather had to be anxiously observed and accommodated. For many artists these temporary studios were only part of the story and, once they had made preliminary sketches or communed with the landscape, they retreated to their studio to make their finishing touches.

Michelangelo's farcical but illuminating sonnet gives some idea of what he suffered during the years that he was working on the Sistine Chapel Ceiling. Michelangelo (1475–1564) had signed the contract for painting the ceiling in May 1508. He had been reluctant to do so because he had fallen out with the quick-tempered Pope Julius II who had commissioned the work. He was also reluctant on artistic grounds: as a sculptor he was sure of himself, but to tackle such a large series of frescoes – containing multiple foreshortened figures – when he had limited experience in the medium, was a daunting prospect. Michelangelo had even suggested that Raphael should do the work. But the Pope had persisted.

The first problem to solve was the scaffolding. The architect Donato Bramante's initial design was rejected by Michelangelo, who then

OPPOSITE: 100. Michelangelo, *The Sistine Chapel Ceiling, Rome,* 1508–12

The painting of the ceiling, which Michelangelo began at the age of thirty-three, was an almost superhuman feat of inspiration and endurance. At its centre lies the sublime *Creation of Adam.* The restoration of the ceiling in the 1980s revealed Michelangelo's vibrant colours in all their glory.

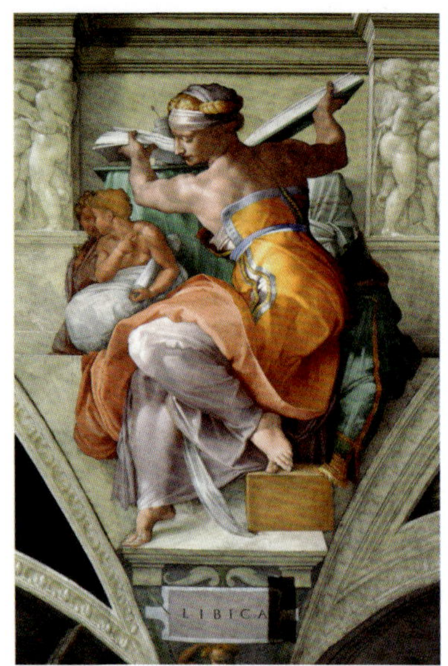

101. Michelangelo, *Study for the Libyan Sibyl, The Sistine Chapel Ceiling, Rome*, 1508–12

This Sibyl is one of five on the ceiling of the Sistine Chapel. The Sibyls were female seers who predicted the incarnation. The ceiling was cleaned in the late 1980s and when the layers of grime were peeled away the true glory of Michelangelo's original vibrant colours was revealed.

invented an ingenious system which in effect consisted of an arched bridge across the top of the chapel, with sufficient clearance to allow him to stand upright. A series of stepladders led him up to his lofty studio; ladders that were sturdy enough to enable the elderly Pope to mount them with – according to Vasari – 'the assistance of Michelangelo' so that he could watch the work in progress.[2]

Suspended on a creaking wooden platform nearly 21m above the floor of the Chapel, his head craned backwards and painting with broad, sweeping brushstrokes in poor or artificial light (candlelight), he could complete a figure well over 3m high in a day.

Only a handful of preparatory drawings for the figures in the Chapel survive. Despite the folds in her drapery, the translucent garment across the thigh of the breathtaking Libyan Sibyl reveals the taut musculature of the male assistant who posed for Michelangelo.

Apart from modelling for some of the figures, the small team of assistants assembled in the little workshop behind the church of Santa Caterina – which was Michelangelo's Roman base – would have mixed the plaster for the frescoes, transferred Michelangelo's cartoons on to the wet plaster and ground his colours. His original plan had been to employ some experienced assistants to do areas of the painting but, always obsessed about money, he balked at having to pay them. His resistance to delegating – a problem throughout his life – and his insistence on supreme quality resulted in him painting the main scenes and figures entirely himself.

The whole ceiling took four years of back-breaking work, including two lengthy interruptions. When the first half was finished, the Pope insisted on people being allowed to view it. 'No sooner was it thrown open than all Rome was drawn to see it,' recounted Vasari, 'and the Pope was the first, not having the patience to wait until the dust caused by the dismantling of the scaffolding had settled.'[3]

The second half of the ceiling was done swiftly, and the finished work was revealed in October 1512, just in time for the ailing Pope to see it before he died four months later. Michelangelo, far from being triumphant that he had completed one of the world's greatest masterpieces, was prostrate with anxiety and exhaustion. Towards the end of the massive project, he had complained to his father: 'I work harder than anyone who has ever lived. I'm not well and worn out with this stupendous labour …'[4]

When Paolo Veronese was commissioned to create a vast painting for the refectory – designed by Palladio – of the Benedictine monastery, San Giorgio Maggiore in Venice, he had one great advantage over Michelangelo: he would not have to work under such fiendish conditions, as the painting would be on canvas. The subject chosen

   SEVEN / IMPROVISATION AND SPONTANIETY

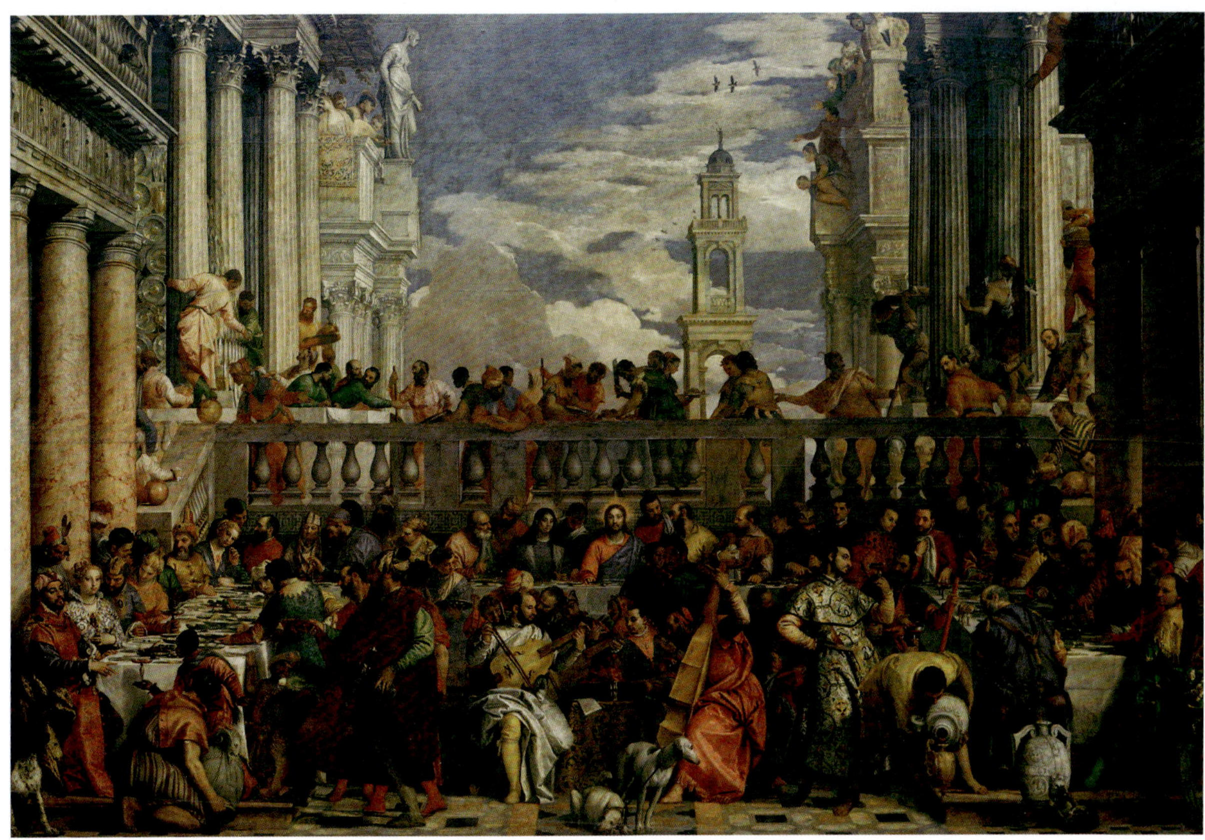

was the biblical story of the *Wedding Feast at Cana* at which Jesus miraculously converts water into red wine.

The contract that Veronese signed in June 1562 stipulated that the artist was to carry out the entire painting himself; that he was to use the 'highest quality pigments and not spare any expense for the finest ultramarine ...'[5] He was not allowed to work on the painting in his workshop near the church of Santi Apostoli, but was to establish a temporary studio in the monastery. Scaffolding would be built to enable him to reach the upper levels of the painting. He would be supplied with the canvas, but it was his responsibility to have it stitched together. As the painting was about the size of a squash court, and the Venetian hand looms could only produce strips close to 1.2m wide, it required six and a half strips which were then stitched together horizontally. The painting was to cover the end wall of the refectory and was designed to give the illusion that the refectory opened on to the terrace, and that the scene depicted was taking place outside. The black-robed monks, who ate their meals at long tables along the walls, would be able to contemplate the painting as they listened to the abbot reading from the Bible. Veronese was to eat his meals with the monks.

102. Paolo Veronese, *The Wedding Feast at Cana*, 1563

Veronese took only one year to complete this stupendous painting. Among the richly-clad guests, two figures stand out: sitting quietly below the balustrade, dressed in simple clothes, are Jesus with his mother Mary. The huge area of sky is painted in the fabulously expensive ultramarine.

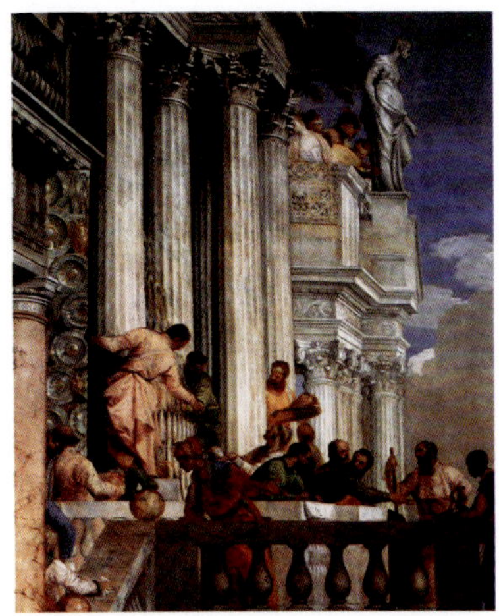

103. Paolo Veronese, *The Wedding Feast at Cana*, 1563 (detail)

This detail, taken from the left hand side of the painting, shows two servants fooling about above the balustrade, their gorgeous costumes catching the light. Above them, the classical columns soar into an ultramarine sky.

Veronese was known as a brilliant draughtsman and colourist. Before beginning the painting, he made numerous drawings with free-flowing, lyrical lines of brown ink, working out the composition, the figures, and their position within the painting. It seems incredible that he crammed in some 130 life-size figures, all of them in natural positions, all relating to each other, and all dressed in sumptuous, vibrant silks. On the painting's far left, resplendent in white with jewels in her hair, sits the bride.

It has been claimed that the violist dressed in white is Veronese himself, and that the other musicians were Venetian artists – Jacopo Bassano on the flute, Tintoretto on the violin, and Titian in red robes on the double bass. The young steward dressed in white, embroidered with black and gold, is raising his glass in astonishment that it is filled not with water but with red wine.

With this sublime work Veronese held up a mirror to the wealth and cosmopolitan life of the Venetian Republic, at that time one of Europe's most prosperous and powerful maritime states. However, 235 years later, the picture was to go on a fantastic journey.

Looted from Venice by Napoleon Bonaparte during his first Italian campaign, *The Wedding Feast at Cana* – together with eighteen other paintings, the winged lion and four bronze horses from St Mark's Basilica – was transported to Paris.

Removing the painting from the refectory wall was only the start of its tribulations. The canvas, badly torn while it was being pried from its stretcher, was then rolled on to a cylinder and encased in a crate for the journey by sea, river and canal. Ten months later, having survived being drenched with rain and salt water and gnawed by rats, the painting arrived in the Louvre. Its trials, however, were not yet over. Before it was hung, the canvas had to be relined and attached to a new stretcher, a delicate and risky business, especially with a canvas of such an enormous size. To facilitate the operation, the restorers split it in two along the line of the balustrade and nailed the two halves on to separate stretchers.[6] Four years after it was stolen from Venice by Napoleon, Veronese's fabulous painting was hung in the Louvre.

The story of the painting's travels does not end there. In 1870, it was again in a crate, being transported to the coast of Brittany to escape the Franco-Prussian War. Restored to its place in the Louvre a year later, in 1939 it was back in its crate once more and on the road, this time to save it from the arch-plunderers, Göring and Hitler. It would spend the following six and a half years secreted in various chateaux and monasteries around France. In 1946, it was returned to the Louvre, where it hangs to this day, despite efforts by the Italians to have it sent back.

To be commissioned to produce huge paintings might be financially

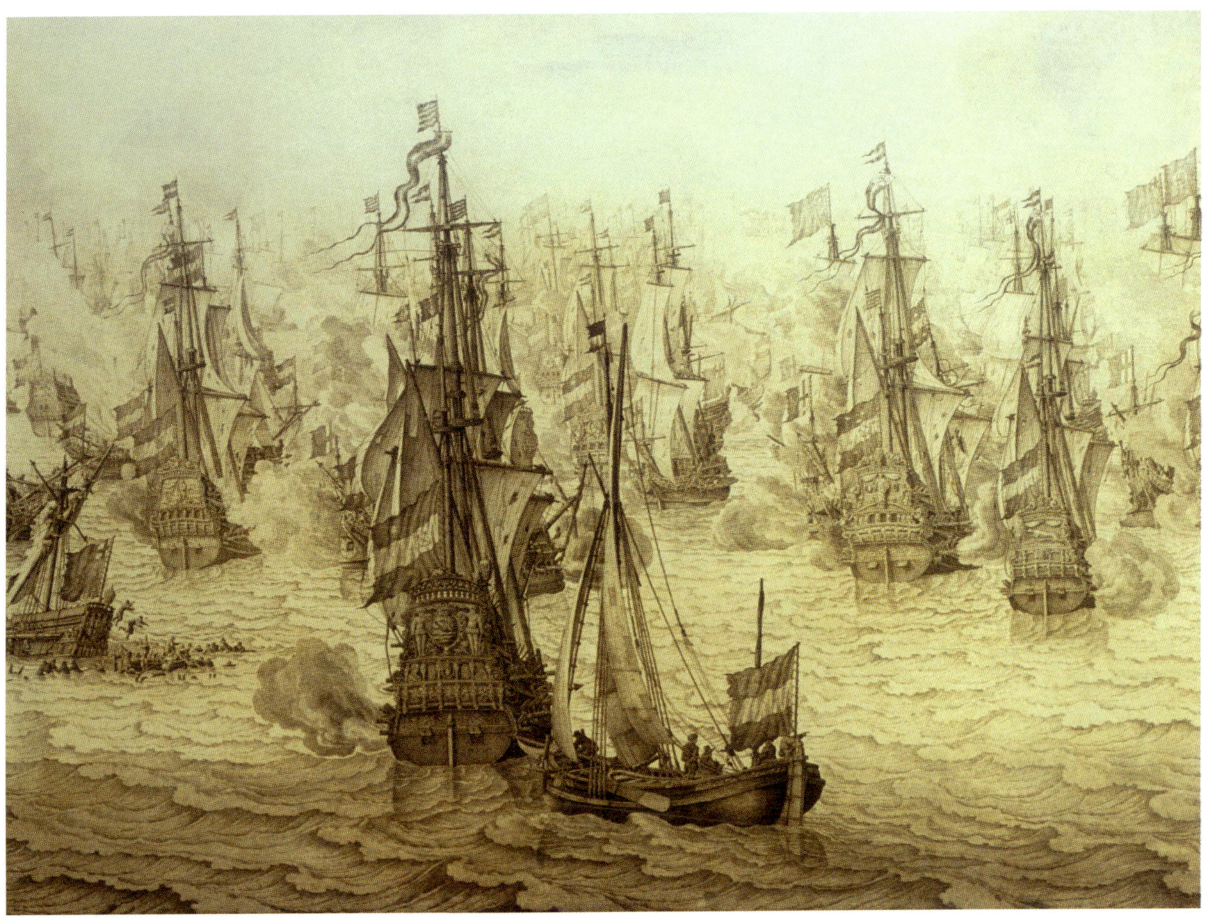

rewarding but few artists had studios sufficiently large in which to paint them. When Jacques-Louis David (1748–1825) was commanded by Napoleon to record his Coronation as Emperor – the painting was to be over 9m long and contain over 100 life-size figures – he was obliged to set up a temporary studio in the empty Église du Collège de Cluny in the Place de la Sorbonne.

The Coronation took place in Notre Dame on 2 December 1804 and David had been assigned a seat at the ceremony so that he could make sketches. Before beginning the painting, he constructed a model of the Cathedral's nave and made little dolls so that he could move them around until he found the positioning and the lighting effect he wanted. Many of those who attended the ceremony posed to David for their portraits. The main problem was to decide which moment of the ceremony to record. Although Napoleon had crowned himself, it was thought prudent for David to show him crowning Josephine instead.

When David had completed the picture, Napoleon, who was constantly enquiring after its progress, paid a visit to the church, accompanied by a large entourage. He stayed one hour – a compliment

104. William van der Velde the Elder, *The Battle of Scheveningen, 10 August 1653* (detail)

This grisaille takes the subject of this chapter to extremes. In the foreground, seated in the centre of the little boat (a galliot) flying a Dutch flag, the artist is sketching the final battle of the First Dutch War, 1652–54. The battle was a disaster for the Dutch.

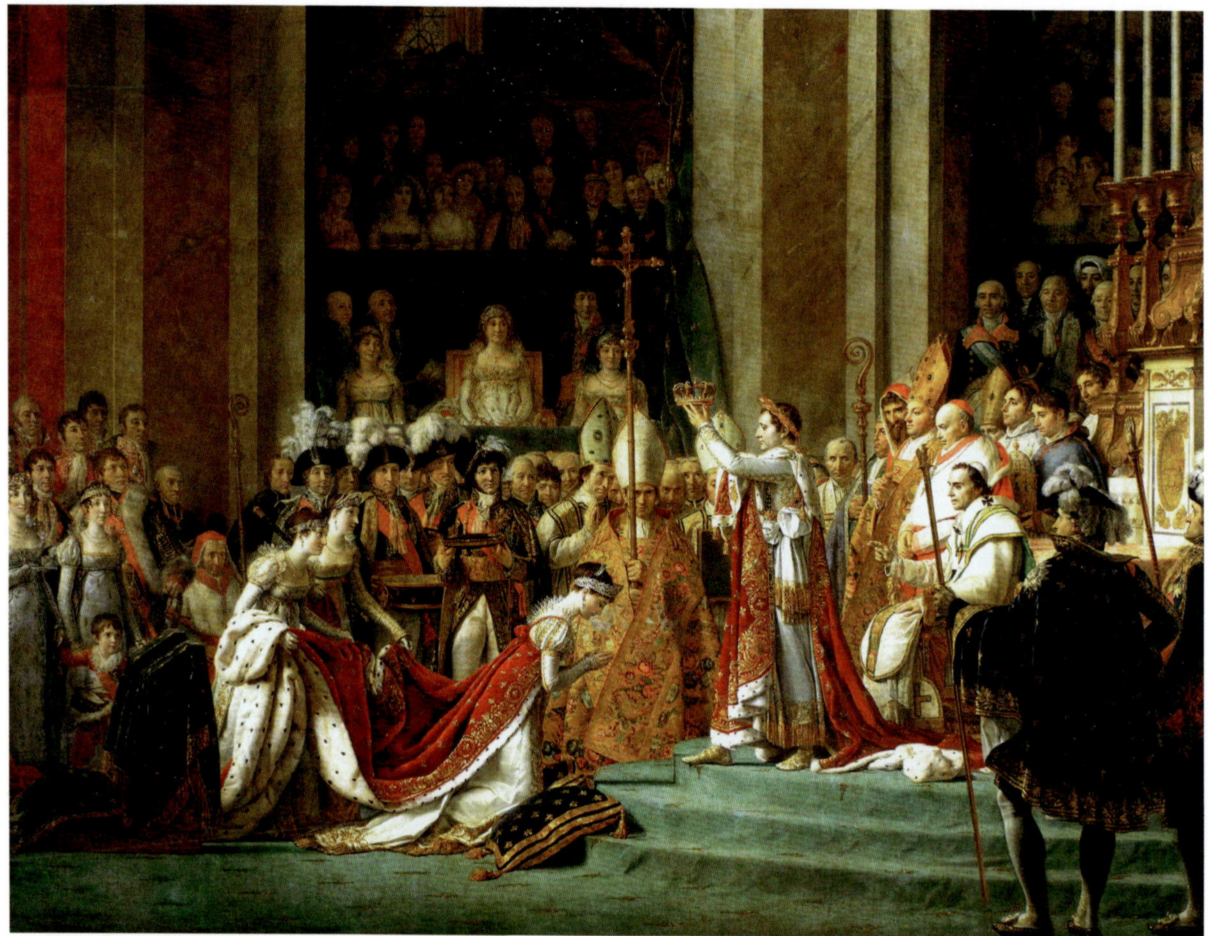

Josephine kneels before her husband as he raises the crown above her head. David included Napoleon's mother, despite her refusal to attend the ceremony. It had snowed the night before and Pope Pius VII, who officiated at the ceremony, took over an hour to travel a quarter of a mile from the Tuileries Palace to Notre Dame.[8]

to David in itself – and then pronounced his verdict: 'This is not a painting; one can walk around in this picture; life is everywhere. Good, very good, David.'[7]

When Jean-Auguste-Dominique Ingres (1780–1867) was commissioned to execute a history painting, *Romulus Conquering Acron*, for Napoleon's residence in the Palazzo Quirinale in Rome, the city in which Ingres had been living since 1806, the church once again came to an artist's rescue. The painting was to be exactly the same size as David's *Coronation of Napoleon* and thus far too large for his modest studio in Rome to accommodate. Santa Trinità dei Monti was made available to him as a temporary atelier. Ingres made a sketch of himself at work that shows him seated on a box, contemplating the acres of canvas before him, a diminutive figure dwarfed by the church's marble arches soaring above him. A ladder stands against the wall to enable him to access the painting's upper reaches.

While he was working in Rome, Ingres regularly sent pictures to the Paris Salon but was angered by their chilly reception by the critics.

In letters home, he expressed his outrage: 'So the Salon is the scene of my disgrace ... The scoundrels, they waited until I was away to assassinate my reputation ... I have never been so unhappy ...'[9] The letter's tone illustrates Ingres' highly emotional character. In his search for perfection, he worked so intensively and became so overwrought that he frequently burst into tears. When Louis Bertin sat to him for what was to prove one of Ingres' most profound and impressive portraits, Bertin recalled: 'Ingres would be weeping and I consoling him.'[10] In an attempt to relax and calm his nerves, Ingres would play his violin.

Following the fall of Napoleon and the departure of the French administration from Italy, Ingres received so few commissions that he was forced to augment his income by drawing portraits of Grand Tourists. For an artist who aspired to a reputation as a history painter, this seemed menial work, and to the visitors who knocked on his door asking, 'Is this where the man who draws the little portraits lives?', he would answer with irritation, 'No, the man who lives here is a painter!'[11]

There were other considerations, apart from a painting's size, that could cause an artist to set up a temporary studio. A house rented by the sea for a summer holiday is highly unlikely to possess a studio, so when Manet painted *Luncheon in the Studio* in Boulogne-sur-Mer, he would have been obliged to improvise. Despite its title, the painting was executed in the dining room, lunch already in progress. (Manet's presence is signalled by the paintbrush on the edge of the table.)

It is an odd, if brilliant picture which has baffled art historians since it was painted. Who are the three figures represented? The rather arrogant young man leaning against the table was originally thought to be the younger brother of Manet's wife, Suzanne Leenhoff, but it has now been concluded that he is her son, probably from a relationship with Manet prior to their marriage. The woman carrying a coffee pot and staring into space, is not Suzanne Leenhoff as was thought, but a servant. The smoking man, whose figure is daringly cropped in the style of a Japanese print, is Joseph-Auguste Rousselin, an artist friend of Manet's (Japanese prints had been a source of inspiration to many artists since they were first exhibited in Paris in 1890). The contents of the table, with the oysters, peeled lemon and glass of wine, is a beautifully painted still life.

Some studios were meant to be permanent but, through causes beyond anyone's control, proved to have a short life. When Paul Gauguin (1848–1903) executed *Vincent van Gogh Painting Sunflowers* in December 1888, he had been living with Van Gogh in Arles for about two months. The previous February, Van Gogh had left Paris for the south of France. Profoundly influenced by the simplicity and clarity of Japanese prints, their designs and the intensity of their colours, he hoped that the blazing light, red earth and blue sea of Provence might give

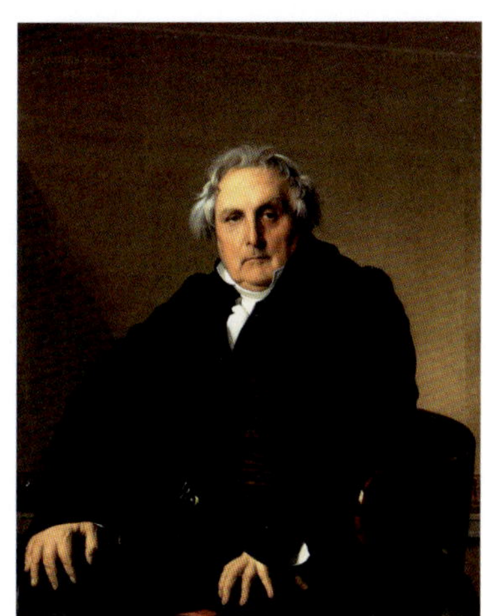

106. Jean-Auguste-Dominique Ingres, *Louis-François Bertin*, 1832

What is now recognised as a superb portrait of a member of the bourgeoisie was met with rejection when it was exhibited at the Salon. Bertin's daughter accused Ingres of having transformed her father from a *grand seigneur* to a *gros fermier* (stout farmer).

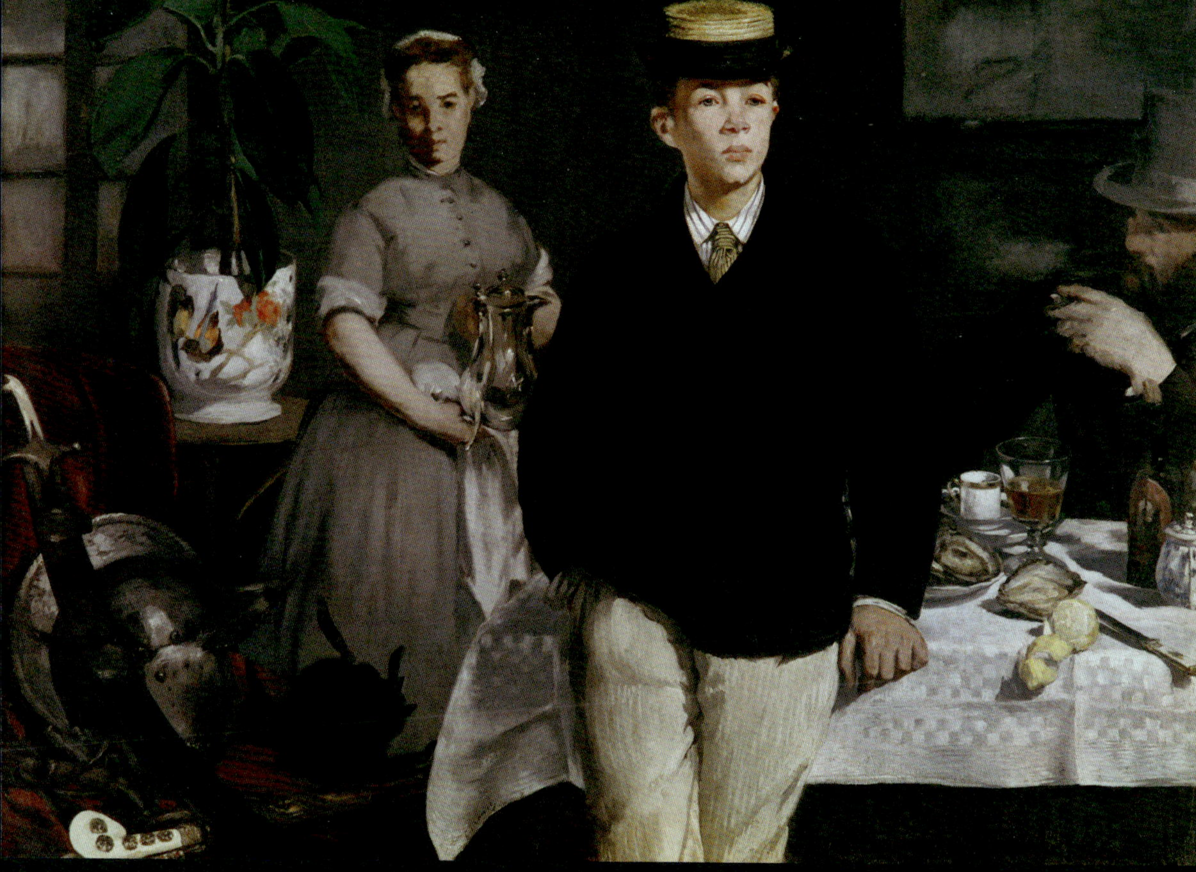

107. Édouard Manet, *Luncheon in the Studio*, 1868

This painting is full of intriguing imponderables. None of the figures relate to each other. What is the armour doing on the chair? Are the knife and the lemon about to fall off the edge of the table? Why is the young man wearing a straw boater indoors? Is it usual to drink coffee and eat oysters at the same time?

him 'a more accurate idea of the way the Japanese feel and draw'.[12] His time in Arles was to prove one of his most prolific periods: he produced some 200 paintings, many of which are now seen as his greatest works.

Van Gogh's dream was to be joined in Arles by other painters and together they would form an artist's colony. Through his younger brother Theo, he persuaded Gauguin to join him in his rented accommodation known as the Yellow House. By that time, Gauguin was just beginning to establish himself as a force while Van Gogh, now aged thirty-five, would sell only one painting during his short life.

In the Yellow House, Van Gogh's studio was in the front room on the ground floor. On seeing it for the first time, Gauguin later recalled: 'I was shocked. His box of colours barely sufficed to contain all those squeezed tubes, which were never closed up.'[13] Van Gogh's bedroom upstairs was sparsely furnished with a deal bed and two chairs. Gauguin's bedroom next door to Van Gogh's was less sparse, but it was Van Gogh's paintings, hung frame to frame around the room, which astonished Gauguin, particularly the two of sunflowers. 'In my yellow room,' he wrote, 'sunflowers with purple eyes stand out on a yellow background ... And the yellow sun that passes through the yellow curtains of my room floods all this fluorescence with gold ...'[14]

The two artists soon established a routine, working side by side – which is what Van Gogh had always longed for. They would set off together, Van Gogh in his paint-daubed working clothes and straw hat, Gauguin dressed as a Breton sailor, both festooned with their artists'

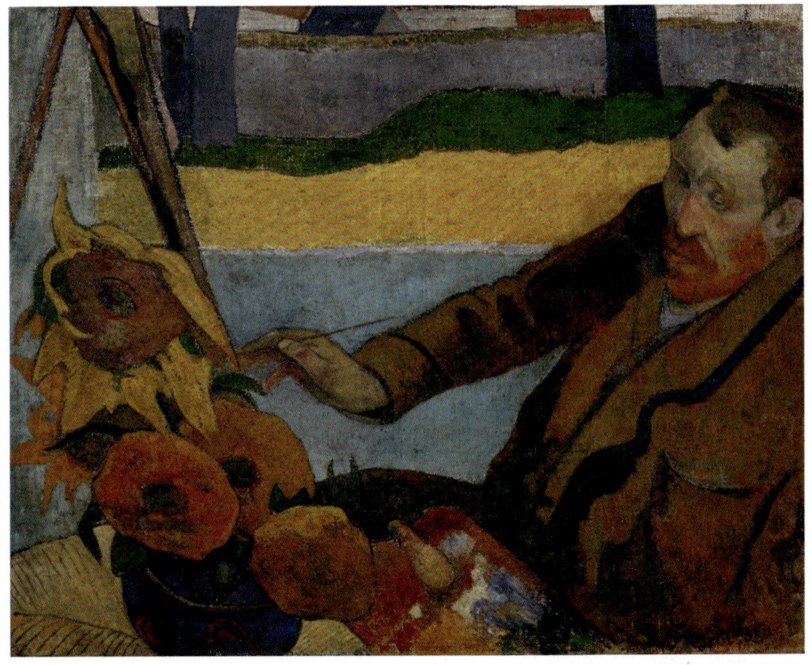

108. Paul Gauguin, *Vincent van Gogh Painting Sunflowers*, December 1888

Gauguin's portrait bears little resemblance to Van Gogh's own view of himself. Also, he looks half asleep; only the hand holding the brush seems alive. Was Gauguin hinting at Van Gogh's deteriorating mental state? It is unlikely that Van Gogh was actually painting sunflowers as they were not in bloom in December.

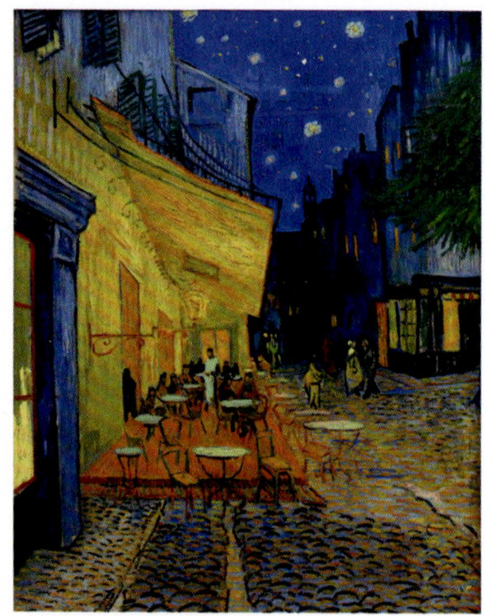

109. Vincent van Gogh, *Café Terrace at Night*, 1888

This was one of the cafés that Vincent visited during the calamitous months he spent with Gauguin at Arles. In a letter to his sister he recounted how much he enjoyed painting at night, although he admitted that it was sometimes difficult to make out the colours clearly.

equipment, to paint scenes around Arles. Initially, the situation was beneficial to them both: they were inspiring each other.

However, this tranquility and singleness of purpose was not to last. It had always been a risk to bring together two such powerful artistic personalities. Vincent's behaviour became increasingly erratic and communication between the two artists broke down completely. Vincent was drinking heavily, which always made him behave oddly, and Gauguin's decision to leave Arles drove him over the edge. On the evening of 23 December, Vincent cut off his ear – or part of it – wrapped it in newspaper and delivered the gruesome package to a girl called Rachel at the brothel he frequented. Gauguin, who had sought refuge in a hotel away from Vincent's madness, returned to the Yellow House next morning to find blood everywhere. 'The blood had stained the two rooms and the little staircase that led up to our bedrooms' he later recalled.[15] Vincent was in bed, curled up in a ball among his gory sheets. Although he recovered, he was soon back in hospital. 'Sometimes moods of indescribable anguish, sometimes moments when the veil of time and fatality of circumstances seemed to be torn apart for an instant,' he wrote two months before he voluntarily entered an asylum at Saint-Rémy in Provence.[16]

For the next eighteen months, he alternated between hospital and the asylum, living with the perpetual fear of another attack of insanity. But he continued to paint with great power and intensity. In May 1890 he left Saint-Rémy and went via Paris to Auvers where 'he enjoyed, for the last time, an astonishing burst of productivity. In little over two months, he painted seventy-six pictures.'[17] On 27 July he shot himself. He lingered for two days, then died. According to Theo, Vincent's last words were: 'The sadness will last forever.'[18]

The landscape and marine painter, Eugène Boudin (1824–98), one of the first French artists to paint *en plein air*, once said: 'Everything painted on the spot has a strength, a power, a freshness that can never be recaptured in the studio.'[19] For those artists who sought to capture this freshness, the studio had become unbearable. They wanted to immerse themselves in some picturesque spot and paint until the light failed. Throughout Europe, remote villages, frequently on the coast, became colonised by artists seeking to record a traditional way of life and the beauties of the environment. The local hotel was often the only place for them to stay.

The Italian painter Ambrogio Raffele (1845–1928), holidaying with his companion John Singer Sargent in the Italian Alps, was obliged to use the cramped conditions of his hotel room to both sleep in and as a studio. In his painting *An Artist in His Studio,* Sargent has pictured Raffele contemplating his large landscape painting that he has propped

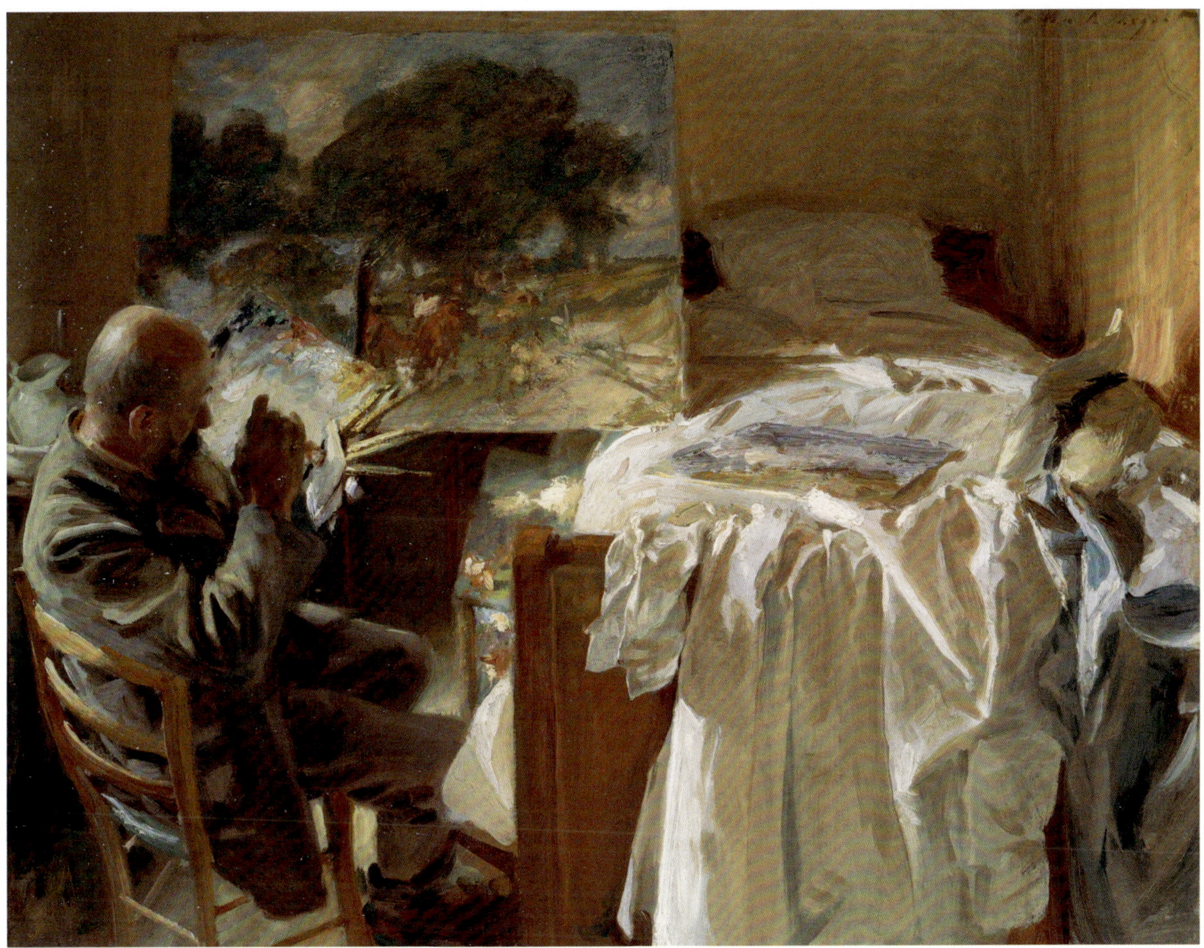

between the washstand and the bed. Sargent's brilliant rendering of light on the unmade bed fills nearly half the canvas. A reviewer in *The Times* wrote admiringly, 'Surely, never were tumbled white sheets so painted before.'[20]

Claude Monet (1840–1926), who for much of his career had been too hard up to afford any kind of permanent atelier, also used a hotel bedroom as a temporary studio. But in his case, it was not some simple hostelry in the Italian Alps but one of the most expensive and luxurious hotels in London: the Savoy. On 5 February 1900 he wrote to his Paris dealer, Paul Durand-Ruel, as follows: 'I count on leaving for London Thursday next. As you know I am going to the Savoy Hotel ... I leave full of ardour with the hope of having suitable weather and of bringing back some good things.'[21]

This was not the first time Monet had visited London. In 1870, he had come as a penniless and unknown exile, fleeing Paris to escape the Franco-Prussian War. On that occasion he had painted scenes around the centre of the city. Further visits followed during the 1880s, his

110. John Singer Sargent, *An Artist in His Studio*, 1904

Although known for working out of doors, Raffele is depicted constructing a painting from a tiny preliminary sketch in his makeshift studio. Another, larger sketch is propped on a chair. There seems hardly space enough for Sargent and his easel.

associations with the city deepening through his friendship with other artists, James Whistler in particular.

In 1899, Monet spent the first of three winters in London and began to paint his great series of views of the Thames, some of the most radical images of his career. By now his finances had improved immeasurably and he could not only afford to stay in the Savoy but found that he was treated by London high society as a celebrity.

For the first of the three winters he took a suite on the Savoy's sixth floor. For his 1900 visit, he informed his wife: 'I'm well installed on the fifth floor, and have two rooms similar to those we had on the 6th: they took the furniture out of room 541 and I sleep in 542, for with all my equipment I would never have been able to move about.'[22] (Much has changed in the hotel since then, but Room 508 is currently named as Monet's room.) Among the Savoy's charms was the food, which is hardly surprising, as the famous French chef, Auguste Escoffier, had just taken over the catering. Judging by Monet's recipe books, he was very partial to English dishes, especially Welsh rarebit and Yorkshire pudding, and was also a devotee of the 'full English' breakfast.[23]

From the hotel balcony, Monet painted the view upstream, with Charing Cross Railway Bridge in the foreground, and downstream, with old Waterloo Bridge.

What he loved about London was the fog: 'It is the fog that gives it its magnificent breadth,' he wrote. 'Those massive, regular blocks become grandiose within that mysterious cloak.'[24] Monet also wanted to paint

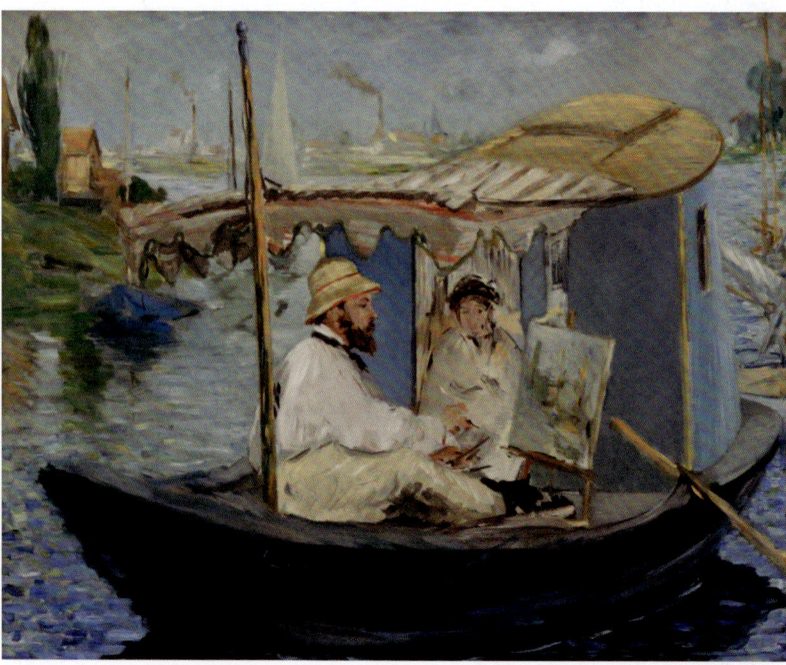

111. Édouard Manet, *Monet working on his Boat in Argenteuil*, 1874

From the 1890s onwards, Monet pushed the technique of painting *en plein air* to its limits. Manet has captured his friend in the boat which had been constructed so that he could evoke the transient beauty of light on water. His second wife, Alice, sits patiently watching him at work.

SEVEN / IMPROVISATION AND SPONTANIETY

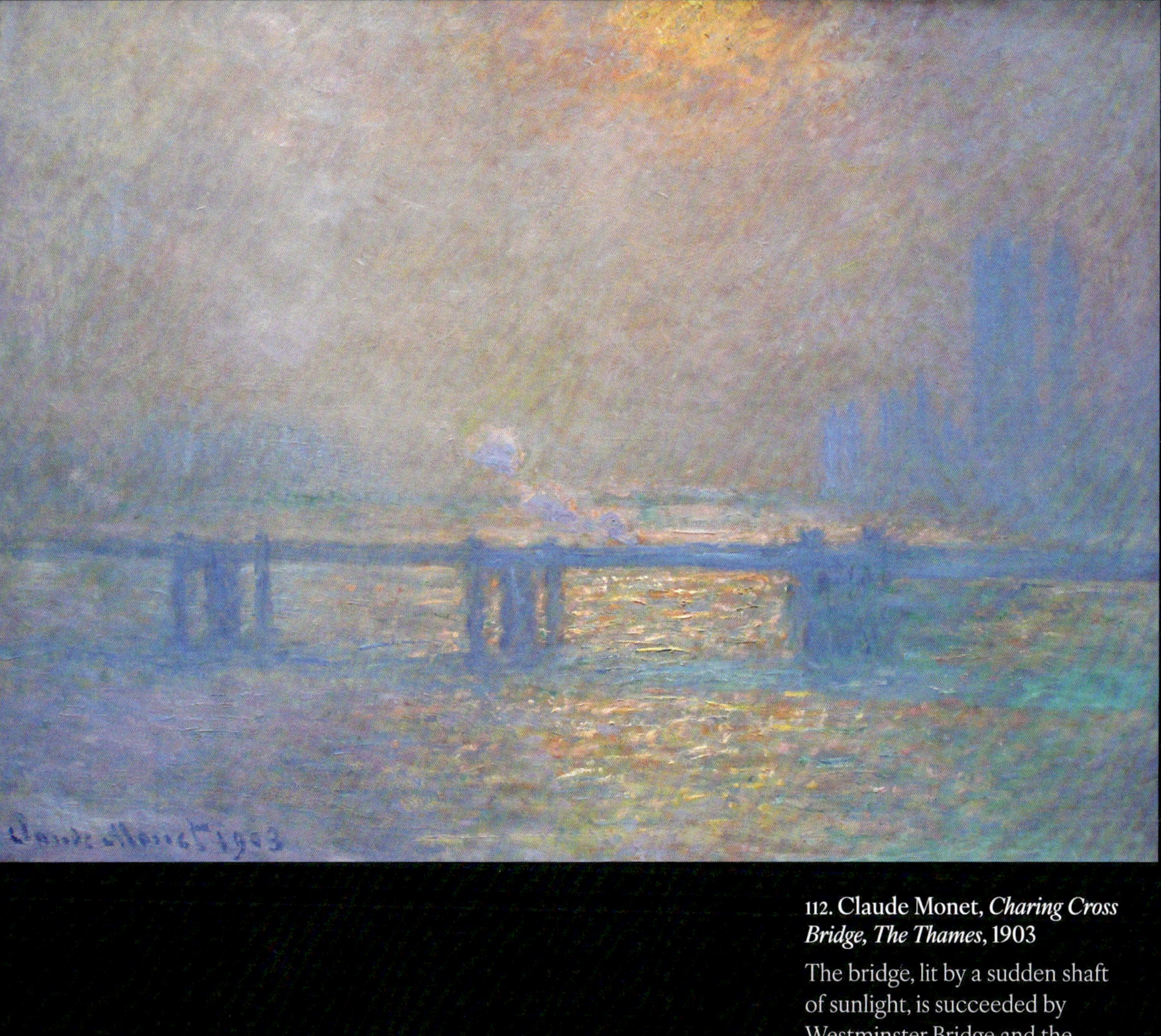

112. Claude Monet, *Charing Cross Bridge, The Thames*, 1903

The bridge, lit by a sudden shaft of sunlight, is succeeded by Westminster Bridge and the grotesque, looming shapes of the Houses of Parliament beyond. Two passing trains add their smoke to the shifting light. This is London at its most shadowy and powerful.

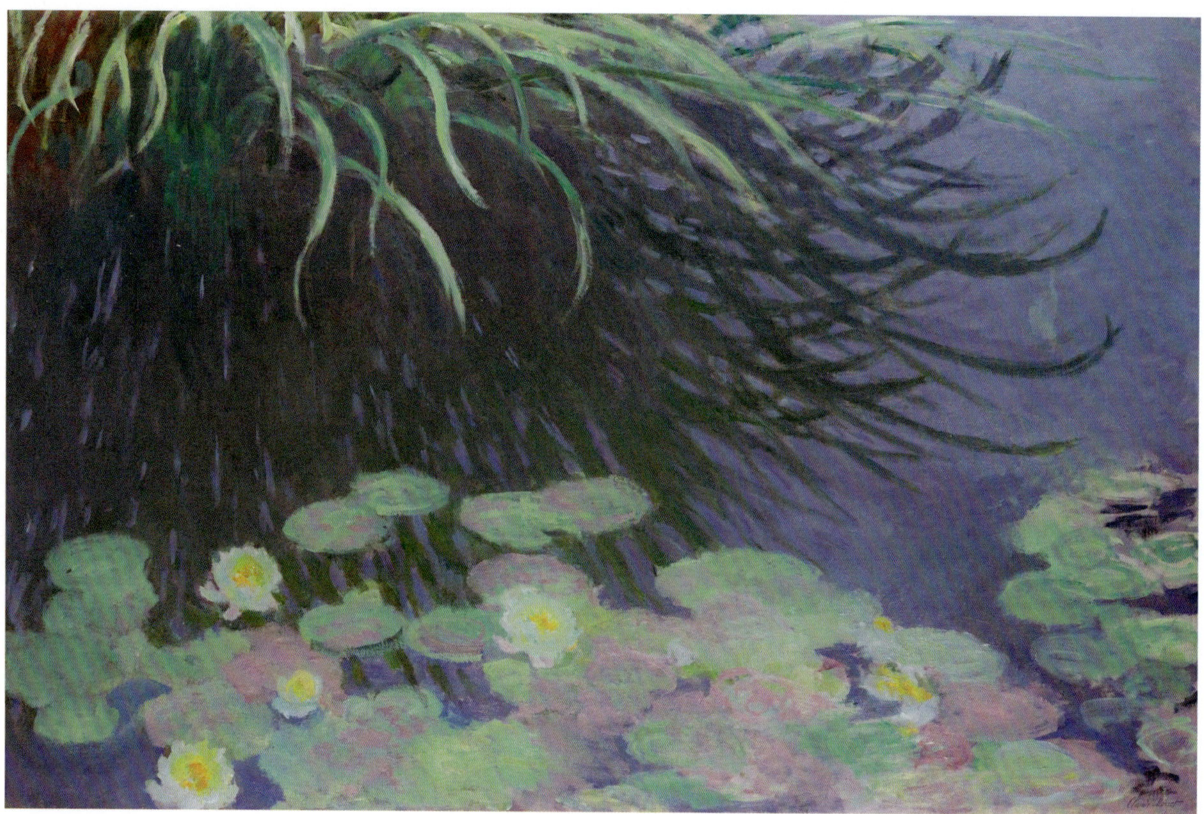

113. Claude Monet, *Water Lilies, Reflections of Tall Grass*, 1914–17

During the last two decades of his career, Monet devoted himself to painting the water lily pond at his home in Giverny. In one extraordinary canvas after another, he captured the constantly shifting reflections and light that transformed the pond's surface with each passing moment.

the Houses of Parliament from *across* the Thames and was allowed to set up his easel on a terrace at St Thomas's Hospital, where he was fed tea and cakes by the kindly hospital treasurer.

From his letters to Durand-Ruel – who was always pressing him to give him more paintings to sell – Monet was continually battling against the changeable weather. As he later told an interviewer, there were times when he had 'up to a hundred canvases on the go – for one single subject'. John Singer Sargent confirmed this by recalling that when he visited Monet at the Savoy, he saw some 'ninety canvases littering the room'.[25] There were some good days, however. On 3 February 1901, he wrote to his wife, Alice, describing the sun coming out at last. 'The Thames was all gold. God it was beautiful, so fine that I began to work in a frenzy, following the sun and its reflections on the water ... I can't begin to describe a day as wonderful as this. One marvel after another, each lasting less than five minutes, it was enough to drive one mad. No country could be more extraordinary for a painter.'[26]

All these 'essays, studies, preparatory sketches', as he called them, were reworked from memory at Monet's home at Giverny where he had abundant space. At that time, he had two studios, one in the house and another in a converted barn in the garden. However, neither studio was large enough when he embarked on his great series of water lily paintings, or *Nymphéas,* so he had a huge tent-like structure erected. There are photographs of him, bearded and venerable, his large palette at the ready, posing within its cavernous space.

Monet was almost sixty when he began transforming the grounds at Giverny into both a flower garden and a water garden. For the pond, he ordered a special type of water lily which he had seen at Exposition Universelle in Paris in 1889. Of the six gardeners, one was solely responsible for keeping the surface of the water clear so that Monet could paint the reflections without them becoming marred by weed.

Despite his age, failing eyesight, the loss of his wife and the thunder of guns as the Great War came ever closer, he was to produce some 250 water lily paintings – some of them monumental in size – before his death at the age of eighty-six. When the Paris art dealer, René Gimpel, visited Monet in his studio in 1919 and found himself surrounded by the water lily canvases, he wrote that 'water and sky have neither beginning nor end. We seem to be present at one of the first hours in the birth of the world. It is mysterious, poetic, delightfully unreal.'[27]

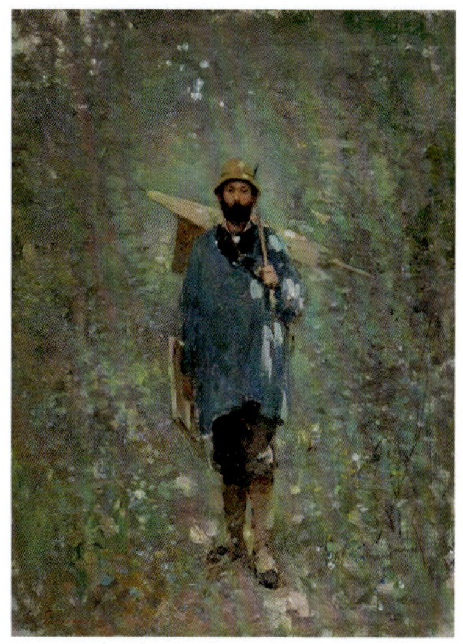

114. Nicolae Grigorescu, *Andreescu la Barbizon, c.*1879

The ultimate temporary studio, carried on the back of this young artist as he heads out into the countryside to spend the day painting a chosen view. Barbizon, just north of Paris, was the first colony to be established by artists in their quest for reality.

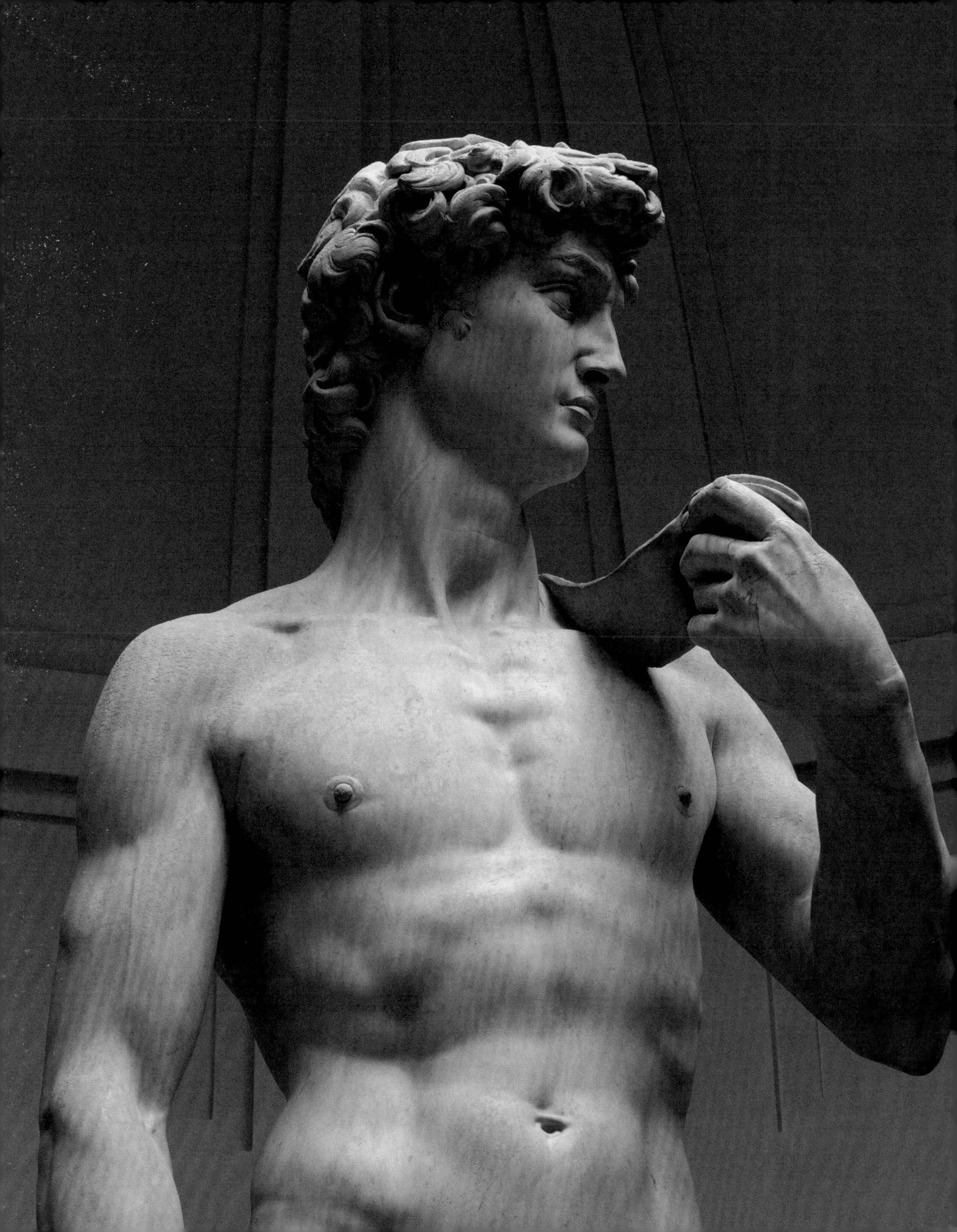

EIGHT

Draped in Beauty

The Sculptor's Workshop

Every young sculptor seems to think that he must give the world some specimen
of indecorous womanhood, and call it Eve, Venus, a Nymph, or any name that
may apologise for a lack of decent clothing …
Nathaniel Hawthorne, *The Marble Faun*[1]

THESE WORDS, SPOKEN BY MIRIAM, one of the main characters
in Hawthorne's novel about American expatriates in mid-nineteenth
century Rome, are addressed to her friend, the sculptor Kenyon who
is about to show her his latest work. She hopes it is not another nude
as she has 'grown weary' of them. Besides, she continues, no-one goes
round naked nowadays, whereas an 'old Greek sculptor, no doubt,
found his models in the open sunshine … and thus the nude statues of
antiquity are as modest as violets, and sufficiently draped in their own
beauty.' In his defence, Kenyon replies: 'But what are we to do? Must
we adopt the costume of to-day, and carve, for example, a Venus in a
hoop-petticoat?'[2]

The same argument about nudity could, of course, be applied to
paintings: artists grew wealthy by filling their canvases with erotic nudes
and maintaining they were nymphs, Eve or Greek gods or goddesses.
Harems and Bacchanalian revels were also useful to legitimise a
rampant display of flesh. Hans Makart painted Diana the Huntress
striding through the forest accompanied by one dog and a bevy of
female nudes. Were they wood nymphs? But as long as artists and their
lascivious buyers were playing the same game, all was well.

Édouard Manet, however, was not playing the game when he
painted *Olympia* – a model lying full length on a couch wearing nothing
but an enigmatic smile – that scandalised the art world (see page 142).
In his book, *The Nude,* Kenneth Clark notes of *Olympia*: 'almost for the

OPPOSITE: 115. Michelangelo,
David, 1501–04

This superb sculpture, carved
from an awkwardly shaped and
previously used block of marble,
involved Michelangelo in formidable
technical difficulties. In only twenty-
one months *David* was ready to be
displayed to the Florentines – an
astonishing achievement.

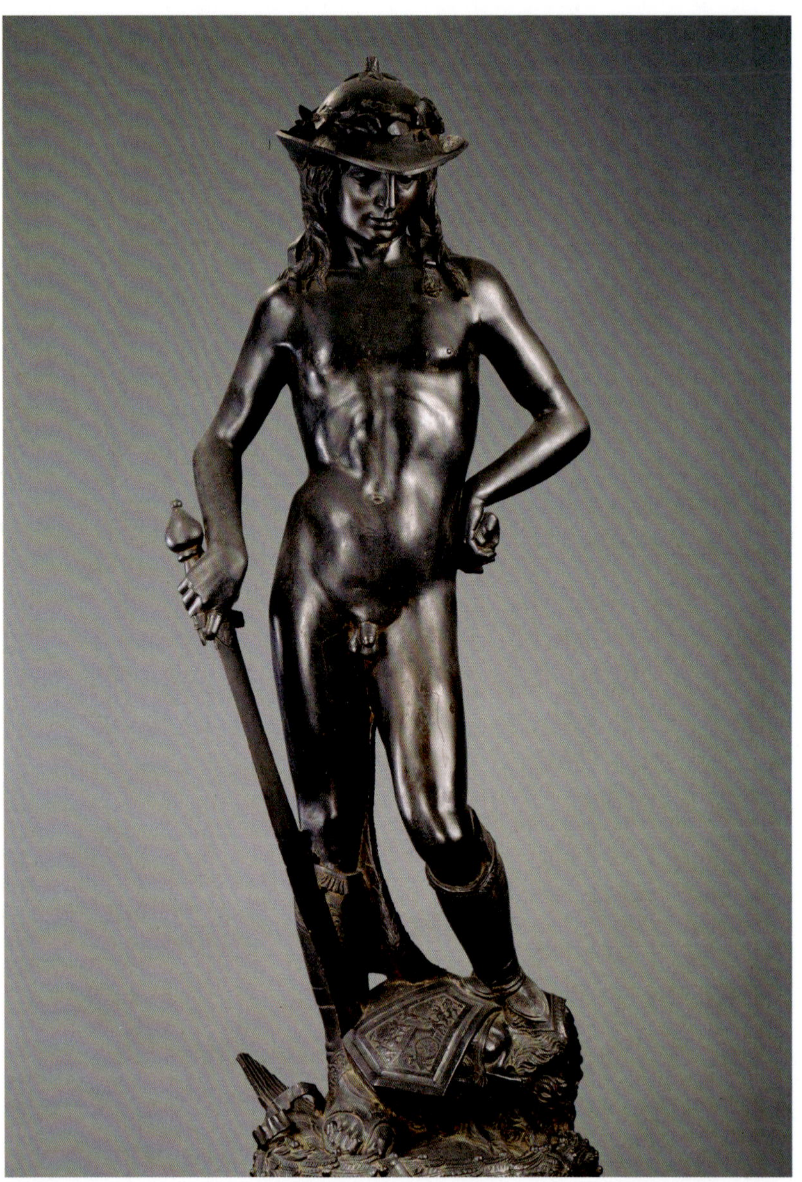

116. Donatello, *David*, c. 1440s

David's vulnerability is emphasised by both his nudity and by the stone he clasps in his left hand, a reminder that he brought down his massive foe with a simple slingshot. The message here is clear: David triumphed not through physical power, but through the grace of God. It is a work of almost incredible originality.

first time since the Renaissance, a painting of the nude represented a real woman in probable surroundings'.[3] Olympia was emphatically not a nymph flitting through a twilit grove or languishing in a harem; she was a *grande horizontale* displaying her charms.

Kenneth Clark maintained that 'in countries where painting and sculpture were practised and valued as they should be, the naked human body was the central subject of art'. Furthermore: 'In the greatest age of painting [the Renaissance], the nude inspired the greatest works ...'[4] Never more so than Donatello's sublime bronze statue of *David*, the first free-standing male nude sculpture made since antiquity. Ever inventive, Donatello (*c.* 1386–1466) depicted him not as the customary venerable king of Israel but as a young Greek god. Wearing a dreamy smile and a saucy little hat, the boy stands triumphant, his foot firmly planted on the severed head of Goliath, the giant's huge sword at his side. In Vasari's opinion, 'This figure is so natural in its vivacity and its softness, that it is almost impossible for craftsmen to believe that it is not moulded on the living form.'[5] Indeed, Donatello was overheard saying more than once to a sculpture that he was toiling over: 'Speak, damn you, speak!'[6]

Donatello would have first made a clay or wax model of his *David* and then cast it into bronze using the lost-wax or *cire-perdue* method, a process that dates to prehistoric times. Modelling in clay or wax is a process of addition and adjustment. By contrast, carving in stone or marble involves irreversible subtraction and enormous labour, accompanied by clouds of dust. When comparing a painter to a sculptor, Leonardo pictures the latter sweating and dirty, 'his face smeared with marble dust so he looks like a baker ... His house is in a mess and covered in chips and dust from the stone.'[7] Brâncuşi complained that 'marble dust penetrates all. I've tried everything, even masks, but still it penetrates into you through the pores.'[8]

Marble dust was not the only problem a sculptor had to deal with. To prevent the clay from drying out, the atmosphere in a studio must be kept constantly cold and moist, the models covered with damp rags. Sculptors devised various methods to cope with such conditions. Italian artist Luca della Robbia (*c.*1400–82) kept his feet warm by standing in a basket full of wood shavings. To prepare his model for the day's work, the English sculptor Joseph Nollekens (1737–1823) used to spit water at it and let it sink in while he had breakfast.[9]

For Michelangelo, who was able to work under the most appalling physical circumstances, the conditions in a sculptor's studio would not have bothered him. Despite earning large sums of money and being admired and valued by powerful men, he always chose to live and work in the most squalid and primitive dwellings. During a temporary stay in Bologna, he informed his father: 'I'm living in a mean room for which I bought only one bed and there are four of us sleeping in it.'[10] He must have made an odiferous bedfellow: his first biographer Ascanio Condivi reported that Michelangelo often slept in his clothes and buckskin boots, keeping the latter on for so long that when he took them off, his skin came with them, like a snake's.[11]

In 1497, at the age of twenty-two, Michelangelo was commissioned 'to make a *Pietà* of marble, that is, a clothed Virgin Mary with the dead Christ, nude in her arms', which was to be installed in the most important church in western Christendom, St Peter's in Rome.[12] For the first time he took a house and workshop of his own while working on the sculpture. Evidence that the house was pretty squalid comes in

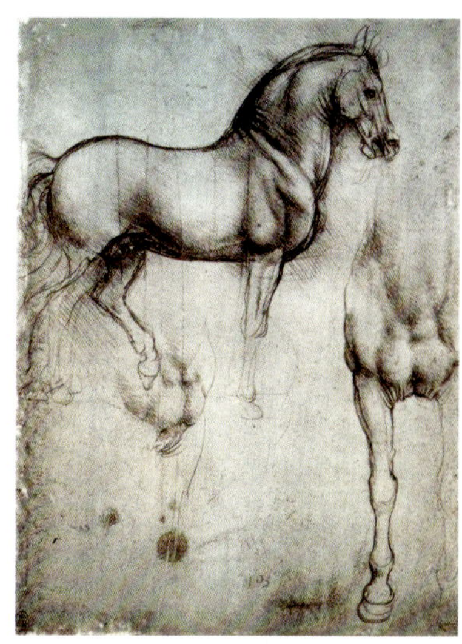

117. Leonardo da Vinci, *Horse Studies*, *c.*1490

Leonardo was particularly interested in horses. This is documented by a large number of studies of their proportions and movements. Some of these studies may have been for two equestrian statues, the Sforza and Trivulzio monuments, both of which were uncompleted.

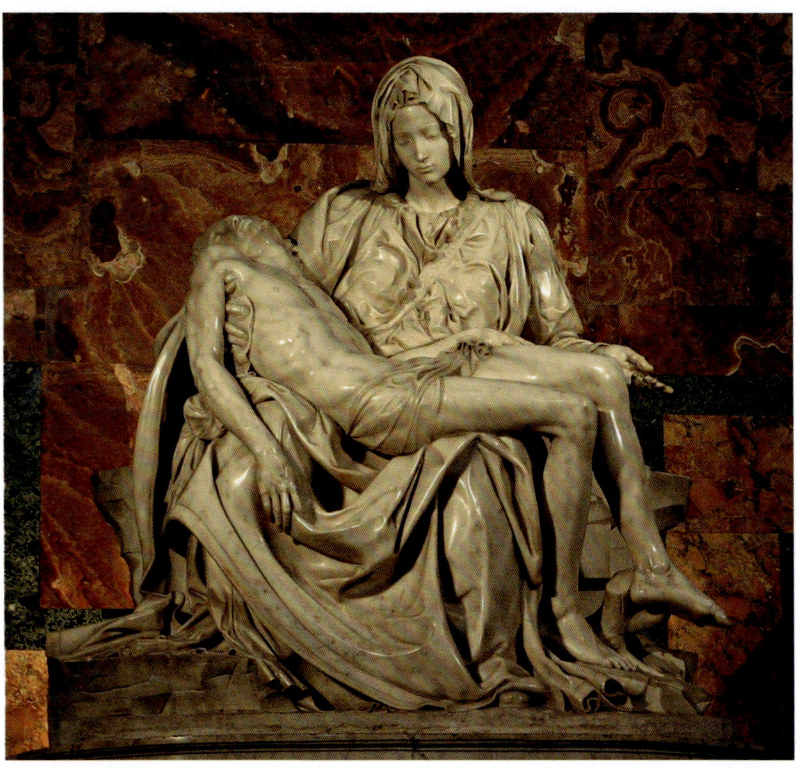

118. Michelangelo, *Pietà*, 1498–1500

It is a measure of Michelangelo's genius that it never occurs to viewers of this breathtaking statue that, should the Madonna stand up, she would be a giantess. Nor does it seem strange that she looks too young to have an adult son. The statue was made to be seen close up, its pure white surfaces shining in the gloom.[15]

a letter from his father: 'Buonarroto (Michelangelo's brother) tells me that you live at Rome with great economy, or rather penuriousness.'[13] He then set off for Carrara's marble quarries in northern Tuscany to choose a block of marble. Once selected, it had to be extracted from the cliff using chisels and wedges – a difficult and dangerous process – then manoeuvered down the precipitous slopes on a sledge-like platform.[14] From there, it took two months for the marble to be carried by cart to the coast, and from thence by boat to the port of Rome.

Michelangelo worked in Rome for two years on this most beautiful and poignant of sculptures. When Lucien Freud visited St Peter's in 2004, and saw the *Pietà*, he commented: 'The church itself is like the most expensive junk shop in the world, with that horrible smell of incense. But in the middle of all that there was this beautiful thing, full of feeling.'[16]

Michelangelo was a mere twenty-six when he began work on the statue of *David*, the first colossal nude since antiquity (see page 126). He had long coveted a giant block of Carrara marble, which had been botched and abandoned in the workshops of Florence's Duomo forty years earlier. In the interim, one sculptor had roughed out a torso, which included hacking a hole between its legs. Another thought he could get round the narrowness of the block by adding extra pieces. Only Michelangelo could see a slim figure trapped within the marble – but it

   EIGHT / DRAPED IN BEAUTY

would have to be naked. In other words, *David*'s nudity was a practical necessity.[17] To protect Michelangelo from the weather and the gaze of curious onlookers while he worked, Vasari reported that a little hut was built: 'an enclosure of planks and masonry, thus surrounding the marble, and, working at it continuously without anyone seeing it, he carried it to perfect completion ... And truly it was a miracle on the part of Michelagnolo (*sic*) to restore to life a thing that was dead.'[18] It seems that Michelangelo made the David in eighteen months – or so he told his biographer, Condivi.[19]

The original plan was to position *David* high up on the wall of the Duomo, but after much discussion it was decided that it should be placed outside the Palazzo Vecchio in Florence's famous Piazza della Signoria. But getting it there – it was 6m high and weighed several tons – would be a feat of engineering. 'The solution was to suspend it from a wooden framework and then slowly pull it over a temporary surface of greased wooden beams.'[20] It took more than forty men four days to drag *David* the few hundred metres from the Duomo to its final position, where a copy of it stands today. However, neither the copy nor the original, which is in the Galleria dell'Accademia, bear the additions that were demanded at the time by the Florentine authorities. Shocked by the statue's nakedness, they insisted that his private parts should be covered with a garland of gilded leaves – and that was how they remained for centuries.

The Florentine authorities were not the only ones to be shocked: when Queen Victoria first saw a cast of David at the Victoria and Albert Museum, she was so offended 'by his nudity that a proportionally accurate fig leaf was commissioned to cover the genitalia. The leaf was kept in readiness for any royal visits, when it was hung on the figure using two strategically placed hooks.'[21]

In 1665, Gian Lorenzo Bernini (1598–1680), celebrated as the foremost Baroque sculptor and architect, the favourite of eight successive popes, was pressurised by Louis XIV to travel from his home in Rome to Paris to advise on the design of the enlargement of the Palais du Louvre. It would be an arduous journey for a man of sixty-seven, since it entailed a hazardous passage over the snow-covered Mont Cenis Pass in a tilting sedan chair, its passenger praying devoutly that the porters were steady on their feet. Indeed, at the foot of the Alps Bernini is alleged to have exclaimed: 'How did I let myself be talked into this?!'[22] But the large retinue of servants and a courier – all paid for by Louis – ensured his comfort and safety. Wherever the party stopped along the way, he was feted by the local population and the town's dignitaries; the journey he had so feared turned out to be virtually a royal progress.[23]

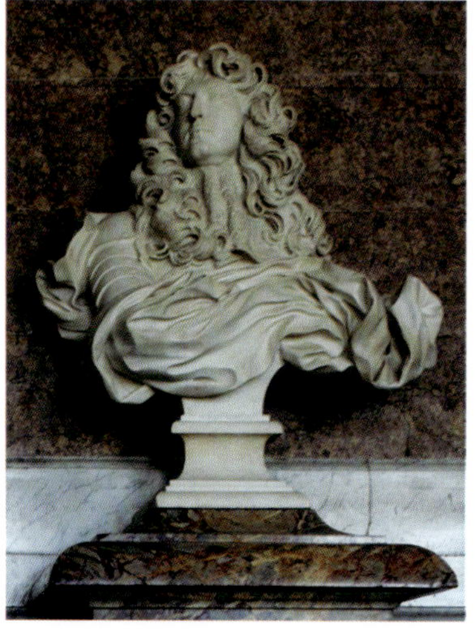

119. Gian Lorenzo Bernini, *Louis XIV*, 1665

Bernini did not enjoy his five months in Paris. His design for the enlargement of the Palais du Louvre was not well received by the French king. He did, however, carve this marble bust of Louis, which required no less than thirteen sittings.

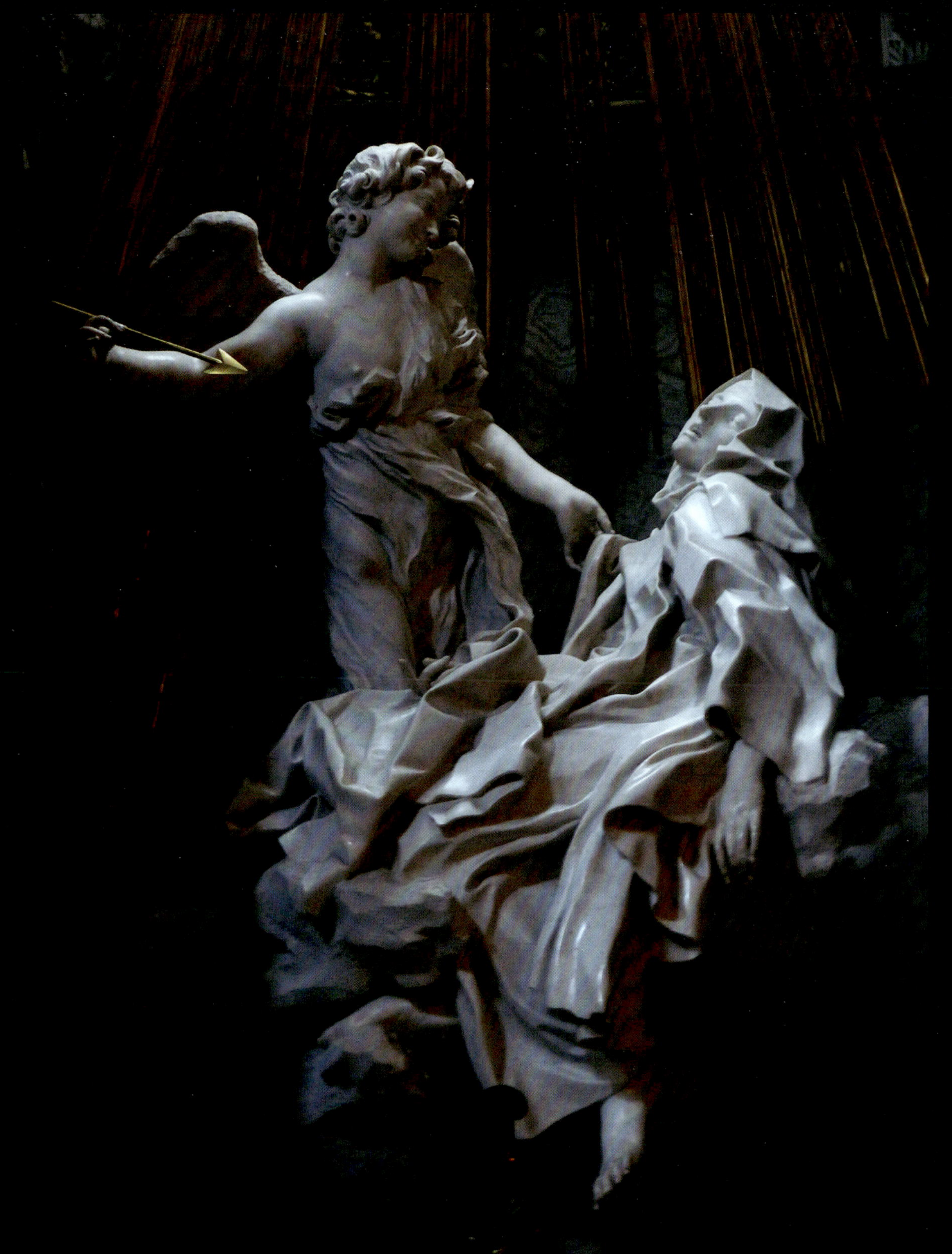

While working on the Louvre design, Louis pressed Bernini to carve his bust in marble. Bernini reluctantly agreed. He had once said: 'If a man whitened his hair, beard, eyebrows, and – were it possible – his eyeballs and lips, and presented himself in this state to those very persons that see him every day, he would hardly be recognised by them … Hence you can understand how difficult it is to make a portrait, which is all of one colour, resemble the sitter.'[24]

Bernini's months in Paris were not a success. He and the king cordially disliked each other; he was obliged to sketch Louis while he played tennis or conducted the business of the court; the room set aside for him as a studio was so cold, he caught a chill and was advised 'to wear a bearskin coat and cotton wool wadding'; in summer it was insufferably hot. Moreover, it was infested with vermin, and he was 'dismayed to find mouse droppings staining his marble'.[25] Bernini did not endear himself, however, by continuously criticising everything French, from the art and architecture of Paris to the interior decoration of the Louvre palace. For a man of Bernini's fiery and arrogant temperament, it is not surprising that he fell foul of many of the courtiers. By the time he left Paris, Louis and the French court had had quite enough of the famous sculptor, and he had certainly had his fill of them – and of France in general.

In 1802, another celebrated Italian sculptor, Antonio Canova (1757–1822), was persuaded to cross the Alps: Napoleon, then First Consul, wanted him to sculpt his portrait – in fact, he *demanded* that he should. Although Canova had lived and worked in Rome for over thirty years, he was a Venetian and, as such, bitterly resented Napoleon's conquest of the city and his looting of art treasures from both Venice and Rome. But, pressed by the Pope to comply in the interests of diplomacy, Canova capitulated.

Like Bernini, Canova disliked carving portraits, but for a different reason: 'When you have produced a portrait, using all our artistic knowledge, what is our reward? The sitter's mistress comes along and tells him: But you are handsomer; I hardly recognised you in it.'[26] Canova avoided this eventuality by narrowing Napoleon's face, lengthening his nose and adding hair to his balding pate, thus giving him the handsome features and intelligent expression of a classical hero.[27] Canova also made a colossal, full-length marble sculpture of the First Consul as 'Mars the Peacemaker', insisting that it should be in the nude. (The statue did not please Napoleon and it ended up in storage.)

Canova created portraits of several members of the imperial family, including Napoleon's mother, sister Pauline Borghese and his second wife, Marie-Louise of Austria. While he was in Paris sculpting the latter, he breakfasted daily with Napoleon and his wife and recorded their

OPPOSITE: 120. Gian Lorenzo Bernini, *The Ecstasy of Saint Teresa*, 1647–52

Bernini created this, the most miraculous and emotionally overpowering of all his works, for the Cornaro Chapel in Santa Maria della Vittoria in Rome. Teresa of Ávila, a sixteenth-century Spanish nun, had described this intensely spiritual encounter with an angel in physical, even sexual terms, in her books.

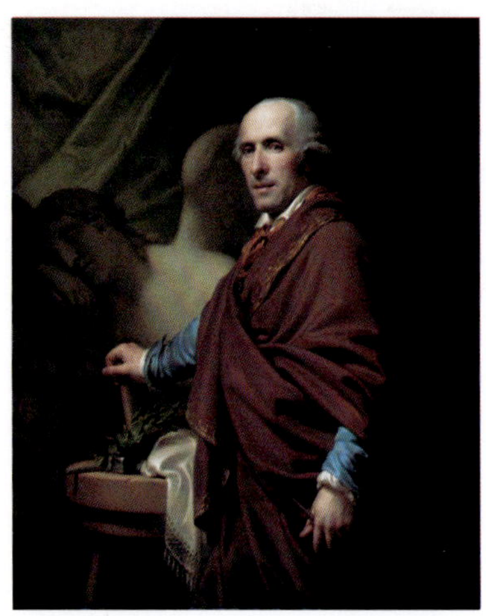

121. Johann Baptist Lampi II, *The Sculptor Antonio Canova*, 1805–06

Depicted in his Rome studio, Canova stands before a lion and the Genius of Death, which were among several figures he carved for the tomb of the Archduchess Maria Christina of Austria. The fiercely independent sculptor fell out repeatedly over the tomb's design with the Archduchess's husband.

conversations together. When the Emperor boasted that all the 'chef-d'oeuvres of art' were in Paris, Canova could have retorted that that was because he had looted so many of them. Instead, he said: 'May it please your Majesty … to leave Italy at least something.' Napoleon's response was that Italy could always 'indemnify herself' by digging up some more antiquities![28]

As the most eminent neoclassical sculptor of his day, Canova ran a large and busy studio in Rome, located in Vicolo delle Colonette. Visiting it was a 'must' for Grand Tourists. One French caller described having to push his way through the crowd of carriages and waiting servants in the street outside before entering the first hall to find it thronged with '*grand personnages et de belles dames*' of many nationalities. Moving on through the series of ateliers, he found assistants working with incredible zeal, 'chips of marble flying about like snowflakes'.[29] Only Canova's friends and fellow artists were allowed into the final studio, where they would find the sculptor at work, dressed like his assistants in a smock and leather leggings, with a paper hat on his head. Everything, including Canova, was white with marble dust.

It was assumed by numerous visitors to Canova's studio that he 'did little more than produce clay models for his statues that his numerous assistants subsequently rendered in marble'.[30] This was only partly true. The model was everything: it was his vision created in clay. Skilled artisans enlarged the model, then built an iron-and-wood armature. Canova checked it, then passed it on to the artisans to be cast into plaster before working it up into marble. Canova then perfected every aspect of the work, an intensely demanding task which often entailed working from a high platform in an atmosphere clammy with the moisture needed to keep the clay used to make the initial models pliable. He generally made the finishing touches by candlelight. Finally, the sculpture was polished with pummice stone, a task Canova often delegated to a specialist.

In 1815, following the battle of Waterloo and Napoleon's abdication, Canova was chosen by Pope Pius VII as the ideal man to negotiate the return of the paintings and sculpture that Napoleon had looted from Italy. 'His main task was to convince the Allied leaders that the 1797 Treaty of Tolentino, which had ceded 100 works of art to the French, was not legally binding.'[31] With the help of the Allies – the British in particular – Canova secured an agreement that many of the looted works should be returned to Italy. 'We are at last,' Canova wrote, 'beginning to drag forth from this great cavern of stolen goods [the Louvre] the precious objects of Art taken from Rome.'[32] One of the few paintings to remain in France was Veronese's *The Wedding Feast at Cana* (see page 113) on the grounds that it was too large and fragile to be moved yet again.

   EIGHT / DRAPED IN BEAUTY

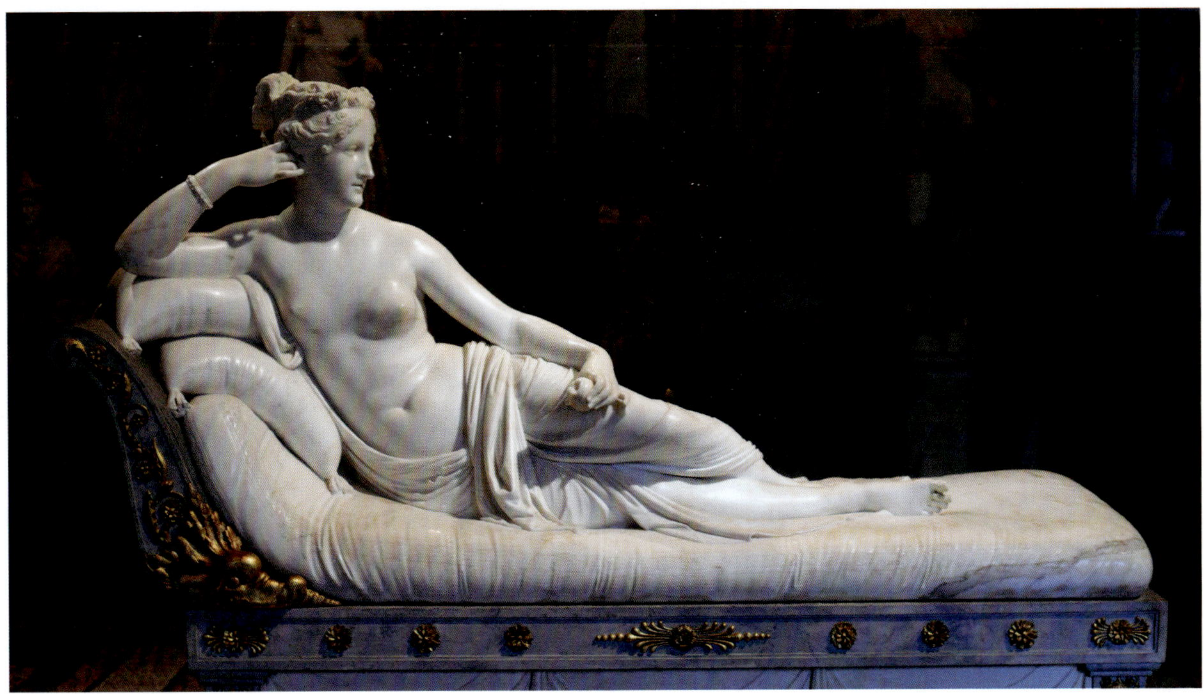

122. Antonio Canova, *Pauline Borghese as Venus Victrix*, 1804–08

At her insistence, Canova carved this statue of Napoleon's sister partially naked. Beautiful and highly intelligent, Pauline was notorious for her extra-marital affairs. When asked how she could have brought herself to pose in this manner, she replied that it had not worried her as there was a stove in the studio.[33]

Canova was so revered as an artist that when he died in 1822, his body was divided into three parts; his heart went to the church of Santa Maria Gloriosa dei Frari and his right hand to the Accademia, both in Venice, while the rest of him went to his native town, Possagno.

Another sculptor with a studio in Rome was an American woman, Harriet Hosmer (1830–1908). At the amazingly young age of twenty-two, she left her home in Massachusetts determined to be trained in the city where she would have access to the most highly skilled carvers, the finest collections of classical sculpture and the best marble. She was the first of several women sculptors to make the journey to Rome in the mid-nineteenth century. The group was so distinctive that it was immortalised by the writer Henry James as 'The White Marmorean Flock'.

The English sculptor John Gibson agreed to take Hosmer on as a pupil and gave her a small studio which had once belonged to Canova. After five years with Gibson, she set up one of her own in via Margutta. One of her earliest visitors was Nathaniel Hawthorne, author of *The Marble Faun*, who described it as 'a lofty room, with a sky-light window; it was pretty well warmed with a stove'.[34] When she could afford it, she moved into luxurious new premises, which boasted no less than nine rooms, a garden, a fountain and stables for her horses. A visitor pronounced it 'the prettiest studio in Rome. The little entrance court, with its beautiful flowers and singing birds, is a delightful change from the hot, dusty streets.'[35]

This depiction of a woodland spirit demonstrates Hosmer's mastery of the neoclassical style, which was inspired by the art of ancient Greece and Rome. The little satyr with furry limbs and cloven hoofs is busy tying the end of the Faun's leopard skin to the tree stump.

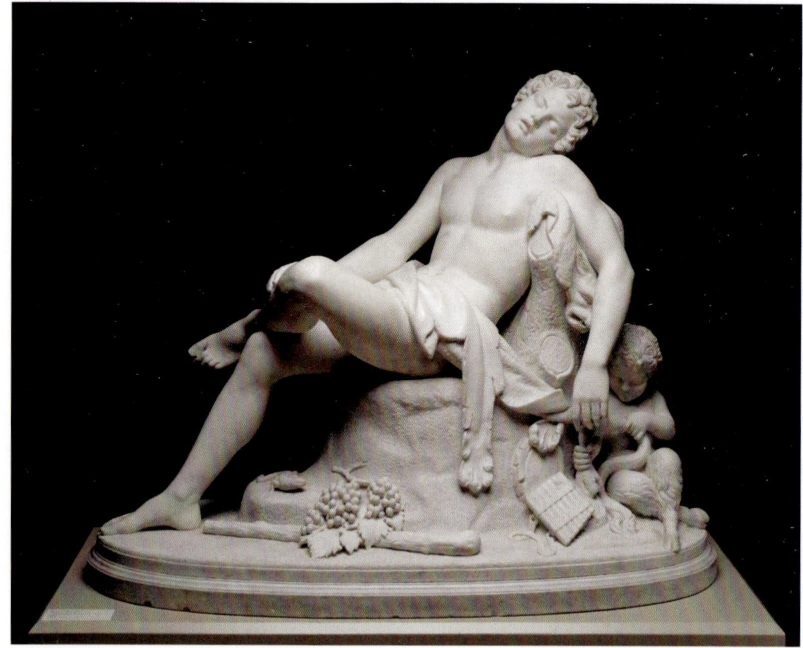

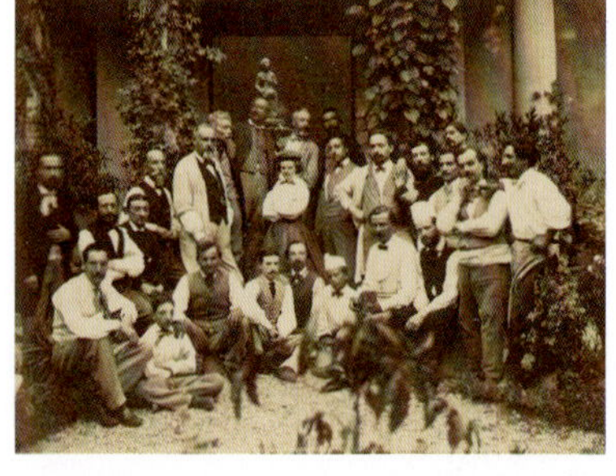

124. Harriet Hosmer with her Italian Workmen, 1867

This photograph shows the diminutive figure of Hosmer with no less than twenty-four of her skilled workmen. They are grouped together in the garden of her studio in Rome. Several of them are wearing the traditional paper hats to protect them from the marble dust.

Hatty – as everyone called her – was an engaging character with a gift for friendship. She became close to Robert and Elizabeth Browning and would visit them in Florence. Describing Hosmer to a friend, Elizabeth wrote: [She] lives here all alone … dines and breakfasts at the caffes precisely as a young man would – works from six o'clock in the morning till night …'[36] Other famous friends included Sir Frederic Leighton, who always dined with Hosmer when he visited Rome. He nicknamed her 'Beloved My Hat' and described her as 'a little American sculptress of great talent, the queerest, best-natured little chap possible'.[37] That Leighton refers to her as a 'little chap' was probably prompted by the fact that she generally wore men's clothes and firmly believed that 'an artist has no business to marry'.[38]

Fortunately for Hosmer, neoclassical sculptors were much in demand in America. The country had no monuments or statues of notable figures to adorn its public buildings, and sculptors were needed to supply them. Particularly popular at the time were mythological, historical and biblical subjects. Hosmer's most successful work was *Zenobia in Chains,* carved in marble (she adopted the same method to create a marble statue as Canova). Hosmer depicted the captive Queen of Palmyra as a bold and dignified woman even though she is manacled. Writing to a friend, she described herself at work: 'I am busy now upon Zenobia, of a size with which I might be compared as a mouse to a camel.' She planned to work wearing the trousers of a Zouave (Zouaves were Algerian members of a French military unit) to avoid breaking her neck 'upon the scaffolding by remaining in petticoats'.[39] The statue was exhibited at the International Exposition in London in 1862, where it took centre place and was viewed by some 600,000 visitors. When it went on tour in America, it made Hosmer famous in her own country.

It is remarkable that Hosmer not only had the courage to challenge the long-held assumption that women were incapable of being professional painters – still less sculptors – but by dint of her talent, ambition and ferociously hard work she became the foremost female sculptor of her time.

Without doubt, Auguste Rodin was the greatest male sculptor of the nineteenth century. In a review of a major Rodin exhibition in Washington in 1981, Robert Hughes wrote: 'Pathos, energy, despair, exhaustion, orgasmic pleasure: every shade of meaning, every sensation that the body can display, found its way into his oeuvre.'[40]

Rodin was thirty-five before he began work on the first free-standing sculpture that was entirely his own work. Entitled *The Age of Bronze,* he created it in Brussels, having left Paris following the Franco-Prussian War. For a model, Rodin chose a young man in the Belgian army, Auguste Neyt, who he described as 'a fine, noble-hearted boy, full of fire and valour'.[41] Together, they tried endless different poses. As Neyt recalled, Rodin 'had a horror of academic poses. He wanted the model to assume a life-like, natural stance'.[42] Neyt managed to train himself so that he could maintain a position for up to an hour at a stretch.

Dissatisfied with his progress with the statue, Rodin went to Italy to study Michelangelo at first hand. In a letter to his long-term mistress, Rose Beuret, he wrote: 'I believe that the great magician is letting me in on some of his secrets ...'[43] When the finished statue was exhibited, its extraordinarily life-like appearance caused a scandal (the first of many) and Rodin was repeatedly accused of simply having made a direct cast from the model. He was stoutly defended in a collective protest signed by a number of his fellow artists.

Rodin had many studios during his prolific career and often, as with his mistresses, several at once. By the end of the century he was so famous that his main studios had become an obligatory port of call for foreign visitors. When he wanted to work in peace, the Austrian poet Rainer Maria Rilke – who briefly worked as Rodin's amanuensis – recalls that there were other studios 'in out-of-the-way places of which no one knew. These rooms were like cells, bare, poor and grey with dust ...'[44]

The studio in which Rodin created his monumental sculpture, *The Burghers of Calais* – commissioned to commemorate the six men whose self-sacrifice saved Calais from the English during the Hundred Years' War – was in boulevard Vaugirard in Montparnasse. In 1886, it was

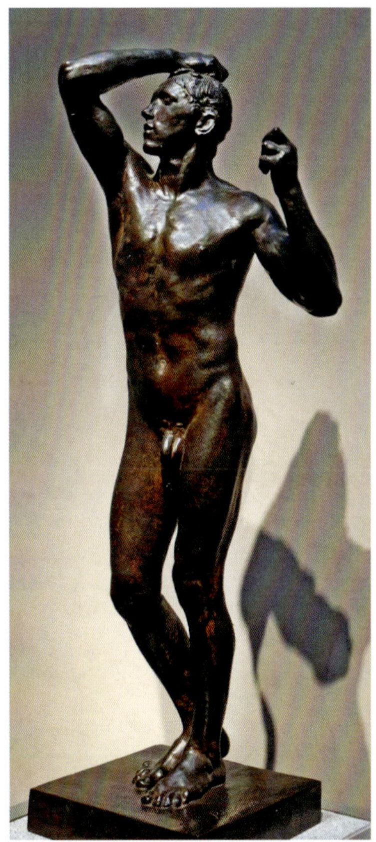

125. Auguste Rodin, *The Age of Bronze*, 1875–76

In retrospect, Rodin felt that this figure was 'the great watershed' of his career – when he at last began to create the life-like figures he wanted. Two of the statue's early titles were 'Man Awakening to Nature' and 'The Vanquished', both of which suit it far better than the prosaic title by which it is known today.

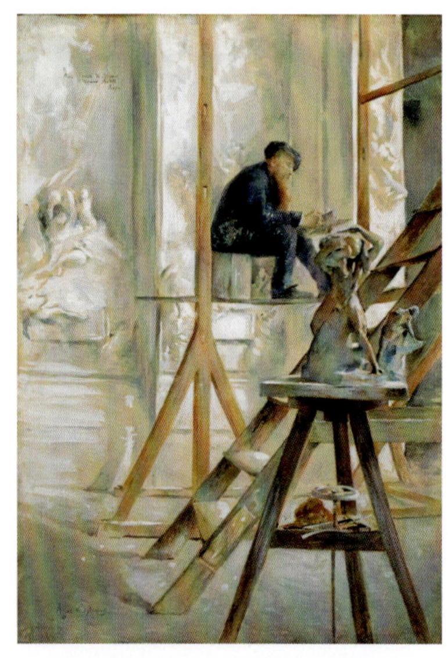

126. Allan Österlind, *Rodin in his Studio*, 1889

With his signature beret and red beard, Rodin is shown hard at work in one of his plaster-spattered studios. As one observer described him, 'he emanated a sense of power that was extraordinary and animal-like ... He had something of the superb architecture of an elephant'.[48]

visited by Edmond de Goncourt, who recalled 'the walls splattered with plaster, its wretched little cast-iron stove, and the cold damp emanating from all these immense *machines* of wet clay, wrapped in rags, and with all these casts of heads, arms, legs, in the middle of which two emaciated cats resemble the effigies of fantastic griffons'.[45]

Rodin's working day began early. 'He enters his atelier at eight,' reported de Goncourt, 'and interrupts his work only for lunch, then continues until nightfall, working on his feet or perched on a stool, which leaves him thoroughly worn out at night ...'[46] He employed numerous models of all ages and types. He liked to have them not posing but moving naked about the studio. When one made a movement that inspired him, he would quickly capture it in plaster. As with Canova, Rodin's genius lay in the conception and creation of the initial model. When he was satisfied with it, he would hand it over to one of his skilled professional sculptors who either carved it in marble, or enlarged or reduced it for casting in bronze. But his artistic control remained absolute.

Rodin was the first artist to receive worldwide acclaim in his lifetime, and it was photography that played an essential part in establishing his fame. He could exhibit a sculpture in Paris and know that in a matter of weeks it would be reproduced photographically from Tokyo to Buenos Aires.[47]

In 1875, the year in which Rodin began to model *The Age of Bronze*, work began on what would be the tallest statue in the world: the Statue of Liberty. Originally called *Liberty Enlightening the World*, it was to commemorate the centennial of America's Declaration of Independence of 1776 and to celebrate the close relationship between France and America. France would build the statue in Paris, then transport it to America to be assembled on a vast pedestal on Bedloe's Island in New York Harbour. America would fund and build the pedestal.

Frédéric-Auguste Bartholdi (1834–1904) designed Liberty, then engaged Gustave Eiffel (yet to build his tower) to devise what proved to be a masterpiece of engineering and technology. To withstand the high winds that sweep through New York Harbour, the apparently solid structure is, in fact, a 'skin' of copper sheets hung on an elegant, invisible skeleton of iron.

Six hundred highly skilled artisans worked in vast workshops on the northwestern boundary of Paris for the eight years it took to build Liberty. Before it was shipped to America, Bartholdi assembled the statue so that Parisians, who had become fascinated by the endeavour, could see the completed work. Photographs show the immense form of Liberty, encased in scaffolding, looming above the city.

For its trans-Atlantic voyage aboard the frigate *L'Isère*, the statue

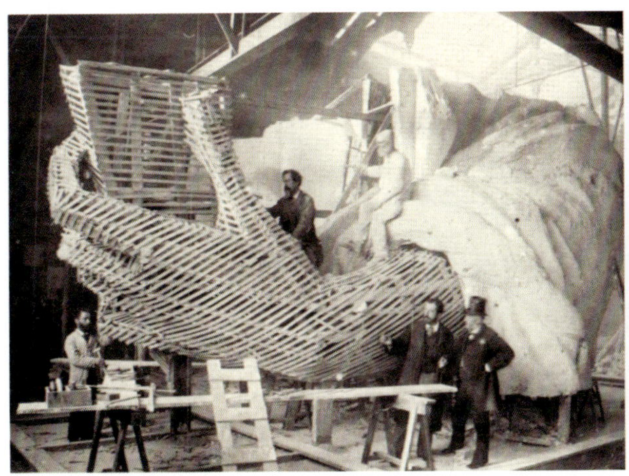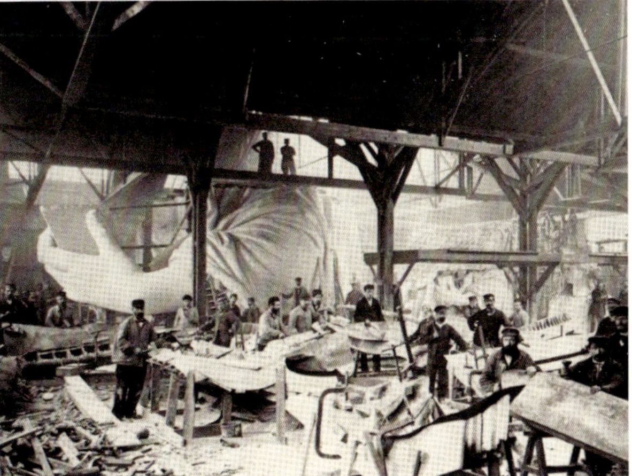

was reduced to 350 individual pieces and packed in 214 crates. The ship arrived in New York Harbour in June 1885, but the statue remained in its crates on Bedloe's Island until the pedestal was completed. Reassembling it took four months. Finally, in October 1886, President Cleveland oversaw Liberty's dedication in front of thousands of wildly cheering spectators – despite the pouring rain.

Leonardo's image of a sweating sculptor working in a dust-laden atmosphere persists to this day. Sculpting anything, be it a small figure in bronze like Donatello's *David* or Rodin's monumental *Burghers of Calais,* required the sculptor to work in an environment of extreme discomfort. The studio must be large enough to accommodate not only the many works in progress but his or her numerous assistants. Some projects entailed enormous investments of time, endurance and physical effort: Rodin's *Gates of Hell* – 6m high and containing some 200 figures – was commissioned in 1880 and yet he was still working on it sporadically when he died thirty-seven years later. Finally, as with Michelangelo's huge, marble *David*, the sculptor was faced with the complex logistics of transporting it safely from the studio to its chosen site. Being a sculptor was not an occupation for the faint-hearted.

127 & 128. Construction of the Statue of Liberty, Paris, *c.* 1882–83

LEFT: The French creator of the statue, Frédéric-Auguste Bartholdi, explains to a top-hatted visitor the construction of Liberty's hand in which she will hold a tablet inscribed 'July 4, 1776', the date of America's Declaration of Independence.

RIGHT: This remarkable photograph shows some of the highly skilled artisans at work in the vast workshops in northern Paris where Liberty was built.

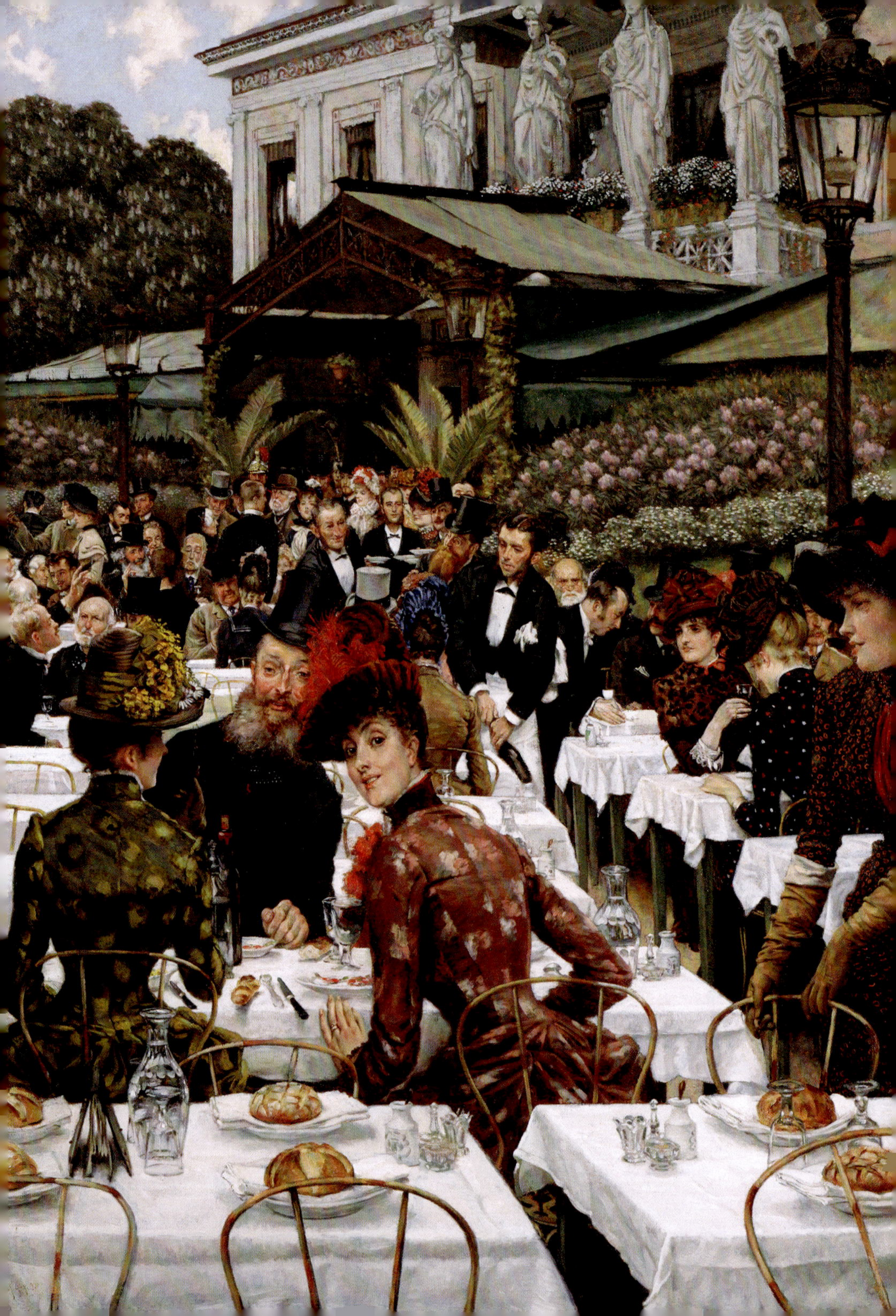

NINE

From Montmartre to Montparnasse

The Studios of Paris

*In sumptuous studios, in wretched garrets, amid affluence,
amid scenes of squalor and hunger, artists of all kinds and
degrees have been squeezing thousands of tubes and daubing
thousands of canvases in preparation for the great day.*[1]

THE 'GREAT DAY' WAS *le Vernissage,* or Varnishing Day, which took place on the eve of the official opening of the annual Salon. For the artists whose work had been accepted for exhibition by the jury, it was their last chance to retouch their work and give it a coat of varnish. The painting by James Tissot shows the artists, their wives and friends celebrating their success on the terrace of the Café Ledoyen. Behind them is the entrance to the Palais de l'Industrie, with its famous caryatid portico, which hosted the Salon. The Ledoyen menu on Varnishing Day was always the same: salmon served with a green dressing and *rosbif à l'Anglaise.*[2]

For the thousands of aspiring artists who gravitated to Paris in the mid-nineteenth century and based themselves in studios in the city, exhibiting at the Salon marked a turning point in their career. For those who had previously exhibited, it was confirmation that their work continued to reach the standards set by the all-powerful Académie Royale. Before art dealers appeared on the scene, which they did in increasing numbers from the mid-nineteenth century onwards, it was virtually the only place artists could show their work. Thus, competition was fierce, and artists vied with each other for lucrative commissions.

In an age when art was considered an essential part of French life, and when there were so few public entertainments, the Salon drew immense crowds, especially on Sundays when entry was free. In 1876, a staggering 518,892 visitors attended. They came, according to the

OPPOSITE: **129.** James Tissot,
The Artists' Wives, 1885

The artists whose work had been accepted for exhibition at the annual Salon are joined by their wives for a grand luncheon on Varnishing Day. Celebrities present include Auguste Rodin, the man with the red beard standing behind a waiter in the centre of the picture.

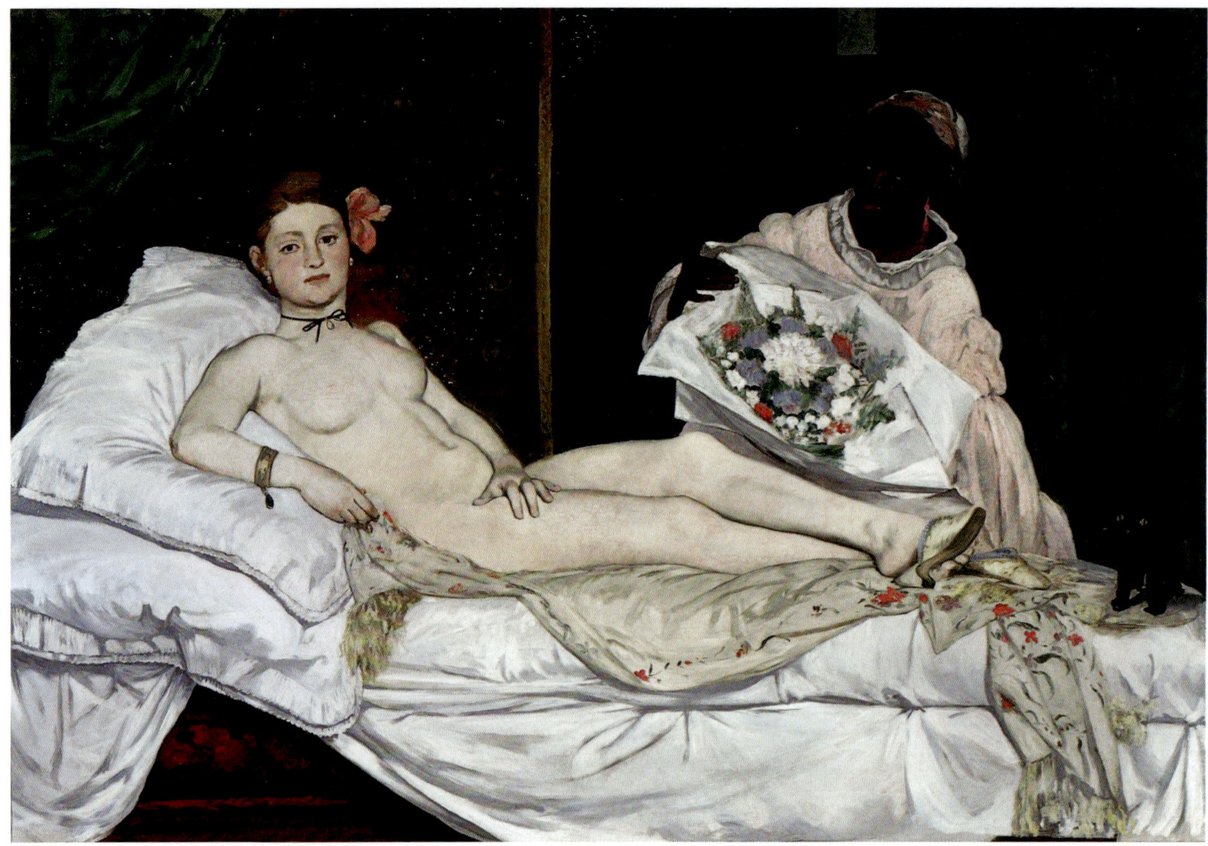

130. Édouard Manet, *Olympia*, 1863

Parisians and critics alike were scandalised by this painting when it was shown at the Salon in 1865. This was no nymph or Venus, but a prostitute brazenly exposing her wares while her maid presents her with a large bouquet from her next customer. Manet had based *Olympia* on Titian's *Venus of Urbino*.

French historian Hippolyte Taine, 'as they would to a pantomime or a circus. They want melodrama or military scenes, undressed women and *trompe-d'oeil;* and they get it: battles and *auto-da-fé*, scenes of slaughter in Roman arenas, Andromeda on the rocks ...'[3]

Until mid-century, the accepted hierarchy in the different categories of art still held firm. History painting – scenes from history, mythology, literature or the Bible – continued to reign supreme, with the other genres trailing some way behind it, and woe betide the artist who deviated from the proscribed path. Continued rejection by the jury could be a mortal blow. In Henri Murger's *Scènes de la Vie de Bohème*, the painter Marcel had submitted a painting to the Salon so many times that it could find its way there by itself.

Increasingly, however, artists had become dissatisfied with the restrictions of the Salon's system of selection. In 1863, more than half of the 5,000 works submitted were thrown out. At this point, Emperor Napoleon III, always wary of unrest, stepped in and instituted an exhibition of rejected pictures, the Salon des Refusés, which became a symbol of rebellion against the increasingly outdated art establishment. The exhibition was not a success, and the critics had a field day. Singled out for particular abuse were Édouard Manet's *Déjeuner sur l'Herbe* and James Abbott McNeill Whistler's *White Girl* (see page 57).

Manet's *Déjeuner,* and his equally scandalous *Olympia,* were signs that change was in the air. Artists were rebelling against the rigid academic style taught at the École des Beaux-Arts and the private academies, and the traditional subjects and subtle blending and polished 'finish' they advocated. The École's entrenched conventional attitude positively encouraged debate and change. In 1864, an essay entitled *The Painter of Modern Life* by Manet's friend, the poet Charles Baudelaire, breathed new life into artists, urging them to abandon history painting and depict instead the everyday world around them: the cafés, bars and dance halls, the new railway system, and Paris itself, which had recently been remodelled by Baron Haussmann.

Despite the lack of success of the Salon des Refusés, many artists realised that such events were their only way of showing their work to the public. Both Manet and Courbet, having suffered repeated rejection by the official Salon, had held one-man shows. In 1874, a group of painters – led by Degas, Monet, Renoir, Pissarro, Sisley and Morisot – followed suit by holding what came to be known as the first Impressionist exhibition. The name was coined by a critic's review of the show in which he labelled some of the artists' work 'Impressionist', taking as his cue the title of a study by Monet: *Impression, Sunrise.* The artists involved were dismissed as 'lunatics', their paintings derided for their sketchiness and their depiction of mundane subjects.

However, the artists – now joined by others such as Mary Cassatt and Gustave Caillebotte – persisted. A sense of community developed

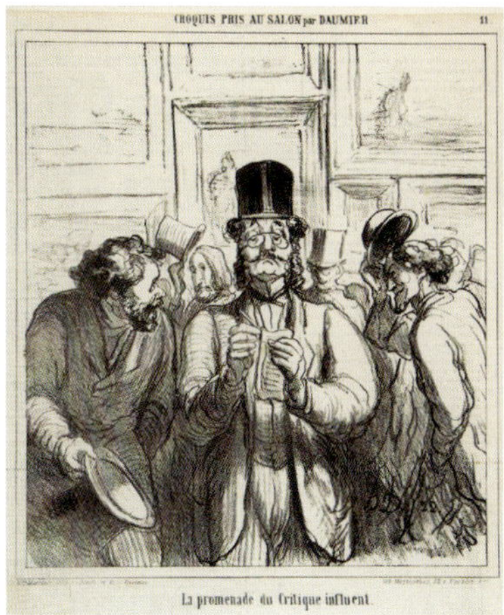

131. Honoré Daumier, *Promenade of the Influential Critic,* 1865

Critics wielded enormous power. Like them or loathe them, they could make or break an artist's reputation. Here, Daumier satirises these painters for the way they are fawning over a stout member of the press, doffing their caps obsequiously in a bid to make him review their work favourably.

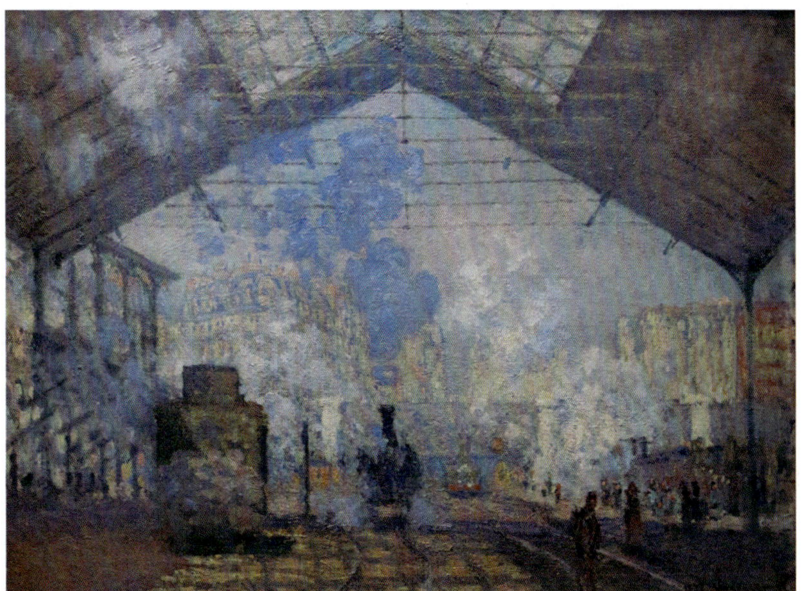

132. Claude Monet, *Gare Saint-Lazare,* 1877

The new railway system opened up the country. Monet, fascinated by the effects created by steam, persuaded the Director of Saint-Lazare to halt all the trains, clear the platforms of people and cram the engines with coal to produce the maximum amount of steam. The result shows that his audacity paid off.

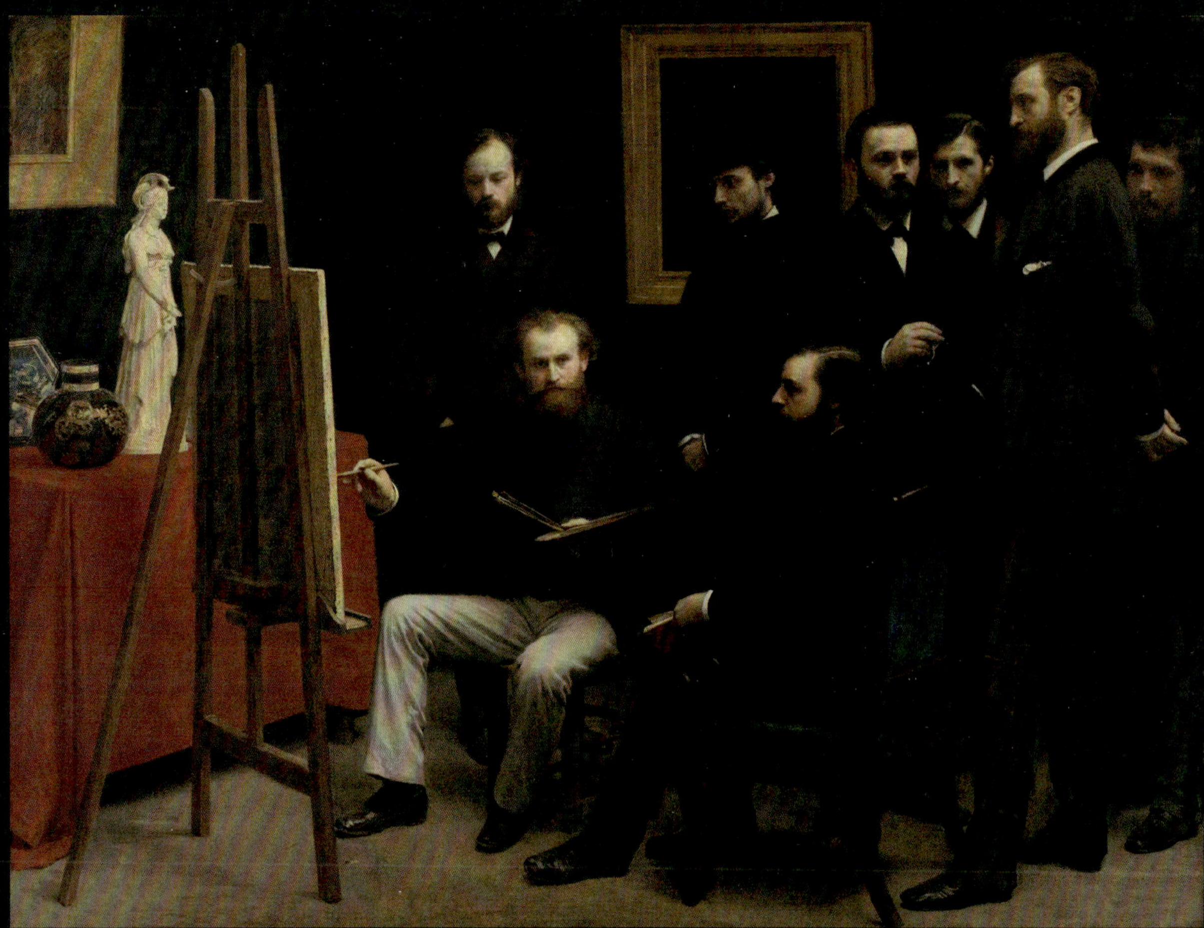

133. Henri Fantin-Latour, *A Studio in the Batignolles Quarter*, 1870

At the centre of the group Manet is painting a portrait of artist and critic Zacharie Astruc. Wearing a hat, Renoir is behind him; to his left is Émile Zola, bearded and holding eyeglasses. Monet peers out behind the tall figure of Frédéric Bazille, who was tragically killed fighting in the Franco-Prussian War.

between them. They were united not so much by their common aims, but by the continual rejection of their work. These aims were thrashed out among them in certain cafés that had become favoured meeting places, such as La Nouvelle Athènes and Café Guerbois.

There were to be eight Impressionist exhibitions in all. But progress towards an appreciation of their work by public and critics was agonisingly slow. An American artist commented after the third exhibition: 'I never in my life saw such horrible things ... They do not observe drawing nor form but give you an impression of what they call nature. It was worse than the Chamber of Horrors. I was there about a quarter of an hour and left with a headache.'[4]

Four years before the first Impressionist exhibition, Henri Fantin-Latour painted *A Studio in the Batignolles Quarter,* one of four enormous group portraits he produced of the artistic and literary avant-garde. The Batignolles district, just north of the Gare Saint-Lazare and west of Montmartre, was a favourite location for the studios of numerous artists at some point in their careers, including Manet, Vuillard, Bonnard and Toulouse-Lautrec.

For any artist, their most urgent task when they arrived in Paris was to find a studio. Its type and location varied according to the status – and pocket – of the artist. A typical studio in the mid-nineteenth century was a large room, often an attic, with a high ceiling and massive windows. Artists tended to congregate in certain areas: on the right (north) bank they stretched from the Grands Boulevards up to Montmartre which, at that date, was still semi-rural. South of the Seine, in the Latin Quarter and deep into Montparnasse, was a particular haunt for students, as it was close to the École des Beaux-Arts. They lived in studio blocks, in cul-de-sacs and courtyards – little islands in a sea of bustle and commerce. The area was peppered with placards reading '*Atelier d'Artiste à Louer,*' the studios advertised ranging in size from cigar-boxes to large draughty barns.

Fantin-Latour's painting shows Manet seated at an easel, the focus of the group gathered around him. Although he never exhibited with the Impressionists, Manet emerged as the guiding light of the movement. Fantin-Latour painted a superb portrait of him that shows him immaculately but soberly outfitted in an elegant jacket, silk top hat, suede gloves and carrying a cane; he is dressed for the boulevards, every inch the dandy or *flâneur*. As Robert Hughes wrote: 'Paris is unthinkable without Manet; Manet unimaginable without Paris.'[5]

The Irish writer George Moore first met Manet in La Nouvelle Athènes (Moore joked that he did not go either to Oxford or Cambridge but he went to La Nouvelle Athènes[6]). Moore admired Manet's 'finely-cut face from whose prominent chin a closely-cut blonde beard came

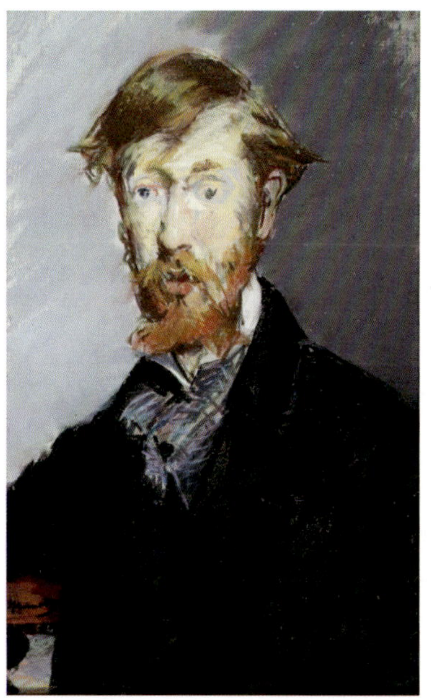

134. Édouard Manet, *George Moore,* 1879

Moore had arrived in Paris from Ireland, intending to become a painter, but abandoned painting for writing. He became an eccentric and familiar figure around Paris, welcome wherever he went 'for his manners were amusing and his French very funny'.

forward; and the aquiline nose, the clear grey eyes, the decisive voice, the remarkable comeliness of the well-knit figure ...'[7] If Moore was enchanted by Manet, Manet was charmed by the Irishman, describing him as having the 'air of a crushed yellow egg', an accurate description judging by his pastel sketch of Moore.[8] Manet was witty and mischievous, but never unkind. Women adored him. He was a valued friend to many, his studio a favourite rendezvous.

Manet's studio was near the Gare Saint-Lazare. George Moore's description of it adds a few bits of furniture to the vast oak-panelled room and 'air of monkish simplicity' described earlier. 'There was very little in his studio except his pictures: a sofa, a rocking-chair, a table for his paintings, and a marble table on iron supports ...'[9] Another source adds some colour to the scene, describing the sofa as crimson and covered with cushions and, behind it, was 'a vast, green Japanese tapestry of birds and flowers'.[10]

Although Degas (1834–1917) loved the life of the streets and cafés, his studio in the Pigalle area – just east of the Batignolles – was sacrosanct. Only intimate friends and the occasional model were allowed to enter the long room under the rooftops that was piled high with the detritus of years of concentrated work. Degas' art dealer, Ambroise Vollard, recorded that 'once an object found its way there, it never left again nor even changed its position, but sank into the visual rubble which the artist knew by heart.'[11] Vollard recorded that on one occasion he had visited Degas carrying a parcel. 'A tiny piece of paper, no larger than a bit of confetti, worked loose from the wrapping and fell on the floor. Degas pounced on it ... and threw it into the stove.

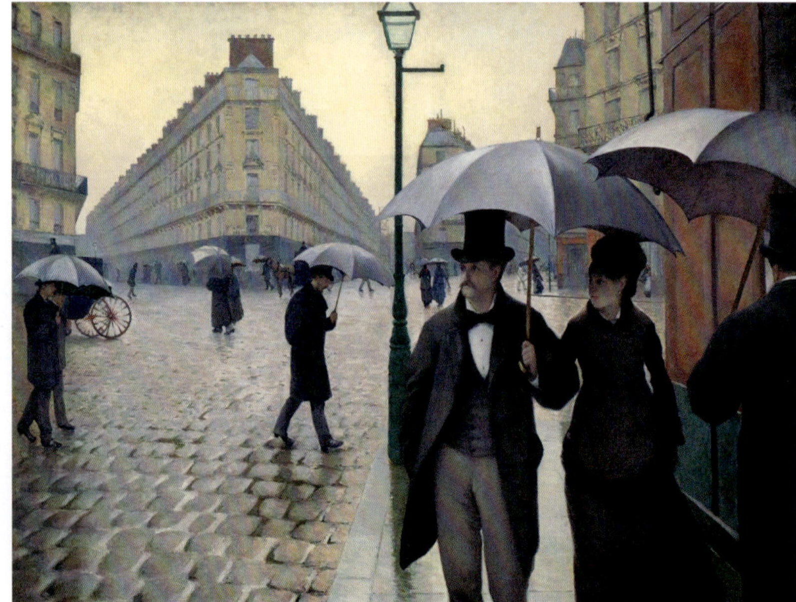

135. Gustave Caillebotte, *Paris Street, Rainy Day*, 1877

This huge painting shows the couple on the right leaving the place de l'Europe, which is built literally *above* the railway lines entering Gare Saint-Lazare. Just to the north lies the Batignolles district. Independently wealthy, Caillebotte was a generous benefactor to his Impressionist friends, helping them to finance their exhibitions.

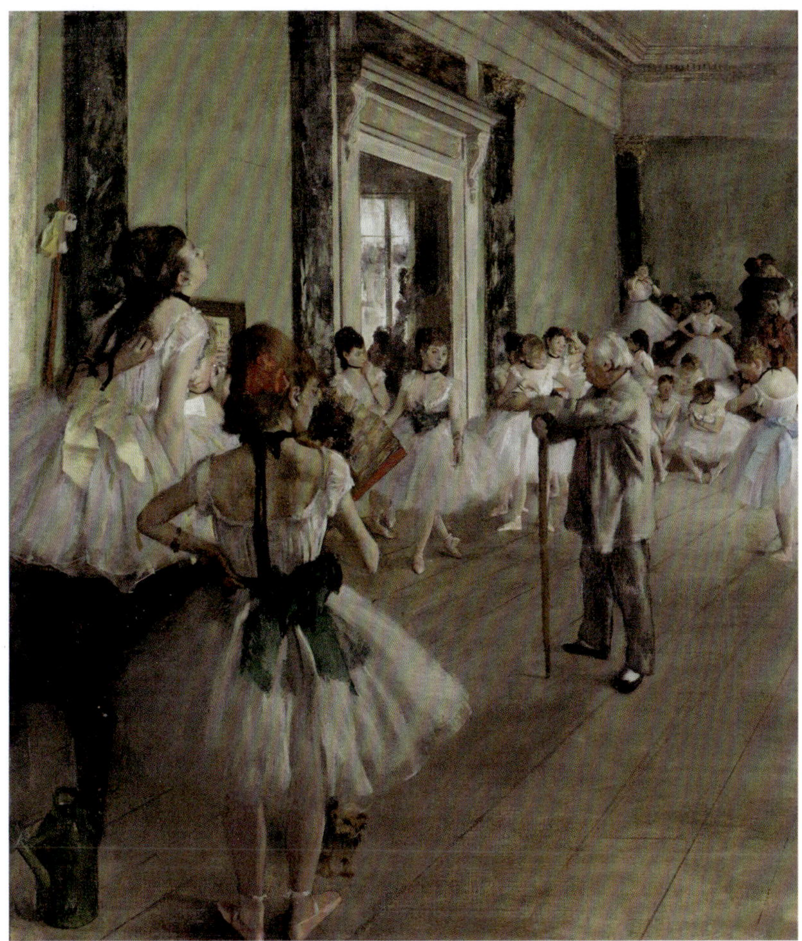

136. Edgar Degas, *The Dance Class*, 1875

Degas was fascinated by life backstage at the Opéra. Here, he pays homage to Jules Perrot, a famous ballet dancer turned teacher. Degas, a master of observation, shows the girl on the left scratching her back. Keeping close watch at the rear of the salle are the girls' mothers. But what is the tiny dog up to?

"I don't like disorder," he said.'[12] No wonder Berthe Morisot called Degas 'paradoxical'.[13]

The numerous works contributed by Degas to the eight Impressionist exhibitions depict contemporary subjects such as scenes from the ballet, horse-racing and café-concerts. In a retrospective view of Degas' work, the novelist and critic J-K. Huysmans wrote: 'A painter of modern life was born, and a painter who derived from no one, who resembled no one else, who brought a totally new flavour to art, totally new procedures of execution.'[14]

Through his friendship with certain influential figures in the world of ballet, Degas was given permission to go backstage at the Paris Opéra where he could observe the dancers at close quarters. He drew hundreds of rapid studies, which were often annotated with details of dress, position, colour and light to enable him to work them up later in his studio. His superb pastels and oils capture every aspect of the ballet: the endless rehearsals set in cavernous rooms; the sweaty exhaustion of the dancers; the easing of ankles, the adjusting of straps; the solicitous mothers chaperoning their children; and the full-blown performances viewed from the wings. Describing Degas' sketches of the young ballet dancers, de Goncourt wrote: 'And there before one, drawn from nature, was the graceful twisting and turning of the gestures of those little monkey-girls.'[15]

Degas rarely painted *en plein air*. For one thing, strong sun hurt his eyes (he was almost blind in his last years). He might make a quick sketch outdoors, but the main work always took place in his studio. 'No art has ever been less spontaneous than mine,' he contended.[16] This is not something that could be said of Claude Monet, whose life was spent trying to capture the transient light and moods of nature.

For much of his career Monet was too hard up to have any kind of permanent studio. There were times when he could barely afford to buy canvases and paints, let alone food. He was at his most content and productive when out in the countryside. For his passion for painting water, he had his boat on the River Seine at Argenteuil, just 12km from the centre of Paris. In 1883, when his finances had improved, he moved to the house at Giverny where he flourished until his death forty-three years later.

By the nineteenth century, painting *en plein air* had been vastly simplified by the technical improvements of painting materials. As they headed into the street or into the country, artists could now shoulder a lighter load: they had collapsible easels and stools, ready-made canvases and paints in metal tubes. In addition, the emergence of synthetic pigments had greatly enlarged their palettes. Manganese-violet was the first pure mauve pigment. Monet favoured it for shadows that he knew were coloured, not just black. A synthetic deep blue was found to replace the fabulously expensive ultramarine. Chrome yellow, one of Van Gogh's favourite pigments, was developed from a new element, chromium.

Impressionism would not have been possible without the invention of either the metal tube or the metal ferrule. The latter replaced the previous method of binding the animal hairs (which could be from 'the tail of a martin, badger, squirrel, or cat or from the mane of a donkey'[17]) on to a stick or inserting them into a quill – a fiddly and highly-skilled process. Flat brushes with metal ferrules changed painting for ever as artists were now able to make rapid, broad brushstrokes. 'Cézanne is probably the most obvious example of a painter for whom a new type of brush provided the potential if not the inspiration for a new vision.'[18]

Cézanne's peripatetic existence was not conducive to the establishment of a permanent studio. The titles of his paintings are a clue to his wanderings: L'Estaque (near Marseille), Pontoise, Auvers, La Roche Guyon, Médan, the Forest of Fontainebleau and Switzerland.

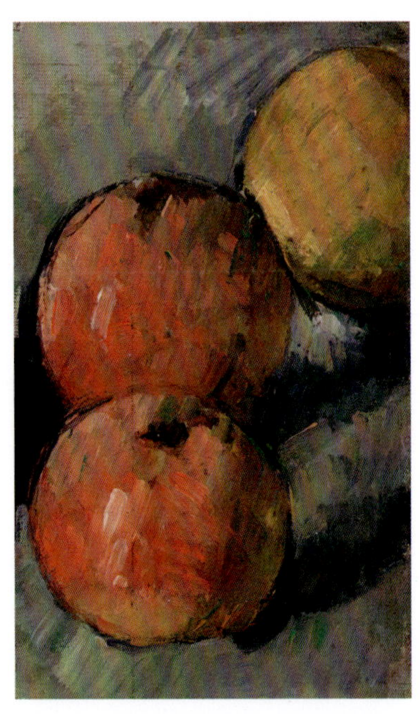

137. Paul Cézanne, *Three Apples*, 1878
Apples were perfect models for Cézanne. When Vollard fell asleep while sitting for his portrait, Cézanne was furious: 'Wretch! You've ruined the pose! I tell you in all seriousness you must hold it like an apple.' The broad brushstrokes on the apples show his use of flat brushes made with metal ferrules.

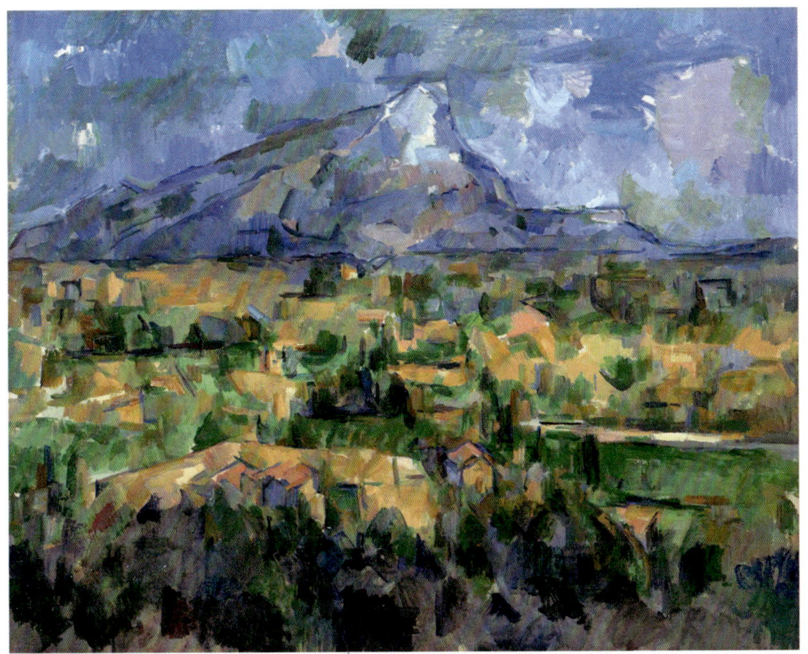

The place he always returned to, however, was Aix-en-Provence, where he was born and spent his childhood. He spent frequent – but always brief – periods in Paris, a requirement for any ambitious artist who wanted to exhibit his work. But he never really adapted to city life, lurking on its fringes and rarely mixing with his fellow artists at Café Guerbois, a secretive bearded figure in his shabby provincial clothes. He had large black eyes 'which rolled in their orbits when he was excited'.[19] When Mary Cassatt first met him, she thought him ferocious looking, but later described him as having 'the gentlest nature possible, *comme un enfant* ...'[20] Émile Zola, a friend since their shared boyhood in Aix, complained of his stubbornness. 'To prove something to Cézanne would be like trying to persuade the towers of Notre Dame to dance a quadrille.'[21]

It was not until Cézanne had turned sixty-three that he found a plot of land just outside Aix, and designed and built a studio specifically for his own use. After years of being scorned in Paris, he increasingly retreated into himself, his life dedicated to his work.

Mary Cassatt, painter of divinely real children and brilliant portrayer of bourgeois family life (see page 76), was independently wealthy and thus able to decorate her apartment with tasteful furniture and *objets d'art*. May Alcott (sister of the famous Louise May Alcott), who was studying art in Paris, had tea with Cassatt. They ate 'fluffy cream cakes ... while sitting on carved chairs, on Turkish rugs, with superb tapestries as a background, and fine pictures on the walls looking down from their splendid frames. Statues and articles of vertu filled the corners, the whole being lighted by a great antique hanging lamp. We sipped

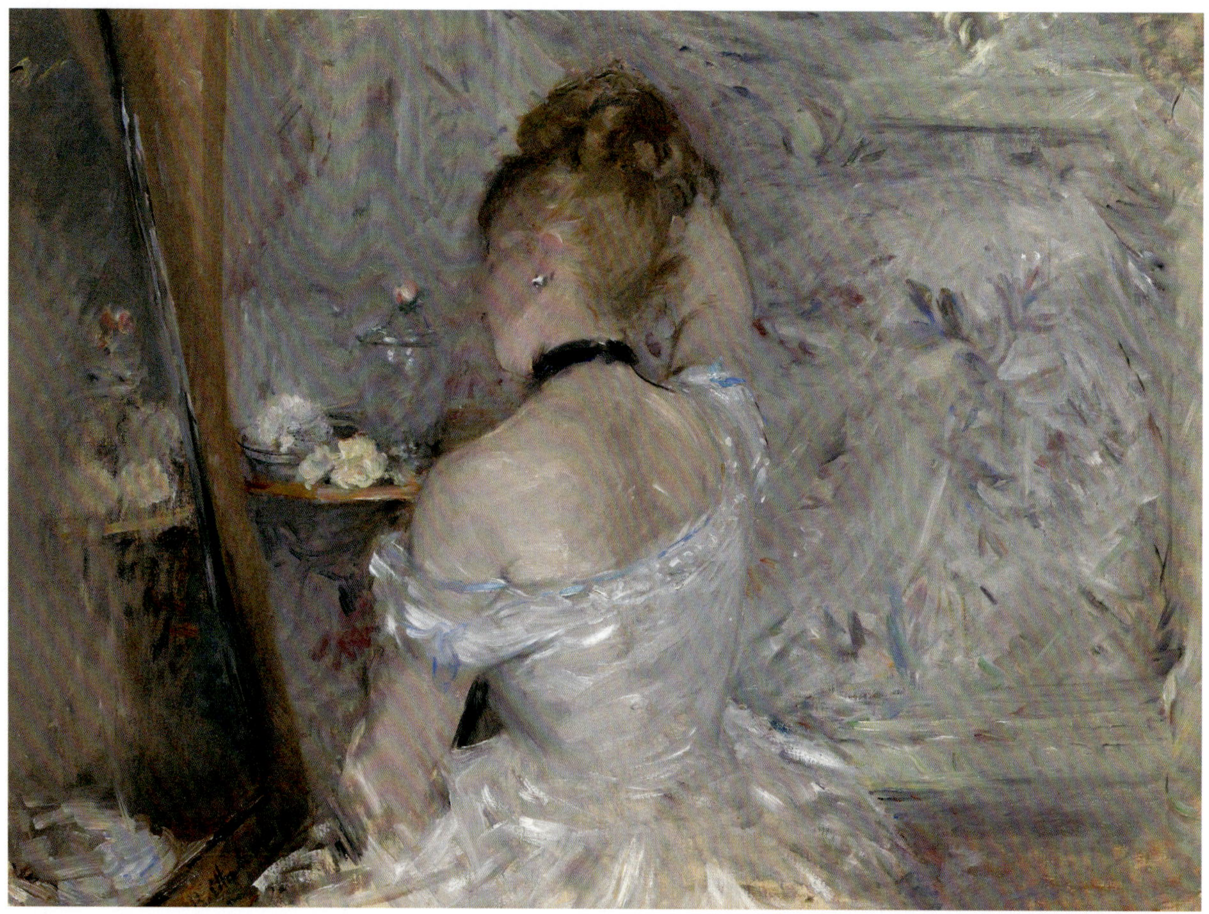

139. Berthe Morisot, *Woman at her Toilette, c.* 1875

Morisot's light, flickering brushstrokes perfectly suit this subject. She was fascinated with the effects of reflected light on white and in this image she tackles both with great skill. Her great friend, the poet Stéphane Mallarmé, described this painting as a 'visual poem'.

chocolat from superior china ... Miss Cassatt was charming as usual in two shades of brown satin and rep, being very lively ...'[22]

All very feminine and elegant, and a far cry from Degas' dust-laden studio. Impressed by the quality of her work, Degas invited her to join the Impressionists for their 1877 exhibition. It was the beginning of her association with the group and of a lifelong friendship with Degas – with a faint suggestion on her part that it might become a romantic one. They shared not only an admiration for each other's work but a fascination with print making, at which Cassatt became an innovative and brilliant exponent.

Berthe Morisot was one of the 'lunatics' whose work appeared in the first Impressionist exhibition, and she continued to contribute pictures to all the shows except one. By dint of her magnetic personality, and the respect she engendered, she was one of the key forces that kept the group together.

Born into the *haute bourgeoisie*, it was assumed that she would spend her life looking decorative until she married and had children. But Morisot was a deeply serious artist. Although constantly assailed by doubt and dissatisfied with everything she produced, she was most at peace when she was working. Like Cézanne, she did not have a studio of her own until towards the end of her tragically short life. She and her artist sister Edma had shared a purpose-built studio in the garden of their parents' house in Passy, but when her family moved into an apartment building, Morisot confined her work to her room, 'a light, cool place' with no bric-a-brac apart from 'a green gauze butterfly net [and] a cage with parakeets ...'[23] Some time after she had married Édouard Manet's brother, Eugène, the couple moved with their daughter into a large house built to their design in rue Villejuste (now rue Paul Valéry) and she transformed the attic into a studio. Morisot's Thursday evening soirées became a focal point for many of the artistic and literary figures of her day, particularly for Manet, the poet Stéphane Mallarmé and her Impressionist friends such as Renoir.

The popular perception of Renoir (1841–1919) is that he spent his time painting plump, rosy nudes, working people dancing in the sunshine at Le Moulin de la Galette or at one of the holiday spots along the Seine favoured by Parisians. One of the latter, the fashionable suburb of Bougival came to be known as the 'cradle of Impressionism', as so many of the artists involved in the movement went there to paint. Renoir's *Dance at Bougival* (see page 50) features Suzanne Valadon who also modelled in the nude for him.

Once he had a bit of money, Renoir acquired a spacious studio in rue Saint-Georges. It was a large rectangular room with one side entirely of glass. It was bare of furniture except for two easels, a few cane chairs, two collapsed old armchairs, a tired divan and a wooden table piled high with his painting apparatus.

When Renoir was painting his famous *Dance at Le Moulin de la Galette*, he moved into an abandoned cottage in rue Cortot, just up the hill from Le Moulin's café-bar and dance hall. Twice a day Renoir and a friend would lug the large canvas down the hill to Le Moulin and then up again in the evening. According to his son Jean, Renoir's only furniture consisted of a mattress on the floor, a table, a deal commode and a stove to keep the models warm.[24]

By his forties, Renoir had settled happily with Aline, who had once been his model, and they had three sons. But he began to suffer from rheumatoid arthritis and moved every winter to the warmth of Cagnes, near Nice. When he found an old farmhouse, he settled there with his family, living out the rest of his days confined to a wheelchair, but still defiantly painting despite his hands being so bandaged that the paintbrush had to be placed between his fingers. He was still painting on the day he died, his last words so typical of him: 'I think I am beginning to understand something about it.'[25]

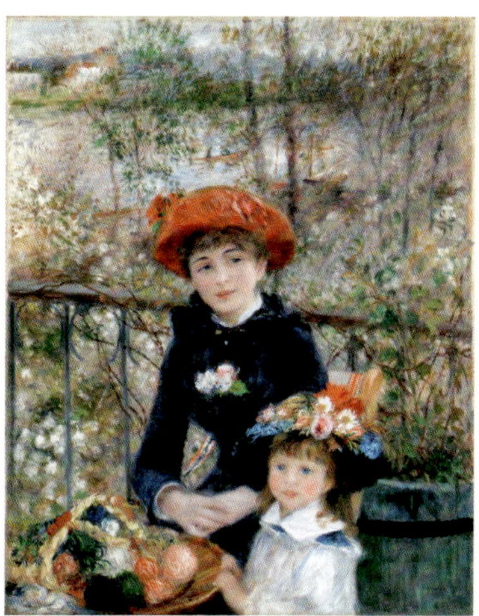

140. Pierre-Auguste Renoir,
Two Sisters (On the Terrace), 1881

The two young girls are on the terrace of a restaurant situated on an island in the River Seine, which is visible behind them. They are holding a basket containing balls of wool.

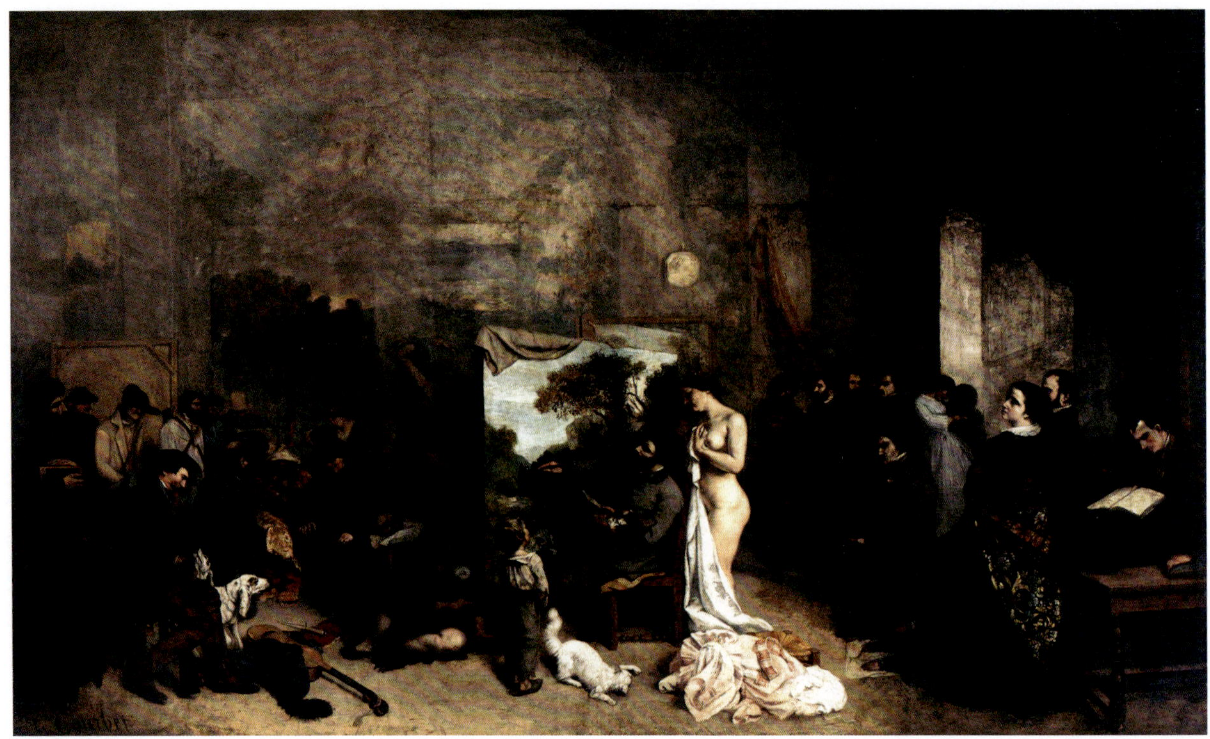

Such modesty was totally alien to Gustave Courbet, who was a
pioneer in self-marketing. At the age of forty-three he called himself,
'the proudest and most arrogant man in France'. Fourteen years later he
pronounced, 'I have astounded the whole world … I triumph not only
over the moderns but over the old masters as well.'[26] But this 'blustering
genius' had plenty to bluster about.

Declaring his contempt for history painting, he depicted peasants
and country folk with a brutal realism previously unknown. His two
tattered labourers in *The Stonebreakers* sweat and strain at their arduous
task; the group of about forty mourners in his *Burial at Ornans* have
worn faces and wear rough homespun black suits. Courbet had been
obliged to paint the huge *Burial* in a two-storey laundry in Ornans that
was barely large enough to accommodate the canvas, let alone allow
him to step back to view his work. In Paris he found a studio in a former
chapel in rue Hautefeuille near the Sorbonne. According to the critic
Castagnary, it was a 'vast, lofty room', lit by a window overlooking the
street. What struck him most was the 'needy, empty look of the place'.
There was very little furniture and 'everything was submerged under an
avalanche of paintings'.[27] Here Courbet would hold court, a Rabelaisian,
black-bearded figure who could smoke his pipe, quaff a tankard of beer,
brag about his achievements and still continue to paint.

Courbet's largest and most mysterious painting, *The Painter's Studio:*

A Real Allegory Summing up a Seven Year Phase of My Artistic Life, was set in his chapel studio. Courbet is in the centre; on the right, as he explained, are 'the people who serve me, support me in my ideas, and take part in my actions'. The figures on the left represented 'the other world of trivial life, the people, misery, poverty, wealth, the exploited and the exploiters, the people who live off death'.[28] Courbet, however, does not explain why he needed a naked model to paint a landscape, or why he is painting a landscape in a studio. And where is the light coming from? Why are none of the figures communicating with each other? Why the dog? And so on. The painting is like a medieval triptych: God (Courbet) at the centre, Heaven and Hell on either side.[29] When it failed to be accepted for the 1855 Universal Exhibition in Paris, Courbet exhibited it in a separate pavilion. On seeing it, Delacroix declared: 'They have rejected one of the most remarkable works of our time ...'[30]

For all his fame and bluster, Courbet came to a sad end. Convicted and imprisoned for his part in the destruction of the Vendôme Column during the Paris Commune, and required to pay towards its restoration, he fled to Switzerland and died soon afterwards.

The cement that kept these artists together, despite their disparate characters, opinions and styles of painting, were the cafés they frequented. On the avenue de Clichy, the tiny Café Guerbois was centred on Manet who would reserve two tables every evening for his group, which included Degas, Renoir, Bazille and occasionally Sisley,

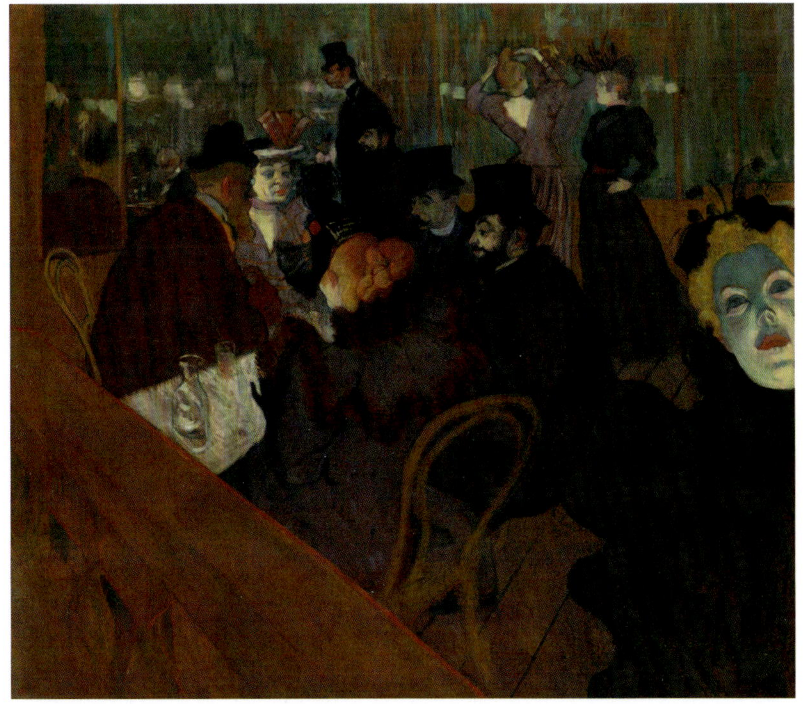

142. Henri de Toulouse-Lautrec, *At the Moulin Rouge*, 1892

Lautrec captures the atmosphere of an evening spent at the legendary nightclub. The diminutive figure in the centre background is Lautrec himself; to his right the dancer La Goulue arranges her hair. The singer May Milton peers out from the right edge of the painting, her face harshly lit and acid green.

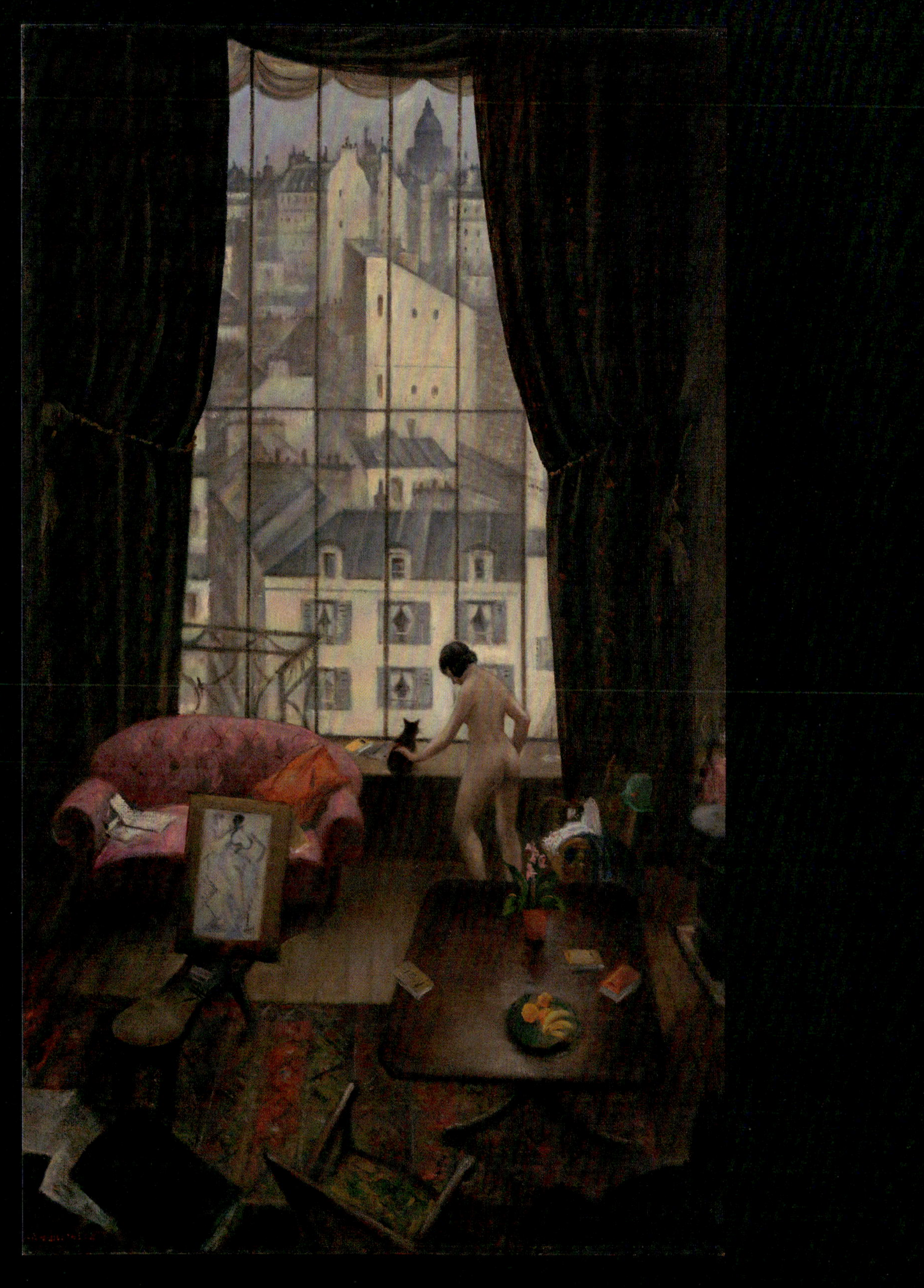

Pissarro and Cézanne. It can be said that within the café's walls 'the theories of realism and impressionism took shape'.[31]

La Nouvelle Athènes was another favourite rendezvous for artists and writers. George Moore recalls how he and his friends would sit around its small marble tables 'aestheticising' until far into the night.

> I can hear the glass door of the café grate on the sand as I open it. I can recall the smell of every hour. In the morning that of eggs frizzling in butter, the pungent smell of cigarettes, coffee and bad cognac; at five o'clock the fragrant odour of absinthe; and soon after the steaming soup ... and as the evening advances, the mingled smells of cigarettes, coffee and weak beer.'

When they finally left the café at 2am, they 'used to stand on the pavements, the shutters clanging up behind us, loath to separate, thinking of what we had left unsaid, and how much better we might have enforced our arguments ... '[32]

There have always been communities of artists – the bustling Renaissance *bottega,* the silent monastery *scriptoria* – but they were primarily practical in purpose, devoted to the business of making art. During the nineteenth century, however, what brought groups of artists together, like the Pre-Raphaelites and the Impressionists, was rejection of their work and their common aims. They were stronger together.

Some artists were able to work in a hotel bedroom, a bobbing boat, the kitchen table or bent double on scaffolding 21m above a stone floor. But the majority needed a place apart, away from the world's clamour, in which to think, to visualise, to create, be it an echoing loft, a pretentious showplace or a squalid garret. They imbued their space with their personalities and filled it with not just the tools of their trade but books, copies of favourite paintings, mementoes of their travels, the odd boa constrictor. The studio was their sanctuary.

Nevinson was a controversial figure, viewed with suspicion by the British art establishment. His painting, with its Parisian rooftops and naked model, epitomises the popular and romantic view of a bohemian artist's studio. It was bought by H.G. Wells who presented it to the Tate Gallery.

Notes

INTRODUCTION

1. Waterfield, p. 11
2. Hall, p. 7
3. Peppiatt & Bellony-Rewald, p. 100
4. Wittkower, p. xix
5. Cole, p. 134
6. Peppiatt & Bellony-Rewald, p. 10
7. Nicholl, p. 127
8. *Ibid.*, p. 126
9. Holman, p. 602, n.5
10. Jacobs & Grabner, p. 39
11. Holman, p. 602
12. Cole & Pardo, p. 3

ONE

1. Cennini, p. 3
2. *Ibid.*, p. 16
3. *Daily Telegraph,* March 2023
4. Brooks, pp. 30–1
5. Cole, p. 137
6. Vasari, vol. 1, p. 628
7. Cole, p. 57
8. Gayford, *Michelangelo,* p. 39
9. *The Story of Painting,* p. 39
10. *Frescoes from Florence,* p. 22
11. Ayres, p. 94
12. *The Story of Painting,* p. 69
13. *Ibid.*, p. 67
14. *Frescoes from Florence,* p. 22
15. Hagen, vol. 1, p. 91
16. *Ibid.*, p. 91
17. *Frescoes from Florence,* p. 31
18. Cole, p. 157
19. Rynck, p. 25
20. Cole, pp. 32–3
21. Peppiatt & Belony-Rewald, p. 100
22. Nicholl, p. 130

TWO

1. Uglow, p. 65
2. Gayford, *Michelangelo,* p. 55

3. Peppiatt & Belony-Rewald, p. 13
4. Syson with Keith, p. 16
5. *The Story of Painting,* p. 121
6. Brooks, p. 106
7. Fenton, p. 43
8. *Ibid.*, p. 43
9. Peppiatt & Belony-Rewald, p. 22
10. Alpers, p. 71
11. Moore, *Modern Painting,* p. 61
12. Shirley Fox, pp. 86–7
13. Lethève, p. 24
14. Breton, p. 164
15. Milner, p. 21
16. Weinberg, p. 227
17. Crow, p. 20
18. Goldstein, p. 56
19. Johnson, p. 40
20. Chapman, *Eighteenth-Century Women Artists,* p. 54
21. Gardner, p. 151–2
22. *Ibid.*, p. 152
23. Peppiatt & Bellony-Rewald, p. 53
24. Milner, p. 11
25. Fehrer, p. 755
26. Perry, G., p. 18
27. Milner, p. 6
28. Lethève, p. 88
29. Chapman, *Eighteenth-Century Women Artists,* p. 55

THREE

1. Postle & Vaughan, p. 9
2. Nicholl, p. 422
3. *Ibid.*, p. 422
4. Gayford, *Michelangelo,* p. 262
5. *Ibid.*, p. 202
6. *Ibid.*, p. 386
7. Borzello, p. 21
8. www.nationalgallery.org.uk
9. Cellini, p. 209
10. Beyer, p. 215

11. Clark, p. 205
12. Bignamini & Postle, p. 65
13. *Ibid.*, p. 82
14. Borzello, p. 38
15. Chapman, *Nineteenth-Century Women Artists,* p. 10
16. Chapman, *Eighteenth-Century Women Artists,* p. 196
17. Postle & Vaughan, p. 96
18. Lethève, p. 74
19. Postle & Vaughan, p. 56
20. Egerton, p. 60
21. Peppiatt & Belony-Rewald, p. 97
22. *Ibid.*, p. 97
23. Elderfield, p. 101
24. Beyer, p. 329
25. Peppiatt & Belony-Rewald, p. 113
26. *Ibid.*, p. 113
27. Vasari, vol. 1, p. 831
28. *Ibid.*, p. 834
29. Weidinger, p. 207
30. Fischer & McEwan, p. 128
31. Weidinger, p. 212
32. Hughes, p. 112
33. Fleming, p. 150
34. Paul, p. 54
35. Prose, p. 15
36. Sooke, *Daily Telegraph,* 19 Jan 2019, p. 6
37. Sooke, *Daily Telegraph,* 20 Oct 2018, p. 14

FOUR

1. Hamilton, p. 260
2. Both these quotes come from Shawe-Taylor, p. 7
3. Beyer, p. 72
4. *Story of Painting,* p. 77
5. Syson, p. 113
6. Nicholl, p. 232
7. Gayford, *Michelangelo,* p. 375
8. Williams, p. 121

9. Peppiatt & Belony-Rewald, p. 15
10. Beyer, p. 202
11. Hearn & Barber, p. 153
12. *The Oldie*
13. Hughes, p. 40
14. *Ibid.*, p. 41
15. Wittkower, pp. 255–6
16. McIntyre, p. 122
17. *Ibid.*, p. 251
18. Hall, p. 167
19. Chapman, *Eighteenth-Century Women Artists,* p. 64
20. Pointon, p. 187
21. Munro, p. 5
22. Chapman, *Eighteenth-Century Women Artists,* p. 65
23. Hamilton, p. 217
24. *Ibid.*, p. 218
25. *Ibid.*, p. 276
26. Mowl, p. 50
27. Chapman, *Eighteenth-Century Women Artists,* p. 79
28. Goodden, p. 75
29. Le Brun, p. 355
30. Wittkower, p. 96
31. Gayford, *Michelangelo,* p. 159
32. *Ibid.*, p. 159
33. Wendorf, p. 164
34. Pollock, p. 79
35. Howard, p. 14

FIVE

1. Milner, p. 27
2. www.lootedart.com, p. 32
3. www.19thc-artworldwide.org Article by C. Muysers
4. Peppiatt & Bellony-Rewald, p. 61
5. en.wikipedia.org/wiki/Jean-Léon_Gérôme
6. Peppiatt & Bellony-Rewald, p. 74
7. Milner, p. 141
8. *Ibid.*, p. 177

9. Lethève, pp. 72–3
10. Peppiatt & Bellony-Rewald, p. 78
11. Mourey, p. 26
12. Milner, p. 45
13. Peppiatt & Bellony-Rewald, p. 83
14. Howard, p. 100
15. Barnes, p. 40
16. *Ibid.*, p. 41
17. Richardson, pp. 132–3
18. Brandon, p. 187
19. Skinner, p. 87
20. Westheider, p. 77
21. Adler, p. 14
22. *William Merritt Chase*, p. 35
23. Robbins, p. 73
24. *Ibid.*, p. 71
25. www.christies.com/en/lot/lot-5728945
26. Peppiatt & Bellony-Rewald, pp. 80–1
27. Fleming, p. 147
28. *Ibid.*, pp. 188–9
29. *Ibid.*, p. 189

SIX

1. Murger, pp. xxix–xxx
2. Price, p. 14
3. Baldick, p. 77
4. Fenton, p. 165
5. *Ibid.*, p. 168
6. Waterfield, p. 43
7. Fenton, pp. 173–4
8. Wilton, p. 10
9. Waterfield, p. 47
10. Wilton, p. 191
11. *Ibid.*, p. 191
12. *Ibid.*, p. 194
13. *Ibid.*, p. 191
14. www.vangoghletters.org Letter 196 to Theo van Gogh, Tuesday 3 Jan 1882
15. Naifeh & White Smith, p. 271
16. Holroyd, p. 158
17. Waterfield, p. 50
18. Schama, p. 425
19. Richardson & McCully, p. 299
20. Olivier, p. 27
21. Perry, p. 59
22. Olivier, p. 48
23. *Ibid.*, p. 168
24. *Ibid.*, p. 27
25. Richardson & McCully, p. 325
26. Clark, pp. 463–4
27. Oliver, p. 135

28. Franck, p. 163
29. Wullschläger, p. 150
30. Peppiatt & Bellony-Rewald, p. 130
31. Franck, p. 165
32. Meyers, p. 127
33. Wullschläger, p. 153

SEVEN

1. Gayford, *Michelangelo*, p. 243
2. Vasari, vol. 2, p. 667
3. *Ibid.*, vol. 2, p. 667
4. Gayford, *Michelangelo*, p. 274
5. Saltzman, p. 36
6. *Ibid.*, p. 145
7. Brookner, p. 156
8. Saltzman, p. 174
9. Jover, p. 54
10. Peppiatt & Bellony-Rewald, p. 54
11. Tinterow, p. 111
12. Gayford, *The Yellow House*, p. 28
13. *Ibid.*, p. 13
14. *Ibid.*, pp. 15-16
15. *Ibid.*, p. 291
16. Hughes, p. 145
17. Gayford, *The Yellow House*, p. 320
18. Sweetman, pp. 342–3
19. *The Story of Painting*, p. 249
20. www.collections.mfa.org/objects/31260/an-artist-in-his-studio
21. Bowness & Callen, p. 37
22. Reed, p. 42
23. *Ibid.*, p. 3
24. Ackroyd, p. 436
25. Peppiatt & Bellony-Rewald, p. 102
26. Kendall, *Monet by Himself,* p. 191
27. Grovier, p. 196

EIGHT

1. Hawthorne, p. 96
2. *Ibid.*, p. 96
3. Clark, p. 224
4. *Ibid.*, p. 23
5. Vasari, vol. 1, p. 368
6. *Ibid.*, vol. 1, p. 367
7. Hall, p. 110
8. *Ibid.*, p. 110
9. Ayres, p. 156
10. Gayford, *Michelangelo*, p. 228
11. *Ibid.*, p. 228

12. *Ibid.*, p. 137
13. *Ibid.*, p. 227
14. *Ibid.*, p. 140
15. *Ibid.*, pp. 144–5
16. *Ibid.*, p. 121
17. *Ibid.*, p. 157
18. Vasari, vol. 2, p. 654
19. Gayford, *Michelangelo*, p. 163
20. *Ibid.*, p. 166
21. collections.vam.ac.uk/item/O85428/fig-leaf-for-idavidi-fig-leaf-d-brucciani
22. Mormando, p. 258
23. Wittkower, pp. 272–3
24. Goldwater, p. 134
25. Hall, p. 9
26. Goldwater, p. 199
27. Saltzman, p. 211
28. *Napoleon & Canova*
29. Honour, Part I, p. 147
30. *Ibid.*, p. 148
31. Saltzman, p. 213
32. *Ibid.*, p. 205
33. Hibbert, p. 366
34. Dabakis, pp. 63–4
35. Hosmer, p. 221
36. Sherwood, p. 97
37. Sherwood, p. 71
38. Chapman, *Nineteenth-Century Women Artists,* p. 163
39. *Ibid.*, p. 168
40. Hughes, p. 130
41. Grunfeld, p. 90
42. *Ibid.*, p. 91
43. *Ibid.*, p. 95
44. Elsen, p. 20
45. Grunfeld, p. 255
46. *Ibid.*, p. 294
47. Elsen, p. 10
48. *Ibid.*, p. 296

NINE

1. Morrow, pp. 72–3
2. Lethève, p. 119
3. *Ibid.*, p. 120
4. Adler, p. 46
5. Hughes, p. 135
6. Moore, *Confessions*, p. 85
7. Moore, *Modern Painting,* pp. 30–1
8. Sturgis, p. 124
9. Moore, *Modern Painting,* p. 31
10. Roe, p. 102
11. Peppiatt & Bellony-Rewald, p. 100
12. Vollard, p. 23

13. Howard, p. 188
14. Lloyd, p. 115
15. Baldick, p. 226
16. Peppiatt & Bellony-Rewald, p. 99
17. Ayres, p. 122
18. *Ibid.*, p. 126
19. Sturgis, p. 106
20. Howard, p. 104
21. Lewis, *Cézanne*, p. 39
22. *Mary Cassatt*, p. 61
23. Higonnet, p. 89
24. Renoir, p. 177
25. *Ibid.*, p. 404
26. Barnes, p. 58
27. Peppiatt & Bellony-Rewald, p. 67
28. Hall, p. 252
29. Barnes, p. 62
30. Howard, p. 10
31. Lethève, p. 181
32. Howard, p. 100

Bibliography

Ackroyd, P., *London: The Biography,* London, 2000

Adler, K., et al., (eds), *Americans in Paris, 1860–1900,* exhibition catalogue, National Gallery, London, 2006

Alpers, S., *The Vexations of Art: Velásquez and Others,* New Haven, *c.* 2005

Ayres, James, *The Artist's Craft,* Oxford, 1985

Barrow, R., *Lawrence Alma-Tadema,* Oxford, 2001

Barnes, J., *Keeping an Eye Open: Essays on Art,* London, 2015

Berenson, E., *The Statue of Liberty: A Transatlantic Story,* New Haven and London, 2012

Beyer, A., *Portraits: A History,* (trans.) S. Lindberg, Munich, 2003

Bignamini, I., and M. Postle, *The Artist's Model: Its Role in British Art from Lely to Etty,* Nottingham, 1991

Borzello, F., *The Artist's Model,* London, 1982

Bowness, A., and A. Callen (eds), *Impressionists in London,* exhibition catalogue, Hayward Gallery, London, 1973

Bowron, E.P., *Pompeo Batoni: A Complete Catalogue of his Paintings,* New Haven, 2016

Brandon, R., *Being Divine: A Biography of Sarah Bernhardt,* London, 1991

Breton, J., *The Life of an Artist: Art and Nature,* New York, 1891

Brookner, A., *Jacques-Louis David,* London, 1980

Brooks, J., *Taddeo and Federico Zuccaro: Artist-Brothers in Renaissance Rome,* exhibition catalogue, J. Paul Getty Museum, Los Angeles, 2007

Burney, C., *Music, Men and Manners in France and Italy, 1770,* London, 1969

Cellini, B., *The Autobiography of Benvenuto Cellini,* Amazon, n.d.

Cennini, C., *The Craftsman's Handbook,* (trans.) Daniel V. Thompson, Jr., New York, 1966

Chapman, C., *Eighteenth-Century Women Artists: Their Trials, Tribulations and Triumphs,* London, 2017

Chapman, C., *Nineteenth-Century Women Artists: Sisters of the Brush,* London, 2021

Clark, K., *The Nude,* Washington, D.C., 1956

Cole, B., *The Renaissance Artist at Work,* Boulder, Colorado, 1983

Cole, M. and M. Pardo (eds), *Inventions of the Studio,* Chapel Hill, 2005

Constable, W.G., *The Painter's Workshop,* London, 1954

Corbeau-Parsons, C. (ed.), *The EY Exhibition: Impressionists in London,* exhibition catalogue, Tate Britain (Gallery), London, 2017

Crow, T.E., *Painters and Public Life in Eighteenth-Century Paris,* New Haven and London, 1985

Dabakis, M., *A Sisterhood of Sculptors: American Artists in Nineteenth-Century Rome,* Pennsylvania, 2014

Elderfield, J., *Manet and the Execution of Maximilian,* exhibition catalogue, Museum of Modern Art, New York, *c.* 2006

Egerton, J., *George Stubbs, Anatomist and Animal Painter,* exhibition catalogue, The Tate Gallery, London, 1976

Elsen, A.E. *In Rodin's Studio: A Photographic Record on Sculpture in the Making,* Oxford, 1980

Esner, R., et al., *Hiding Making – Showing Creation: The Studio from Turner to Tacita Dean,* Amsterdam, 2013

Fehrer, C., 'Women at the Académie Julian in Paris', *Burlington Magazine,* vol. 136, Nov., 1894

Fenton, J., *School of Genius: A History of the Royal Academy of Arts,* London, 2006

Fischer, W.G. and D. McEwan, *Gustav Klimt & Emile Flöge: An Artist and his Muse,* London, 1992

Fleming, G.H., *James Abbott McNeill Whistler: A Life,* Moreton-in-the-Marsh, Glos., 1991

Franck, D., *The Bohemians: The Birth of Modern Art: Paris 1900–1930,* London, 2001

Frescoes from Florence, exhibition catalogue, Hayward Gallery, London, 1969

Gardner, J., *The Louvre: The Many Lives of the World's Most Famous Museum,* New York, 2020

Gayford, M., *Michelangelo: His Epic Life,* London, 2013

Gayford, M., *The Yellow House: Van Gogh, Gauguin and Nine Turbulent Weeks in Arles,* London, 2006

Goldstein, C., *Teaching Art: Academies and Schools from Vasari to Albers,* Cambridge, 1996

Goldwater, R. and M. Treves, *Artists on Art: from the XIV to the XX century,* London, *c.* 1945

Goncourt, E, and J. de, *Pages from the Goncourt Journal,* (ed. and trans.) Robert Baldick, London, 1980

Goodden, A., *The Sweetness of Life: A Biography of Elisabeth Louise Vigée Le Brun,* London, 1997

Grovier, K., *A New Way of Seeing: The History of Art in 57 Works,* London, 2018

Grunfeld, F. V., *Rodin: A Biography,* London, 1988

Hagen, R-M. and R., *What Great Paintings Say,* London, 2005

Hall, J., *The Artist's Studio: A Cultural History,* London, 2022

Hamilton, J., *Gainsborough: A Portrait,* London, 2018

Hawthorne, N., *The Marble Faun,* Oxford, 2008

Hearn, K. and T. Barber (eds), *Van Dyck and Britain,* exhibition catalogue, Tate Britain Gallery, London, 2009

Hibbert, C., *Rome: The Biography of a City,* Harmondsworth, 1985

Higonnet, A., *Berthe Morisot: A Biography,* London, 1990

Holman, B., Review of 'Inventions of the Studio, Renaissance to Romanticism by M. Coe and M. Pardo', *The Art Bulletin,* Sept., 2006, vol. 88, no. 3

Holroyd, M., *Augustus John: The Years of Innocence,* vol. 1, London, 1975

Honour, H., 'Canova's Studio Practices', *Burlington Magazine,* Part 1 and 2, March, April, 1972

Hosmer, Harriet, *Letters and Memories,* New York, 1913

Howard, M. (ed.), *The Impressionists by Themselves: More than Twenty Artists, their Works, and their Words,* London, 1991

Hughes, R., *Nothing if not Critical: Selected Essays on Art and Artists,* London, 1990

Jacobs, M.J., and M. Grabner (eds), *The Studio Reader: On the Space of Artists,* Chicago, 2010

Johns, C., *Antonio Canova and the Politics of Patronage in Revolutionary and Napoleonic Europe,* Berkeley, Los Angeles and London, 1998

Johnson, D. (ed.), *Jacques-Louis David: New Perspectives,* Newark Delaware, 2006

Jover, M., *Ingres,* Paris, 2005

Kendall, R. (ed.), *Cézanne by Himself,* London, 1988

Kendall, R. (ed.), *Monet by Himself,* London, 1989

Lethève, Jacques, *Daily Life of French Artists in the Nineteenth Century,* (trans.) H.E. Paddon, London, 1972

Levey, M., *The Painter Depicted – Painters as a Subject in Painting,* London, 1981

Lewis, M.T., *Cézanne,* London, 2000

Lloyd, C., *Edgar Degas: Drawings and Pastels,* London, 2014

Mary Cassatt: Modern Woman, exhibition catalogue, Art Institute of Chicago, 1998

McIntyre, I., *Joshua Reynolds: The Life and Times of the First President of the Royal Academy,* London, 2003

Meyers, Jeffrey, *Modigliani: A Life,* London, 2006

Millar, Oliver (ed.), *Van Dyck in England,* exhibition catalogue, National Portrait Gallery, London, *c.* 1982

Milner, J., *The Studios of Paris,* New Haven, 1988

Moore, G., *Confessions of a Young Man,* London, 1928

Moore, G, *Modern Painting,* London, 1898

Mormando, F., *Bernini: His Life and His Rome,* Chicago and London, 2011

Morrow, W. C., *Bohemian Paris of To-day,* London, 1899

Mourey, G., 'Some French Artists at Home', *The Studio,* vol. 7, 1896

Mowl, T., *Horace Walpole: The Great Outsider,* London, 1996

Munro, J., *Silent Partners: Artist and Mannequin from Function to Fetish,* Cambridge, 2014

Murger, H., *Scenes of Bohemian Life,* London, 1883

Muysers, C., 'Physiology and Photography: The Evolution of Franz von Lenbach's Portraiture', *Nineteenth-Century Art Worldwide,* vol. 1, Issue 2, Autumn, 2002

Naifeh, S. and G. White Smith, *Van Gogh: The Life,* London, 2011

Napoleon and Canova: Eight Conversations held at the Chateau of the Tuileries, in 1810, London, 1825

Nicholl, C., *Leonardo da Vinci: The Flights of the Mind,* London, 2005

Olivier, F., *Picasso and His Friends,* London, 1964

Paul, C., 'A Model of a Muse', *Royal Academy of Arts Magazine,* 23 Feb., 2022

Peppiatt, M. and A. Bellony-Rewald, *Imagination's Chamber: Artists and Their Studios,* London, 1983

Perry, G., *Women Artists and the Parisian Avant-Garde,* Manchester and New York, 1995

Pevsner, N, *Academies of Art, Past and Present,* Cambridge and New York, 1940

Pointon, M., 'Portrait-Painting as a Business Enterprise in London in the 1780s', *Art History,* vol. 7, no. 2, June, 1984

Pollock, G., *Mary Cassatt: Painter of Modern Women,* London, 1998

Postle, M. and W. Vaughan, *The Artist's Model: From Etty to Spencer,* London, exhibition catalogue, York City Art Gallery, 1999

Price, J.M., *My Bohemian Days in Paris,* London, 1913

Prose, F., *The Lives of the Muses: Nine Women and the Artists they Inspired,* London, 2003

Reed, N., *Monet and The Thames,* Kent, 1998

Renoir, J., *Renoir, My Father,* London, 1962

Richardson, J., *Sarah Bernhardt and her World,* New York, 1977

Richardson, J. and M. McCully, *A Life of Picasso,* London, 1991–2007

Robbins, D., *Leighton House Museum,* London, 2011

Roe, S., *The Private Lives of the Impressionists,* London, 2007

Rynck, P., *How to Read a Painting: Decoding, Understanding and Enjoying the Old Masters,* London, 2004

Saltzman, C., *Napoleon's Plunder and the Theft of Veronese's Feast,* London, 2021

Schama, S., *The Face of Britain: A History of the Nation Through its Portraits,* London, 2015

Shawe-Taylor, D., *The Georgians: Eighteenth-Century Portraiture and Society,* London, 1990

Shirley Fox, J., *An Art Student's Reminiscences of Paris in the Eighties,* London, 1909

Skinner, C., *Madame Sarah,* London, 1967

Sooke, A., 'Madame Bonnard's Eternal Bathtime', *Daily Telegraph,* 19 Jan., 2019

Sooke, A, 'Maman, c'est ma muse', *Daily Telegraph,* 20 Oct., 2018

The Story of Painting: How Art was Made, Dorling Kindersley, London, 2019

Sturgis, A., et al., (eds), *Rebels and Martyrs: The Image of the Artist in the Nineteenth Century,* exhibition catalogue, National Gallery, London, 2006

Sweetman, David, *The Love of Many Things: A Life of Vincent Van Gogh,* London, 1990

Syson, L. with L. Keith, *Leonardo da Vinci: Painter at the Court of Milan,* exhibition catalogue, National Gallery, London, 2011

Taylor, B., *George Stubbs,* exhibition catalogue, Walker Art Gallery, Liverpool, 1957

Tinterow, G. et al. (eds), *Portraits by Ingres: Image of an Epoch,* exhibition catalogue, National Gallery, London, 1999

Uglow, J., *Hogarth: A Life and a World,* London, 1997

Vasari, G., *Lives of Painters, Sculptors and Architects,* (trans.) G. du C. De Vere, London, 1996

Vigée Le Brun, É., *The Memoirs of Elisabeth Vigée Le Brun,* (ed. and trans.) S. Evans, London, 1989

Vollard, A., *Degas: An Intimate Portrait,* (trans.) R.T. Weaver, New York, 1986

Waterfield, G. (ed.), *The Artist's Studio,* Compton Verney, 2009

Wedd, K., *Creative Quarters: The Art World in London from 1700 to 2000,* London, 2001

Weidinger, A. (ed.) *Gustav Klimt,* London, 2007

Weinberg, H.B., *The Lure of Paris: The Nineteenth-Century American Painters and their French Teachers,* London, 1991

Wendorf, R., *Sir Joshua Reynolds: The Painter in Society,* London, 1986

Westheider, O. (ed.), *High Society: American Portraits of the Gilded Age,* exhibition catalogue, Hamburg, 2008

White, Christopher, *Peter Paul Rubens: Man and Artist,* New Haven, 1987.

William Merritt Chase: A Modern Master, exhibition catalogue, Museum of Fine Arts, Boston, 2016

Williams, J., *The World of Titian, c. 1488–1576,* New York, 1968

Wilton, A., *Turner in his Time,* London, 2006

Wittkower, R. and M., *Born under Saturn: The Character and Conduct of Artists: A Documented History from Antiquity to the French Revolution,* London, *c.* 1963

Wullschläger, J., *Chagall: Love and Exile,* London, 2008

Illustration List

Front cover: Jean Alaux, *Studio of Ingres in Rome,* 1818. Oil on canvas, 55.4 x 46 cm. Musée Ingres Bourdelle, Montauban, France

Back Cover: Gustave Courbet, *The Painter's Studio,* 1855 (detail). Oil on canvas, 361 x 598 cm. Musée d'Orsay, Paris

Title page: Johannes Vermeer, *The Art of Painting,* 1666–68. Oil on canvas, 120 x 100 cm. Kunsthistorisches Museum, Vienna, Austria

1. Rogier van der Weyden, *Saint Luke Drawing the Virgin, c.* 1435–40. Oil and tempera on panel, 137.5 x 110.8 cm. Museum of Fine Arts, Boston

2. Illumination from Giovanni Boccaccio, *On Famous Women, c.* 1400. Bibliothèque Nationale, Paris

3. January from *Les Trés Riches Heures du duc de Berry, c.* 1416. Tempera on vellum, 22.5 x 13.6 cm. Condé Museum, Paris

4. Gerard Dou, *The Painter in his Studio,* 1632. Oil on panel, 59.1 x 43.2 cm. Museum de Lakenhal, Leiden, The Netherlands

5. Louis-Léopold Boilly, *A Painter's Studio, c.* 1800. Oil on canvas, 73.5 x 59.5 cm. National Gallery of Art, Washington, DC

6. Jan van Eyck, *Portrait of a Man with a Red Turban,* 1433. Oil on panel, 26 x 19 cm. National Gallery, London

7. Jan van der Straet, *The Invention of Oil Paint, c.* 1590. Engraving, 27 x 20 cm. Metropolitan Museum of Art, New York

8. Workshop of Maso Finiguerra, *A Youth Drawing,* 1450s. Pen and ink with wash on paper, 19 x 11.3 cm. British Museum, London

9. Andrea del Verrocchio, *The Baptism of Christ, c.* 1472–75. Tempera and oil on poplar, 177 x 151 cm. Uffizi Gallery, Florence

10. Antonio Pisanello, *Two Horses,* 15th Century. Pen and ink on paper, 20 x 16.5 cm. Louvre Museum, Paris

11. Leonardo da Vinci, *Drapery Study for a Seated Figure,* 1470–80. Brush and grey distemper on grey canvas, 26.6 x 23.3 cm. Louvre Museum, Paris

12. Anon, *Wilton Diptych c.* 1395–99 (detail). Tempera on panel, overall 53 x 37 cm. National Gallery, London

13. Michelangelo, *The Manchester Madonna, c.* 1494. Tempera on panel, 104.5 x 77 cm. National Gallery, London

14. Gerard David, *The Rest on the Flight into Egypt, c.* 1510. Oil on panel, 41.9 x 42.2 cm. National Gallery of Art, Washington, DC/ Andrew W. Mellon Collection

15. Fresco from the Villa of the Mysteries, Pompeii, before 79 CE

16. Federico Zuccaro, *Taddeo Zuccaro Decorating the Facade of Palazzo Mattei*, *c.* 1595. Drawing, pen and brown ink, 25 x 42.2 cm. Getty Centre, Los Angeles

17. Scrovegni Chapel, Padua, Italy, *c.* 1300

18. Benozzo Gozzoli, *The Procession of the Magi*, Palazzo Medici, Florence, 1459–63. Fresco

19. Giovanni di ser Giovanni Guidi (called Scheggia), *Cassone Adimari*, 1450. Painted wood, 88.5 x 303 cm. Galleria dell'Accademia, Florence

20. Robert Campin, *The Mérode Altarpiece*, *c.* 1427–32. Oil on oak panel, overall 64.5 x 117.8 cm. Metropolitan Museum of Art, New York/The Cloisters Collection, 1956

21. Giovanni di ser Giovanni Guidi (called Scheggia), *A Birth Tray*, *c.* 1449. Tempera, silver and gold on wood, overall diameter 92.7 cm. The Metropolitan Museum of Art, New York

22. Matthew Pratt, *The American School*, 1765. Oil on canvas, 91.4 x 127.6 cm. Metropolitan Museum of Art, New York/ Gift of Samuel P. Avery, 1897

23. Enea Vico after Baccio Bandinelli, *Bandinelli's Night Class*, 1545–50. Engraving, 30.6 x 43.8 cm. Metropolitan Museum of Art, New York/Purchase, Joseph Pulitzer Bequest, 1917

24. Agostino Carracci, *Male Nudes and Other Studies*, *c.* 1590 (detail). Pen and ink on paper.

25. Paolo Uccello, *The Battle of San Romano*, 1456. Tempera on wood, 182 x 320 cm. National Gallery, London

26. Charles-Joseph Natoire, *Life Class at the Royal Academy of Painting and Sculpture*, 1746. Drawing, 45.3 x 32.2 cm. The Courtauld, London / Bridgeman Images

27. Élisabeth Vigée Le Brun, *Peace Bringing Back Abundance*, 1780. Oil on canvas, 103 x 133 cm. Louvre Museum, Paris

28. Thomas Rowlandson, *A Dutch Academy*, *c.* 1792. Pencil, pen and ink and watercolour, 18.7 x 28.6 cm. Houghton Library, Harvard University, Cambridge

29. Johann Zoffany, *The Academicians of the Royal Academy*, 1771–72. Oil on canvas, 101.1 x 147.5 cm. Royal Collection Trust, London

30. Jean-Henri Cless, *David's Studio*, *c.* 1804. Pen and ink on paper, 46.5 x 58.3 cm. Musée Carnavalet, Paris

31. Marie Bashkirtseff, *In the Studio*, 1881. Oil on canvas, 154 x 186 cm. Dnipropetrovsk State Art Museum, Ukraine

32. Maria Wiik, *In the Attic Studio*, 1889. Oil on canvas, 52 x 61 cm. Private Collection

33. Édouard Manet, *Eva Gonzalès Painting in Manet's Studio*, 1870. Oil on canvas, 56 x 46 cm. Private Collection

34. Hubert Robert, *The Grande Galerie in the Louvre*, 1796. Oil on canvas, 115 x 145 cm. Louvre Museum, Paris

35. Adélaïde Labille-Guiard, *Self-Portrait with Two Pupils*, 1785. Oil on canvas, 210.8 x 151.1 cm. Metropolitan Museum of Art, New York/Gift of Julia A. Berwind, 1953

36. Rembrandt van Rijn, *Hendrickje Bathing*, 1654. Oil on wood, 61.8 x 47 cm. National Gallery, London

37. Michelangelo, *Study for an* Ignudo *for the Sistine Chapel*, 1504–05. Red chalk, lead point on paper. Teylers Museum, Haarlem, The Netherlands

38. Michael Sweerts, *The Drawing Class*, 1660. Oil on canvas, 103.4 x 136.5 cm. Frans Hals Museum, Haarlem, The Netherlands

39. Eugène Delacroix, *The Massacre at Chios*, 1824 (detail). Oil on canvas, 419 x 354 cm. Louvre Museum, Paris

40. Elizabeth Southerden Thompson (Lady Butler), *Scotland Forever!*, 1881. Oil on canvas, 101.6 x 194.3 cm. Leeds Museum and Galleries

41. Pierre-Auguste Renoir, *Dance at Bougival*, 1882–83. Oil on canvas, 182 x 98 cm. Museum of Fine Arts, Boston

42. Henri de Toulouse-Lautrec, *Yvette Guilbert Salutes her Audience*, 1894. Gouache on cardboard, 48 x 28 cm. Musée Toulouse-Lautrec, Albi, France

43. George Stubbs, *Anatomy of the Horse*, 1766. Pencil on paper, 47 x 29 cm. Royal Academy of Arts, London

44. Théodore Géricault, *The Raft of the Medusa*, 1818. Oil on canvas, 491 x 716 cm. Louvre Museum, Paris

45. George Stubbs, *Whistlejacket*, *c.* 1762. Oil on canvas, 292 x 246.4 cm. National Gallery, London

46. Édouard Manet, *The Execution of Emperor Maximilian*, 1867–68. Oil on canvas, 193 x 284 cm. National Gallery, London

47. Andrea del Sarto, *Lucrezia di Baccio del Fede, the Artist's Wife*, *c.* 1514. Oil on panel, 73 x 56 cm. Prado, Madrid

48. Gustav Klimt, *The Kiss*, 1907–08. Oil on canvas, 180 x 180 cm. The Belvedere, Vienna, Austria

49. James Abbott McNeill Whistler, *Symphony in White, No. 1: The White Girl*, 1862. Oil on canvas, 213 x 107.9 cm. National Gallery of Art, Washington, DC

50. Édouard Vuillard, *Mme Vuillard in a Drawing Room*, 1893 or 1898. Oil on canvas, 27.5 x 28.2 cm. Hermitage Museum, Moscow

51. Pierre Bonnard, *La Grande Baignoire*, 1937–39. Oil on canvas, 94 x 144 cm. Private Collection

52. Antonio Pisanello, *Portrait of Leonello d'Este, Marquess of Ferrara*, *c.* 1441. Tempera on panel, 28 x 19 cm. Accademia Carrara di Belle Arti, Bergamo, Italy

53. Thomas Gainsborough, *The Morning Walk*, 1785. Oil on canvas, 236 x 179 cm. National Gallery, London

54. Leonardo da Vinci, *Portrait of Cecilia Gallerani ('The Lady with an Ermine')*, 1483. Oil and tempera on panel, 54.8 x 40.3 cm. Czartoryski Museum, Kraków, Poland

55. Michelangelo, *Portrait of Andrea Quaratesi*, 1528–31. Black chalk, 41 x 29 cm. British Museum, London.

56. Hans Holbein the Younger, *Charles de Solier, Sieur de Morette*, *c.* 1534. Oil on panel, 92.5 x 75.4 cm. Staatliche Kunstsammlungen Dresden, Gemäldegalerie Alte Meister, Germany

57. Titian, *Ranuccio Farnese*, 1542. Oil on canvas, 89.7 x 73.6 cm. National Gallery of Art, Washington, DC/Samuel H. Kress Collection

58. Anthony van Dyck, *Queen Henrietta Maria*, 1632. Oil on canvas, 109 x 86.2 cm. Royal Collection

59. Joshua Reynolds, *Portrait of Jane Fleming*, 1778. Oil on canvas, 235.6 x 145 cm. The Huntington Library, Art Museum and Botanical Gardens, San Marino, USA

60. Joshua Reynolds, *Lady Cockburn and her Three Eldest Sons*, 1773. Oil on canvas, 141.5 x 113 cm. National Gallery, London/ Bequeathed by Alfred Beit, 1906

61. Thomas Gainsborough, *Ann Ford, Mrs Philip Thicknesse*, 1760. Oil on canvas, 134.9 x 197.2 cm. Cincinnati Art Museum

62. Rosalba Carriera, *Louis XV as a Boy*, 1720–21. Pastel on paper, 50.5 x 38.5 cm. Staatliche Kunstsammlungen, Dresden

63. Edgar Degas, *Portrait of Henri Michel-Lévy*, 1878. Oil on canvas, 40 x 28 cm. Calouste Gulbenkian Museum, Lisbon

64. Pompeo Batoni, *Sir Wyndham Knatchbull-Wyndham, 6th Bt*, 1758–59. Oil on canvas, 233 x 161.3 cm. Los Angeles County Museum of Art/Gift of the Ahmanson Foundation

65. Élisabeth Vigée Le Brun, *Marie-Antoinette en Gaulle*, 1783. Oil on canvas, 92.7 x 73.1 cm. National Gallery of Art, Washington, DC

66. Diego Velázquez, *Las Meninas*, c.1656. Oil on canvas, 318 x 276 cm. Prado Museum, Madrid

67. Marie-Gabrielle Capet, *Studio Interior*, 1808. Oil on canvas, 69 x 83.5 cm. Neue Pinakothek, Munich

68. Mary Cassatt, *Lady at the Tea Table (Portrait of Mary Dickinson Riddle)*, 1883–85. Oil on canvas, 73.7 x 61 cm. Metropolitan Museum of Art, New York

69. Edgar Degas, *Six Friends at Dieppe*, 1885. Pastel on paper, 114.9 x 71.1 cm. Rhode Island School of Design Museum, Providence, USA

70. Eduard Charlemont, *Hans Makart in his Studio in Vienna*, c.1875. Oil on canvas, 140 x 85 cm. Vienna Museum

71. Rudolf von Alt, *Hans Makart's Studio in Vienna*, 1885. Oil on canvas. Historisches Museum der Stadt, Vienna

72. Franz von Lenbach, *Portrait of Otto von Bismarck*, 1871. Oil on panel, 121 x 87.5 cm. Walters Art Museum, Baltimore

73. Jean-Louis-Ernest Meissonier, *Napoleon on Campaign, 1814*, 1864. Oil on canvas, 51.5 x 76.5 cm. Musée d'Orsay, Paris

74. Jean-Léon Gérôme, *The Pelt Merchant, Cairo*, 1869. Oil on canvas, 61.5 x 50 cm. Private Collection

75. John Singer Sargent, *Portrait of Carolus-Duran*, 1879. Oil on canvas, 116.8 x 96 cm. Clark Art Institute, Williamstown

76. Marie-Desirée Bourgoin, *The Actress Sarah Bernhardt in her Studio*, 1879. Watercolour and gouache over graphite, 67.8 x 53.1 cm. Private Collection/Fine Art Images/Heritage Images

77. Annie Traquair Lang, *William Merritt Chase*, 1910. Oil on canvas, 76.2 x 63.5 cm. Metropolitan Museum of Art, New York/ Gift of Margaret and Raymond J. Horowitz, 1977

78. William Merritt Chase, *A Friendly Call*, 1895. Oil on canvas, 76.5 x 122.5 cm. National Gallery of Art, Washington, DC

79. The Arab Hall, Leighton House, London

80. James Tissot, *Caricature of Frederic Leighton*, 1872. Colour lithograph. Private Collection

81. James Tissot, *In the Conservatory (Rivals)*, n.d. Oil on canvas, 38.4 x 51.1 cm. Private Collection

82. Lawrence Alma-Tadema, *The Poet Gallus Dreaming*, 1892. Oil on panel, 24.2 x 16.5 cm. Private Collection

83. James Abbott McNeill Whistler, *Nocturne: Blue and Gold – Old Battersea Bridge*, c.1872–75. Oil on canvas, 66.6 x 50.2 cm. Tate Gallery, London

84. James Abbott McNeill Whistler, *Nocturne: Black and Gold – The Falling Rocket*, c.1875. Oil on panel, 60.3 x 46.4 cm. Detroit Institute of Arts

85. Octave Tassaert, *Interior of a Studio*, 1845. Oil on canvas, 46 x 38 cm. Louvre Museum, Paris

86. Paul Cézanne, *The Stove in the Studio*, 1865–70. Oil on canvas, 41 x 30 cm. National Gallery, London

87. Adriaen van Ostade, *The Painter in his Studio*, 1663. Oil on oak wood, 38 x 35.5 cm. Gemäldergalerie Alte Meister, Dresden

88. Rembrandt van Rijn, *The Artist in his Studio*, 1629. Oil on panel, 24.8 x 31.7 cm. Museum of Fine Arts, Boston

89. James Barry, *Self-Portrait with Dominique Lefèvre and James Paine the Younger*, c.1767. Oil on canvas, 60.5 x 50 cm. National Portrait Gallery, London

90. Thomas Rowlandson, *The Artist's Studio*, 1814. Watercolour, 26.7 x 21.4 cm. Yale Center for British Art, New Haven

91. Hubert Robert, *The Artist's Studio*, 1760. Oil on canvas, 56.5 x 72.7 cm. Städel Museum, Frankfurt

92. J.M.W. Turner, *The Burning of the House of Lords and Commons*, 1835. Oil on canvas, 92.1 x 123.2 cm. Cleveland Museum of Art, Ohio

93. Vincent van Gogh, *View from the Window of Vincent's Studio*, 1883. Pen, ink and pencil on paper, 20.7 x 13.5 cm. Private Collection

94. John Peter Russell, *Vincent van Gogh*, 1886. Oil on canvas, 60.1 x 45.6 cm. Van Gogh Museum, Amsterdam

95. Gwen John, *A Corner of the Artist's Room in Paris*, 1907–09. Oil on canvas on board, 31.2 x 24.8 cm. National Museum, Wales

96. Picasso in his Studio at Bateau Lavoir, 1908. Photograph. Size and whereabouts unknown

97. Pablo Picasso, *Au Lapin Agile*, 1905. Oil on canvas, 99.1 x 100.3 cm. Metropolitan Museum of Art, New York/Art Resource/ Scala, Florence

98. Robert Delaunay, *Simultaneous Windows on the City*, 1912. Oil on canvas, 40 x 46 cm. Kunsthalle Hamburg

99. Amedeo Modigliani, *Portrait of Chaïm Soutine*, 1916 or 1917. Oil on canvas, 100 x 65 cm. Private Collection

100. Michelangelo, *The Sistine Chapel Ceiling, Rome*, 1508–12

101. Michelangelo, *The Libyan Sibyl, The Sistine Chapel Ceiling, Rome*, 1508–12

102. Paolo Veronese, *The Wedding Feast at Cana*, 1563. Oil on canvas, 677 x 994 cm. Louvre Museum, Paris

103. Paolo Veronese, *The Wedding Feast at Cana*, 1563 (detail). Oil on canvas, 677 x 994 cm. Louvre Museum, Paris

104. William van der Velde the Elder, *The Battle of Scheveningen, 10 August 1653*, 1655 (detail). Grisaille, 114.3 x 156.2 cm. Royal Museums, Greenwich

105. Jacques-Louis David, *The Coronation of Napoleon*, 1807 (detail). Oil on canvas, 621 x 979 cm. Louvre Museum, Paris

106. Jean-Auguste-Dominique Ingres, *Louis-François Bertin*, 1832. Oil on canvas, 116 x 95 cm. Louvre Museum, Paris

107. Édouard Manet, *Luncheon in the Studio*, 1868. Oil on canvas, 118.3 x 154 cm. Neue Pinakothek, Munich

108. Paul Gauguin, *Vincent van Gogh Painting Sunflowers*, December 1888. Oil on hessian, 73 x 91 cm. Van Gogh Museum, Amsterdam, The Netherlands

109. Vincent van Gogh, *Café Terrace at Night*, 1888. Oil on canvas, 81 x 65.5 cm. Kröller-Müller Museum, Otterlo, The Netherlands

110. John Singer Sargent, *An Artist in His Studio*, 1904. Oil on canvas, 56.2 x 72.07 cm. Museum of Fine Arts, Boston

111. Édouard Manet, *Monet Working on his Boat in Argenteuil*, 1874. Oil on canvas, 82.7 x 105 cm. Neue Pinakothek, Munich, Germany

112. Claude Monet, *Charing Cross Bridge, The Thames*, 1903. Oil on canvas, 100 x 73.5 cm. Museum of Fine Arts of Lyon, France

113. Claude Monet, *Water Lilies, Reflections of Tall Grass*, 1914–17. Oil on canvas, 130 x 200 cm. Private Collection

114. Nicolae Grigorescu, *Andreescu la Barbizon, c.* 1879. Oil on canvas, 61 x 46 cm. National Museum of Art of Romania, Bucharest

115. Michelangelo, *David, c.* 1501–04. Marble, 517 x 199 cm. Galleria dell'Accademia, Florence

116. Donatello, *David, c.* 1440s. Bronze, height 135 cm. Bargello Museum, Florence/Bridgeman Images

117. Leonardo da Vinci, *Horse Studies, c.* 1490. Silverpoint on paper, 25 x 18.7 cm. Royal Library, Windsor Castle

118. Michelangelo, *Pietà*, 1498–1500. Marble, 174 x 195 x 69 cm. St. Peter's, Rome

119. Gian Lorenzo Bernini, *Louis XIV*, 1665. White marble, 105 x 99 x 46 cm. Palace of Versailles

120. Gian Lorenzo Bernini, *The Ecstasy of Saint Teresa*, 1647–52. Marble. Church of Santa Maria della Vittoria, Rome

121. Johann Baptist Lampi II, *The Sculptor Antonio Canova*, 1805–06. Oil on canvas, 113 x 94 cm. Liechtenstein. The Princely Collections, Vaduz-Vienna

122. Antonio Canova, *Paolina Borghese as Venus Victrix*, 1804–08. Marble. Galleria Borghese, Rome

123. Harriet Hosmer, *The Sleeping Faun*, 1865. Marble, overall 127 cm. Cleveland Museum of Art, USA/Leonard C. Hanna, Jr. Fund

124. Harriet Hosmer with her Italian Workmen, 1867. Photograph. Schlesinger Library, Radcliffe Institute for Advanced Study, Harvard, Cambridge

125. Auguste Rodin, *The Age of Bronze*, 1875–76. Bronze, 180.5 x 68.5 x 54.5 cm. Musée Rodin, Paris

126. Allan Österlind, *Rodin in his Studio*, 1889. Oil on canvas, 73 x 51.5 cm. Finnish National Gallery, Helsinki

127 & 128. *Construction of the Statue of Liberty, Paris, c.* 1882–83. Albumen prints. The New York Public Library.

129. James Tissot, *The Artists' Wives*, 1885. Oil on canvas, 146.1 x 101.6 cm. Chrysler Museum of Art, Norfolk, VA/ Gift of Walter P. Chrysler, Jr., and The Grandy Fund, Landmark Communications Fund, and 'An Affair to Remember' 1982

130. Édouard Manet, *Olympia*, 1863. Oil on canvas, 130 x 190 cm. Musée d'Orsay, Paris

131. Honoré Daumier, *Promenade of the Influential Critic*, 1865. Lithograph. Metropolitan Museum of Art, New York/ Rogers Fund, 1922

132. Claude Monet, *Gare Saint-Lazare*, 1877. Oil on canvas, 75 x 105 cm. Musée d'Orsay, Paris

133. Henri Fantin-Latour, *A Studio in the Batignolles Quarter*, 1870. Oil on canvas, 204 x 273.5 cm. Musée d'Orsay, Paris

134. Édouard Manet, *George Moore*, 1879. Pastel on canvas, 55.2 x 35.2 cm. Metropolitan Museum of Art, New York/ H.O. Havemeyer Collection, Bequest of Mrs. H.O. Havemeyer, 1929

135. Gustave Caillebotte, *Paris Street, Rainy Day*, 1877. Oil on canvas, 212.2 x 276 cm. Art Institute of Chicago

136. Edgar Degas, *The Dance Class*, 1875. Oil on canvas, 85 x 75 cm. Musée d'Orsay, Paris

137. Paul Cézanne, *Three Apples*, 1878. Oil on canvas, 16.5 x 10.2 cm. Barnes Foundation, Philadelphia

138. Paul Cézanne, *Mont Sainte-Victoire from Les Lauves*, 1902–04. Oil on canvas, 69.8 x 89.5 cm. Philadelphia Museum of Art

139. Berthe Morisot, *Woman at her Toilette, c.* 1875. Oil on canvas, 60.3 x 80.4 cm. Art Institute of Chicago

140. Pierre-Auguste Renoir, *Two Sisters (On the Terrace)*, 1881. Oil on canvas, 100.4 x 80.9 cm. Art Institute of Chicago/ Mr and Mrs Lewis Larned Coburn Memorial Collection

141. Gustave Courbet, *The Painter's Studio,*1855. Oil on canvas, 361 x 598 cm. Musée d'Orsay, Paris

142. Henri de Toulouse-Lautrec, *At the Moulin Rouge*, 1892. Oil on canvas, 123 x 140.5 cm. Art Institute of Chicago, Illinois

143. Christopher Nevinson, *A Studio in Montparnasse, c.* 1926. Oil on canvas, 127 x x 76.2 cm. Tate Gallery/Tate Images

Index

Acknowledgements

The debt I owe to Gosia Lawik and her team in Country Orders at the London Library is incalculable. They not only parcelled up and sent me over 150 books, but during Covid – and subsequently – they did not even charge postage. Without this access to other people's erudition, there is no way that this book would have come to pass. Nor would it have been possible without the constant support of my family: the generosity of my sister-in-law Jan Conway; the ability of my husband Roger to put up with three years of brooding silence from my end of the house; the perspicacity of my daughter Catherine whose wise advice altered the shape of the book.

The manuscript was skilfully moulded and trimmed by my peerless editor Liz Wyse; beautifully designed by a consistently patient and resilient Felicity Price-Smith; and forensically proofread to within an inch of its life by Ramona Lamport. The whole team was gently choreographed by Unicorn's Publishing Director, Lucy Duckworth. Finally, my thanks go to Unicorn's Chairman, Ian Strathcarron, for accepting the book for publication.

Published in 2023 by Unicorn, an imprint of Unicorn Publishing Group
Charleston Studio, Meadow Business Centre, Lewes BN8 5RW
www.unicornpublishing.org

Text © Caroline Chapman
Images see p. 160 Illustration List

ISBN 978-1-911397-68-7
10 9 8 7 6 5 4 3 2 1

Designed by Felicity Prce-Smith
Printed in Turkey by Fine Tone Ltd